THOUGHTS ON THE UNION
BETWEEN ENGLAND AND SCOTLAND

THOUGHTS ON
THE UNION BETWEEN
ENGLAND & SCOTLAND

BY

ALBERT V. DICEY, K.C.

M.A., Hon. D.C.L. Oxford, LL.D. (Hon.) Cambridge, Glasgow and Edinburgh
FELLOW OF ALL SOULS' COLLEGE, OXFORD

AND

ROBERT S. RAIT, C.B.E.

HISTORIOGRAPHER-ROYAL FOR SCOTLAND
PROFESSOR OF SCOTTISH HISTORY AND LITERATURE, IN THE UNIVERSITY OF GLASGOW

GREENWOOD PRESS, PUBLISHERS
WESTPORT, CONNECTICUT

Originally published in 1920
by Macmillan and Co., Ltd., London

First Greenwood Reprinting 1971

Library of Congress Catalogue Card Number 77-114510

SBN 8371-4785-9

Printed in the United States of America

PREFACE

In 1603 James VI. of Scotland succeeded on the death of Elizabeth to the English crown as James I. of England.[1] Hence arose the so-called union of Crowns. Under this union the King of England was the same person as the King of Scotland. But, as King of England, he had, constitutionally, no authority in Scotland, and as King of Scotland, he had no authority in England. Hence it resulted that no law passed by the English Parliament had operation in Scotland, and no law passed by the Scottish Parliament had operation in England. In 1707 was passed first by the Parliament of Scotland, and then by the Parliament of England, the Act of Union. This statute abolished the separate Parliament of England and also the separate Parliament of Scotland, and brought into existence the Parliament of the United Kingdom of Great Britain and, from a legal point of view,[2] the United Kingdom of Great Britain. Hence the Parliament of Great Britain had, after the Union, authority to legislate for every part of Great Britain and for every country which had immediately before the

[1] When in the following pages a King is mentioned simply as James, the monarch thus named is James VI. of Scotland, who became James I. of England.

[2] The term "Great Britain" was used, e.g., on the coins issued by James after the Union of Crowns, though there was really no United Kingdom of Great Britain before 1707. Cf. p. 121, post.

Union been subject either to the King of England
or to the King of Scotland, or, to use a modern
expression, for every part of the British Empire.

This essay is concerned in one way or another
wholly with the Act of Union, and treats of (1) the
Scottish parliamentary government from 1603 to
1707; (2) the passing of the Act of Union, 1703–
1707; (3) the results of the Act of Union, 1707–
1832.[1]

This book, though it deals, from different points
of view, with the Union between England and Scotland, is not in strictness a work of history; it is
rather an attempt to comment upon the nature and
the results of a great legal or political transaction.
It contains Thoughts upon the Act of Union, but
it does not profess to be a history of Scotland, even
during the period with which these Thoughts are
specially concerned. This period may broadly be
described as the years from 1603 to 1707, or, if we
take the widest possible view, from 1603 to 1832.
From the special character and the limited scope of
these Thoughts upon the Act of Union flow several
results which may conveniently be here noted.

In reading this essay it must in the first place be
borne in mind that there is an essential difference
between the work of a writer who comments upon
and explains (as in this essay) the gradual development of the Union between England and Scotland,
the passing of the Act of Union, its character and
its results, and the work of an historian who intends

---

[1] The parliamentary constitution of Scotland remained to a great
extent in force after the abolition of the Parliament of Scotland till
1832, when almost all the remains thereof were, in substance,
abolished by the Reform Act of that year.

to tell the story of Scotland, even. during the very same years with which this essay is mainly concerned (1603–1707).[1] Such a commentator must on the one hand of necessity emphasise some matters or events with which the historian of Scotland is but slightly, or secondarily, concerned. Thus the commentator must of necessity emphasise the points of likeness, and still more the points of unlikeness, between the Parliament of England and the Parliament of Scotland. He must also lay the strongest emphasis upon the essential difference between the parliamentary constitution of Scotland in 1603 and the parliamentary constitution of Scotland in 1690. Nor can he fail to examine with care the position and the influence of the committee known as the Lords of the Articles. For all these things are of vital importance for the understanding either of the almost insuperable difficulty up to 1703 of passing an Act of Union or the possibility of passing it in 1707. But some of these matters, and especially the elaborate comparison and contrast between the Parliament of England and the Parliament of Scotland, only in a secondary degree concern the historian of Scotland. Such a commentator, on the other hand, is relieved from the careful examination of some matters which are of primary importance to the Scottish historian. He may rightly omit the careful investigation of the steps by which the anomalous authority of the Lords of the Articles came into existence, though such an examination is from an antiquarian or merely historical point of view of first-

[1] The revolutionary years between 1638 and 1660 being for the most part omitted.

rate interest and importance.   So again our commentator is rightly dispensed from passing judgement on the strange hesitations or, as foes would
say, tergiversations of the Duke of Hamilton, which
contributed as much as did the parliamentary skill
of the Duke of Queensberry towards the passing of
the Act of Union.   For the personal motives by
which a Scottish statesman may have been actuated
in opposing, or sometimes in supporting, the Act
have in themselves little importance as regards the
growth or the understanding of the Act of Union,
except in so far as they may occasionally give insight
into the state of public opinion during a political
crisis in which the Duke of Hamilton and others
played a conspicuous part.

In the next place, from the scope of this essay
it will soon appear to any thoughtful reader that it
is a work not of research but, in the main at least,
of inference.   This distinction is a real one, though
it is sometimes overlooked.   An author who tries to
ascertain new, important, or startling facts about
the history of Scotland ought to possess rare powers
not only of historical investigation but of historical
narrative, so that he may be able to make visible
to all students the results of the discoveries made
by his industry and insight.   These are the legitimate
rewards of research when combined—which it sometimes is not—with a gift for impressive narrative.
A commentator on the Act of Union, on the other
hand, has neither the aim nor the claim to reveal
new or unknown facts.   His object is to take the
ordinary facts as to the Act of Union which are the
common knowledge obtained by the labours of men

devoted to historical research, and, assuming these facts to be in the main established, to draw from them more or less obvious inferences which may often escape the attention both of Scotsmen and Englishmen, but especially of Englishmen, who have become so accustomed to the political and the moral unity of every part of Great Britain as never to have known, or else to have forgotten entirely, the labour, the forethought, the skill, and the wisdom through which the inhabitants of the south and of the north of the British Isles, who had been for centuries bitter enemies, were at last and slowly blended into the one united Kingdom of Great Britain.

It is, lastly, plain that such success as may be attained in the attempt to lay before the British public thoughts on the Union must, at bottom, depend upon the labours of men who for the last sixty years and more have investigated with infinite care the many different and important aspects of Scottish history, and who have thrown year by year more and more light on the parliamentary history of Scotland both up to and after the passing of the Act of Union. On the facts established by this patriotic and successful effort the commentary put forward in this essay depends.

It is here both a pleasure and a duty to acknowledge the infinite help given in the preparation of this book by friendly communications, by men competent to speak—one of them, alas, is now for ever silent—with special authority as to different subjects on which these Thoughts at times touch. We are specially indebted to the late Professor Hume Brown,

Historiographer Royal for Scotland; to Professors J. H. Millar and R. K. Hannay, of the University of Edinburgh; to Professor William L. Davidson, of the University of Aberdeen; to Dr. C. H. Firth, Regius Professor of Modern History at Oxford; and to Professor J. Swift MacNeill.

We have also pleasure in thanking the owners of the *Quarterly Review* and of the *Scottish Historical Review* for allowing the use, in this Essay, of Thoughts on the Parliament of Scotland, and on the General Assembly of the Church of Scotland under the Constitution of 1690, by A. V. Dicey, which have already appeared in these reviews.

A. V. DICEY.

ROBERT S. RAIT.

December 1919.

CONTENTS

INTRODUCTION

PART I

THE PARLIAMENTARY GOVERNMENT OF SCOTLAND, 1603–1707

CHAPTER I

THE CONSTITUTION OF 1603—(THE NON-SOVEREIGN PARLIAMENT)

First Thought.—*Under the Constitution of 1603 the Parliament of Scotland was the recognised organ through which the King exercised his legislative authority over all his Scottish subjects. The Parliament took, when acting together with the King, a real part in legislation, but it was a non-sovereign legislature, owing to its authority being limited by the existence of two institutions, viz.* (1) *the Committee of the Articles ;* (2) *the Conventions of Estates* 32-44

Comment

THE AUTHORITY OF PARLIAMENT . . . 32

RESTRICTIONS ON THE AUTHORITY OF PARLIAMENT . 33

Committee of the Articles 33
Conventions of Estates 42

Second Thought.—*The Constitutions both of 1603 and of 1690 were governed by a principle which lay at the basis of the whole Scottish parliamentary system, namely that no man who was not a King's freeholder (tenant in capite) had a right to appear in Parliament either personally or by his elected representative (Commissioner)*

The King's freeholders who were entitled to appear in Parliament were—

(A) *King's freeholders who were entitled and under the obligation to appear in Parliament individually in virtue of their being individually summoned. They were either—*

(a) *Nobles, whatever their title, or*

(b) *Bishops, when Episcopacy was legally recognised in Scotland*

CHAPTER II

PART II

THE PASSING OF THE ACT OF UNION

CHAPTER III

THE STATE OF OPINION ON THE EVE OF THE UNION

CHAPTER IV

THE WAR BETWEEN THE PARLIAMENTS

CHAPTER V

THE COMMISSIONERS AND THE TREATY OF UNION

CHAPTER VI

THE PASSING OF THE ACT OF UNION BY THE TWO PARLIAMENTS

PART III

THE ACT OF UNION AND ITS RESULTS

CHAPTER VII

THE ACT OF UNION—ITS GENERAL CHARACTERISTICS AND LEADING PROVISIONS

CHAPTER VIII

OBJECTIONS TO THE WORKING OF THE ACT OF UNION

CHAPTER IX

THE GRADUAL ACCEPTANCE OF THE ACT OF UNION

CHAPTER X

THE SUCCESS OF THE ACT OF UNION

*First Thought.—The permanent success of the Act of
Union is shown in—*
    (A) *The creation thereby of the United Kingdom of Great
Britain and*
    (B) *The preservation thereby of English and of Scottish
Nationalism*   319-345

Comment

INTRODUCTION

It is well to note in this Introduction two leading duction. considerations : Intro-

First Consideration.— The ignorance, even of educated Englishmen, with regard to the Act of Union 1707.

The Imperial Parliament[1] of to-day has been created by the union of three legislative bodies belonging to three different countries—the Parliament of England, the Parliament of Scotland, and the Parliament of Ireland. Every well-read Englishman is convinced, often quite erroneously, that he understands the growth and the working of England's Constitution. Through the course of recent events the story of the Irish Parliament, though he generally reads it wrongly, has been forced upon his attention ; and the knowledge thereof, slight though it be, is made the easier because the Parliament of Ireland was, like so many other constitutions, an imitation, though a misdeveloped copy, of the Parliament of

[1] The word "Parliament" is throughout the following pages, when the contrary does not appear from the context, used, in accordance with popular phraseology, as meaning, when applied to Scotland, the House of Parliament, and, when applied to England, or to Ireland, the two Houses of Parliament. In regard to the technically correct use of the word "Parliament" as including the King and the Houses of Parliament, see Dicey, *Law of the Constitution* (8th ed.), p. xviii.

1

England. Of the old Parliament of Scotland our educated English gentleman till recently knew little or nothing, and he would often be found to confuse the Union of Crowns [1] with the Union of Parliaments.

The ignorance of Englishmen has been encouraged, if not excused, by the want of interest in Scottish affairs displayed by eminent English writers. Hallam was an author in advance of his time. But in his *Constitutional History of England* — a work of about 1300 pages—he dedicates but thirty-six pages to the Constitution of Scotland. Freeman's admirable *Growth of the English Constitution* contains little, if any, reference to either of the great Acts of Union which gave birth, first to the one kingdom of Great Britain, and next to the United Kingdom of Great Britain and Ireland. Macaulay, the most brilliant, the most parliamentarian, and still, in virtue of his genius, the most influential among the historians of England, though he knew the facts of Scottish history, had even in 1852 not discovered, until it was revealed to him by Burton, the now open secret that one main explanation of the Union between England and Scotland lies in the desire of Scotland for a full share in English trade and commerce.

"I remember," writes Burton, "upwards of twenty "years ago, a talk with the great historian of the "English Revolution . . .; he said he believed I had

[1] "It is amazing," said Johnson in 1769, "what ignorance of "certain points one sometimes finds in men of eminence. A wit about "town, who wrote Latin bawdy verses, asked me how it happened that "England and Scotland, which were once two kingdoms, were now "one" (Boswell, *Life of Johnson*, iii. 92, Croker's ed., 1859). If the Act of Union passed in 1707 was forgotten in 1769, no wonder it is not remembered in 1919.

INTRODUCTION

INTRODUCTION

"been studying the Union; he was yet far off from
"that period, but he saw some points of difficulty.
"One was that although the Union was notoriously
"unpopular in Scotland, yet there were symptoms of
"pressure on the side of Scotland in its direction.
"He had thought whether this might be the action
"of the Episcopalian party to obtain protection from
"England, but that did not seem a satisfactory
"explanation. I said I believed he would find a
"simple solution in the urgency of the Scots for
"participation in the English trade, and that he
"would find his way to this solution in the laws
"of the Protectorate and those of the Restoration.
"I find in a short letter from him, dated 20th Nov-
"ember 1852, immediately on returning to his own
"books—'I have looked into the question of the
"commercial relations between England and Scotland
"after the Restoration. You were quite right, and
"the subject is full of interest.' How affluently he
"would have made the world a participator in this
"full interest had his days not then been numbered,
"can only be matter of regretful conjecture."[1]

Bagehot, the most original among the thinkers
of insight who, since the time of Burke, have

[1] Burton, 2nd ed., viii. 3, note 1. Macaulay had, however, by or
before 1855, fully mastered the relation between Scotland's need for
free trade and the passing of the Act of Union. See Macaulay, *History*,
iii. 253-4, where he mentions his obligation to the seventh chapter
of Burton's valuable *History of Scotland*. See also quotation from
Macaulay, Chap. III. Second Thought, *post*.

Professor Firth has pointed out that Macaulay in the writing of the
last volume of his *History* had not before him a mass of additional
information as to Scottish History which has been accumulated during
the last sixty years, nor the use of numerous and excellent works in
which, during the same period, the results of such information have
been placed before every reader.

analysed the working of the English Constitution,
though he lived till 1877, seemingly took little notice
of the way in which these two Acts of Union have
told upon the development, or occasionally the mis-
development, of representative institutions which
were, at one time, of purely English growth, but
have subsequently been influenced by Scottish or
Irish wants or ideals. And this remark applies in
substance to the excellent work of Mr. A. Lawrence
Lowell, which gives the most thoughtful, the most
complete, and the most impartial picture of the working of the British Constitution as it stood at the time
when he published his *Government of England.*
In truth, the success of the Union has concealed
from the thinkers of to-day the all but insuperable obstacles which opposed its creation, and has
propagated an idea, for which there is no true
justification, that the political unity of separate
countries, each endowed with a representative Parliament, is a matter of easy accomplishment.

*Second Consideration.—The marked likeness, and
even more the unremarked unlikeness, between the
Scottish Parliament and the English Parliament.*

On this point Englishmen and Scotsmen are both
exposed to error, but the mistake in each case is due
to a different cause. An English student is prone to
assume, without much inquiry, that the Parliament
of Scotland either reproduced or was an attempt
to reproduce all the characteristics of the English
Parliament. A Scottish student knows the important
part which the Parliament, or rather the parliamentary constitution of England, has played throughout
the whole of English history in promoting English

delusive. In the one country, as in the other, though
some important qualifications, which will soon become obvious, must be made with regard to Scotland, the Parliament contained before 1603 (i.) the Peers; (ii.) the Bishops, Abbots, and Priors; (iii.) the County members, and (iv.) the Burgh members. Every person who belonged to class (i.) or (ii.) attended Parliament because he had a right to receive, and did receive, from the King a personal summons, which he was bound to obey, requiring him to attend, whilst the persons who belonged to classes (iii.) and (iv.), that is the representatives of the burghs (borough members) and of the shires (county members), appeared in virtue of a summons from the King ordering the counties and the burghs to appear in Parliament by their elected representatives, or, to use a Scottish expression, Commissioners.

(3) *Functions.*—The functions of the Scottish, no less than of the English Parliament were judicial as well as legislative. From 1603 to 1707 in Scotland, and to a considerably later time in England, the judicial aspect of Parliament had a political importance which we have now all but forgotten. An Impeachment in England, and Acts of Attainder in both countries were during the seventeenth century a real though extreme method of enforcing the liability of public men for high crimes and misdemeanours.

Neither in England nor in Scotland was the Parliament originally in any sense a supreme or sovereign legislature; it was rather the organ by which the King regularly exercised his legislative power. In Scotland, from 1603 to 1690, the Parliament did little more than ratify or register the laws laid before it by the King or by the Government acting in the King's name. In England, the Parliament in 1603 played an essential and even a dominant part in legislation.[1]

(4) *The Mode of Growth and Termination of Existence.*—To the Parliament of each country may with equal truth be applied the statement that it was "not made, but grew." This current expression, like most popular phrases, lacks accuracy, and is marked by ambiguity, but it contains a real, and more or less important, significance. It means that the constitution of Scotland, no less than the constitution of England, was not deliberately made or created by any man, or body of men, and thus did not, as did the Constitution of the United States, come into existence on a given day. The phrase means also that the constitution neither of England nor of Scotland was framed in accordance with some foreign model, as were most of the constitutional monarchies which have abounded in modern Europe, and betray the wish of their creators to imitate, though the endeavour has often failed, the well - known constitution of England. From both these points of view, the parliamentary constitution of Scotland may be considered, no less than the English constitution itself, to be the natural and, so to speak, unconscious outgrowth of the historical circumstances of the country wherein it came into existence.

The parliamentary constitution, lastly, both of Scotland and of England came to a similar end. Each of them was absorbed and united into the new

[1] See Chap. I. pp. 32-44, *post.*

Parliament of Great Britain. This statement, which,
if properly understood, is the most undeniable of
truisms, may seem to many Scotsmen an unmeaning
paradox ; yet the history of the United Kingdom, at
all events since 1800, has made manifest to every constitutionalist that you cannot combine the legislative
bodies of two hitherto independent countries without
creating a legislature which may exhibit essentially
different characteristics from those which marked the
separate Parliament of each country. The Scottish
members of the British Parliament did from the first,
in one way or another, change the character of the
Parliament sitting at Westminster, and from the days
following the Reform Act of 1832 it has always been
possible, and has in fact sometimes been the case,
that the Parliament at Westminster should support
policies or legislation opposed to the wishes entertained by the majority of Englishmen, and in this
sense enforce upon the inhabitants of England respect
for un-English ideas.

Points of Unlikeness

(1) *Form of Parliament.*—The Scottish Parliament was a unicameral, or a one-House Parliament,
and not, like the English Parliament, a bicameral,[1] or
two-House Parliament. This difference is no mere
matter of form ; it certainly affected the character of
the Scottish legislature.[2]

---

[1] Modern experience has pronounced almost decisively in favour of
a bicameral, as against a unicameral legislature. There are indica-
tions of deliberation by the Scottish Estates separately, but only in a
more or less informal manner.

[2] See Chap. I. pp. 32, 56-58, *post.*

Intro-
duction.

(2) *Presence of Officers of State in Parliament.*—
Such officers were nominated by the King to have a
seat, be present, speak, and vote in Parliament. Till
1617, the right to nominate them probably depended
on usage;[1] after 1617 the King could not appoint
more than eight of such officers to take part in
Parliament.[2]

In the English Parliament nothing like such
nominated officers existed. A Lord Chancellor, though
presiding over the House of Lords as Chancellor, had
a right to speak and to vote not because he was
Chancellor, but because he had been created a Peer.[3]
An Attorney-General is not necessarily a member of

---

[1] The right of officers to attend is probably a vestige of the
attendance of lairds and lower clergy, which died out during the
sixteenth century as a general practice, until the attendance of the
lairds was renewed in another form.

[2] A.P.S. iv. 236. The attendance of such officers was abolished
during the revolutionary period, beginning in 1638, but was substantially restored by the General Act Rescissory in 1661 (c. 18, A.P.S.
vii. 16).

After 1690 an Officer of State could be elected to a committee if
he was a member of any of the Estates, but not if he was merely a
member *ex officio*. Thus any officer who was also a Peer was eligible to
a committee. In 1690, the King was empowered to appoint officers to
sit and debate in committees without the power of voting, and no
Officer of State who was not a Peer could vote in a committee (1690,
c. 3, A.P.S. ix. 113). In 1696, when the member for Cullen was
made Secretary of State, he was held to have vacated his seat, and
to sit *ex officio*. See Rait, "Lower Clergy, Lairds, and Officers in
Parliament," *Scot. Hist. Rev.*, Jan. 1915.

[3] A man created Lord Keeper of the Great Seal and remaining a
Commoner held in relation to the House an anomalous position, which
has thus been described : " If he be a commoner, notwithstanding a
" resolution of the House that he is to be proceeded against for any
" misconduct as if he were a peer, he has neither vote nor deliberative
" voice, and he can only put the question, and communicate the
" resolutions of the House according to the directions he receives. . . .
" Lord Keeper Henley, till raised to the peerage, used to complain
" bitterly of being obliged to put the question for the reversal of his
" own decrees, without being permitted to say a word in support of

the House of Commons, but he cannot for any length
of time perform his duties unless he is a member of
the House. He sits in the House, however, not
because he is Attorney-General, but because he has
been elected to represent some county or borough.

(3) *The Representative System.*[1]—The representative system was introduced into the Scottish
constitution at a comparatively late date, and the
rigid application of the principle that no man was
entitled to appear in Parliament who was not either
a King's freeholder, or a person chosen to represent
the King's freeholders, produced a much narrower
and proportionally smaller electorate than that
of England from 1603 down to the Reform Act
1832.[2]

(4) *The Absence of General Elections.*—A minor,
though not unimportant, difference between the
Scottish and the English parliamentary system is
that the English plan of holding general elections at
irregular intervals was, certainly till after the Restoration, unknown in Scotland. The Acts which provided
for the representation of the small barons or landowners in the counties ordered the election of their
Commissioners to be made annually at the Michaelmas
Head Courts. The published records of the Sheriff
Court of Aberdeen show that this was the custom
until the middle of the seventeenth century. The
election was made "for keeping of Parliaments and
" other His Majesty's general conventions that should

"them" (*Lives of the Lord Chancellors of England,* by John Lord
Campbell (5th ed.), pp. 14, 15. See also "Henley, Robert, first Earl
of Northington," *Dict. Nat. Biog.* xxv. 417).

[1] See Chap. I. pp. 47-56, *post*, and Burton, viii. p. 187.

[2] On this point see Chaps. I. and II. pp. 32, 59, *post*.

" happen to be before the next Michaelmas Court." [1]
There is no reason to believe that burghal elections
ever took place annually. An annual election was
convenient for the small barons who met only at
long intervals, but the Town Councils, who were
in constant session, made their elections as necessity
arose. Burgh records always speak of an election
for a Parliament or Convention already summoned
to meet at a given date. Fresh elections were
made after a prorogation of Parliament.[2] Both
in the shires and in the burghs, Commissioners were
eligible for re-election, and were in fact frequently
re-elected. In 1661, the practical effect of re-
election was destroyed by the first of a series of Acts
of Adjournment which were thereafter regularly
passed when the Parliament was prorogued. These
Acts ordered that there should be no new choice
of Commissioners during the existence of a Parliament, "except upon the death or incapacity of
" the present commissioners." Another Act, passed in
1681, contemplated that the election of Commissioners
for the shires should take place " either at the
" Michaelmas Court or at the calling of Parliaments or
" Conventions," and it made a special provision " that
" sufficient advertisement may be given to all parties
" having a vote in Election who are to vote at the
" calling of a Parliament or Convention " *i.e.* at a
special meeting and not at the Michaelmas Head
Court, for which no special advertisement was
required. The older method of annual election,

---

[1] *Records of the Sheriff Court of Aberdeenshire*, ed. Littlejohn, New
Spalding Club, i. 372, ii. 11.

[2] Extracts from Aberdeen Burgh Records, Spalding Club, ii. 269.

though useless in that there was, after 1661, no opportunity of changing a representative, was not abolished, and the actual practice seems to have varied.[1] But the tradition of an annual election in the counties survived till the Union, for Harley, writing to Godolphin in August 1702, stated that " the constitution of Scotland requires them to elect " members for the counties at Michaelmas, but not for " the burghs till a Parliament be actually called."[2] In the period from 1661 to 1707, there were only five new Parliaments, elected respectively in 1661, 1669, 1681, 1685, and 1703, and four Conventions, elected respectively in 1665, 1667, 1678, and 1689. The last of these became a Parliament and sat as a Parliament from 1690 to 1702, its meeting being interrupted by a series of prorogations, which reduced the total period of its sitting to some seventeen months in the course of twelve years. If we neglect the three comparatively unimportant Conventions of 1665, 1667, and 1678, there were in the forty-seven years from 1660 to 1707, six General Elections, and in the eighteen years from 1689 to 1707 only two. The custom of electing annually in the shires and of making *ad hoc* elections for each session of Parliament in the burghs had provided an opportunity of keeping the Commissioners in touch with their constituencies, and the effect of the Adjournment Acts in and after 1661 was to destroy this opportunity, and to create what were virtually General Elections at long intervals, the duration of which was determined by the Government.

[1] Cf. Terry, *The Scottish Parliament*, pp. 28-29.
[2] *Letters relating to Scotland in the Reign of Queen Anne*, ed. P. Hume Brown, p. 142 (Scottish History Society).

(5) *Legislative Power.*—Up to 1690 the Scottish Parliament as a whole did not exercise anything like the predominant authority in the making of laws which had long been obtained by the English Parliament.

This restriction on the legislative power of the Scottish Parliament in the main arose from the existence of a parliamentary committee, called the "Lords of the Articles," or more briefly, even in statutes, "the Articles."[1] This Committee prepared the Acts, or to use English expressions, the Bills, to be submitted to Parliament, and until 1690 the Parliament had, at times, no authority to discuss or vote upon any Bill not submitted to it by this Committee, and when a Bill was thus submitted, had no power to do anything but either accept or reject it. The Committee of the Articles was formally elected by Parliament, but for a long time back, and certainly between 1603 and 1690 (the revolutionary period of 1638–1660 being excluded), was elected in accordance with the authoritative suggestions of the King. Hence from 1603 to 1690, the King assuredly controlled the legislative power of Parliament, and this control limited, if it did not absolutely prevent, Parliament from transferring to itself the administrative power of the King.[2]

(6) *Taxation.*—The Scottish Parliament rarely exercised the power of taxation, as it was constantly employed by the English Parliament, to limit the

[1] As to the Lords of the Articles see Chap. I. pp. 33-42, *post.*
[2] As to conventions of Estates, which, though not strictly Parliaments, exercised a good deal of legislative power, see Chap. I. pp. 42-44, *post.*

authority of the King, or rather to increase the
authority of Parliament.[1]

What, we· naturally ask, is the cause of this undoubted difference ? or, to put the same inquiry in other words, How does it happen that disputes about taxation between the King and the English Parliament are from the time of Edward I., at any rate, down almost to the Revolution of 1688, of constant recurrence, whilst such disputes between the King and the Scottish Parliament rarely occur till the end of the seventeenth and the beginning of the eighteenth century ?

The reply to this question, in whatever form the inquiry be put, is not easy to find. Two possible answers suggest themselves :

First Answer. — The Scottish Parliament was, through the existence of the Committee of the Articles, so much under the control of the King[2] that it was little likely that there should be a dispute as to taxes between the King and the Parliament, or, in other words, the Parliament was not a body which could freely use the taxing power to limit royal authority.

Second Answer.—The King of Scotland must in general have possessed a smaller revenue than the

[1] The extent of this difference may be measured by a comparison of the index to Stubbs's *Constitutional History of England* with Burton's index to his *History of Scotland,* as regards references to the subject of taxation or of taxes. In Stubbs's work such references fill up at least two full pages (iii. 648, 649). In Burton's work they fill at most five or six lines (see index vol. p. 595). The difference is the more remarkable, as Stubbs's *Constitutional History of England* brings us down only to the death of Richard III., whilst Burton's *History of Scotland* goes down to 1748.

[2] Or rather of the person or persons who at a given moment possessed executive power.

contemporary King of England, but it is possible
that the King of England may usually have found it
harder to live on his own than did the contemporary
King of Scotland.

This conclusion, though it sounds a strange one,
is suggested by an examination of the revenues on
which a Scottish King could rely, and of the expenses
which he was forced to incur.

During the Middle Ages the revenues of the King
consisted mainly of the rents and other returns of
Crown lands, together with the feudal prestations,
incidents, and casualties, etc., and the customs and
rents paid by the Royal Burghs. The imposition
of a tax was occasional. When it was imposed, the
" Cess," or land-tax, was levied *quoad* one-half upon
Kirk lands, *quoad* one-third upon counties, and
quoad one-sixth upon Royal Burghs. By the Act
1587, c. 8 (29), Kirk lands were annexed to the
Crown, and 1587, c. 109 (119) enacts that, in spite
of that change, " the taxation of free burrows shall
" na-ways be altered, but shall stand as the same
" stood in all times preceding : That is to say, their
" part of all general taxations in time coming shall
" extend to the saxt part thereof allanerly [only]."

In the seventeenth century the " Cess " became
a regular institution. So much was allocated on
each county on a valuation which became stereotyped
in 1670. The sixth levied on the Royal Burghs was
allocated among these burghs by the Convention
of the Royal Burghs, and in each Royal Burgh its
proportion was allocated among the burgesses by
stentmasters appointed by the magistrates. A pro-
prietor in a burgh of barony or a burgh of regality

would pay the share allocated upon him by the
commissioners of supply in the county, who did for
the county what the stentmasters did for the Royal
Burghs.[1]

After the Union the "Cess" was incorporated
with the English land-tax, which seems to have
been assessed and levied on pretty much the same
principle—its possibilities being always lessened by
the fact that it was based upon a stereotyped
valuation of ancient date.

It would therefore appear that the Scottish King
had a more or less fixed revenue from the rents of
land owned by him, from feudal dues, from the
annual payments made by the Royal Burghs, and
from customs received by the Royal Burghs and
payable to the Crown.[2] It is also, at any rate, likely
that the pecuniary expenses of government were in
the case of the Scottish King comparatively small.
The English King, on the other hand, must have
found at all times the expenses of government great
and constantly increasing. The wars carried on
abroad involved large pecuniary cost. We may also
fairly assume that the early development of a complete judicial system must, though a great benefit
to England, have involved a great deal of governmental expense. Hence it is at least intelligible
that the King of Scotland with a limited but more
or less certain revenue may have found it more
possible to "live on his own" than the King of
England, who, with a much larger revenue, had to

---

[1] See Bell's *Principles*, ss. 1123-1130, and Rankine, on *Land
Ownership*, 4th ed. pp. 834-840.

[2] There is no evidence that the King could raise the customs
payable on imports received by the Royal Burghs.

carry on a far more costly system of government and administration. To put the same conclusion in other words, the King of England had almost of necessity to demand taxation to meet the ever-increasing cost of government which the King of Scotland might more or less meet from his own revenues independently of grants from Parliament.

There are very few instances of the imposition of special taxation by the Great Council or by Parliament before the sixteenth century. Before the War of Independence, the sum paid to Richard I. of England for the abrogation of the Treaty of Falaise was raised by taxes upon both ecclesiastical and temporal lands, and the catalogue of Scottish documents removed to England by Edward I. shows the existence of land valuations. After the conclusion of the War of Independence, Parliament voted Robert I. a tax on all rents and profits of land, and special taxes were imposed for carrying out the provisions of the Treaty of Northampton (1328); for the ransoms of David II. (1367) and James I. (1424); for the marriage of James III. (1467); for the despatch of an army to France (1471); for the defence of the Kingdom in 1481, 1488, and 1535; and on a few other occasions. General taxations became more frequent in the English War of Queen Mary's minority.[1] Up to this date taxation was imposed solely upon tenants-in-chief of the Crown, *i.e.*, Royal Burghs and lay and ecclesiastical lands held by the recognised feudal tenures. The burden was doubtless transferred in one way or another, and such transference was occasionally contemplated,

[1] For the circumstances of this war, cf. Chap. III. Second Thought, *post.*

although one of the Acts expressly states that the taxation is not to fall on the common people. In 1580 this principle was abandoned. Direct taxation was imposed upon tenants who held royal lands in feu, *i.e.*, by the payment of a fixed annual ground rent, which, owing to the deterioration in the value of Scottish money, no longer represented the value of their holdings. The same Act gave barons and freeholders the right of reclaiming the proper proportions from their sub-vassals. In the seventeenth century, this liability of sub-vassals was recognised, but the State actually received, directly, no taxes from others than royal tenants or feu-holders until 1643, when a general taxation was imposed upon all lands. This system was abandoned in 1661, but was permanently revived in 1667. From this date, taxation was no longer restricted, even in theory, to tenants-in-chief, although the share of taxation imposed on the estate of burgesses was paid only by Royal Burghs, which continued to possess special trading privileges.

(7) *Parliament not the Centre of Scottish Public Life.*—The Parliament of Scotland never during the whole of its existence became the centre of Scottish public life in the sense in which the Parliament of England has normally from the accession of Henry IV. (1399) and indeed from a much earlier date, been the centre of English public life.[1]

(8) *The Sovereign Power of Parliament.*[2]—There exists a somewhat subtle unlikeness between the

[1] See for the full treatment of this most important fact, Chap. II. Third Thought, *post*.
[2] Compare Chap. VII. (D), *post*.

Parliament of Scotland and the Parliament of England
which it is somewhat hard to describe in definite
terms.   The difference lies in the fact that the
Scottish Parliament never felt itself to be, nor in
fact ever was, a sovereign power in the sense in
which the English Parliament certainly from a very
early time did feel itself to be a sovereign power, or
at any rate an essential and most important part of
a strictly sovereign power, namely the King and the
Houses of Parliament acting 'together.   To see the
extent of this difference we may well, in treating of
this particular point, use the word " Parliament" in
a more extensive sense than is generally given to it
in this essay.   We may employ it as meaning in
Scotland the King and the House of Parliament, as
it strictly means in England the King and the two
Houses of Parliament.   Having thus defined the
terms used, we can say with truth that Parliament
for centuries has exerted what Blackstone calls
" omnipotence," by which is meant that Parliament
could from a legal point of view override every other
authority in the land.   The historical causes of this
acknowledged supremacy are noteworthy.   The first
of these causes is that when in England a King was
weak and the Houses of Parliament were strong, the
latter increased their own power, not by abolishing
the authority of the King, but by claiming to act for
the King and in effect acting in his name.   This was
on the whole the policy of the Houses under the
Lancastrian dynasty whose title rested upon the
revolution of 1399.   When the King was strong, as
was Henry VIII., the King reversed this policy.   He
did not abolish the power of the Houses, but he used

the Houses for extending the power of the Crown.
Hence, in theory at least, the King and the Houses,
however they divided sovereignty between them,
became in their own eyes and in those of the
nation the omnipotent sovereign of England. The
second cause which must be taken into consideration
is this : The Crown from the time almost of the
Norman Conquest, and certainly from the time of
Edward I., has exercised through the Law Courts
and other governmental bodies actual authority in the
whole of England. There was no place where, in
technical language, the "King's writ did not run."
He was, in fact, to a degree hardly then existing in
any other country than England, the real ruler of every
part of the country, and of every person nominally
owing allegiance to the King, and, as in one way or
another the power of the King became identified with
that of the Parliament, a parliamentary sovereignty
unknown to other countries came into existence. For
this purpose, odd as the statement sounds, it does not
matter whether the King, as under the Tudors, turned
the Houses of Parliament into his instrument for
legislation and also in many cases for judicial punishment, or whether the Houses of Parliament claimed
for themselves sovereignty under the form of exercising the Royal prerogative. There was no place, and in
normal circumstances no class, which could defy the
national sovereignty, whether in reality exercised by
the Crown or by the Parliament. In Scotland it was
far otherwise. It may be doubted whether before
the Union of Crowns the King himself for practical
purposes could exercise his authority without great
difficulty among the Border Families. It is certain

that neither the judicial nor the legislative power of
the King could before, say, 1745 be always effectively
exercised among the Highland clansmen. This weakness of the Crown obtained a certain kind of recognition from the existence of hereditary jurisdictions
held by landowners, nobles, and chiefs, which to a
considerable extent competed with the jurisdiction of
the King's Court. Hence, from historical circumstances, the Parliament of Scotland never had, or felt
that it had, the omnipotence of the English Parliament. Indeed, the Scottish Parliament almost at all
times acknowledged some power which restrained
or competed with parliamentary authority. Up to
1690, except in revolutionary periods, the competitor
was the King acting through the Lords of the
Articles. After 1560, during the revolutionary
period from 1638 to 1651, and even between 1690
and 1707, the competitor was the established Church
of Scotland. Neither the Parliament of Scotland itself
nor the Church of Scotland fully realised the effect
produced by the Parliament of Scotland becoming
part of the British Parliament which had inherited for centuries the tradition of parliamentary
sovereignty. And half the difficulty experienced by
the British Parliament in dealing with the Church of
Scotland lies in the fact that the British Parliament
could not, even in imagination, grasp the idea that, as
regards the Church of Scotland, Parliament was not,
in the eyes of many Scotsmen, as truly a sovereign
power as it is by every English lawyer regarded in
respect of the Church of England. Walpole was a
great, and by no means a rash statesman; he caused
the suspension for more than a century of Convocation.

Was any Minister ever rash enough, after the Constitution of 1690 was fully established, to suspend by a single year the meetings of the General Assembly of the Church of Scotland ?

SUMMARY OF COMPARISON

The essential points of similarity and of dissimilarity between the Scottish and the English Parliament may, omitting minor circumstances, be thus summed up :

The resemblances arose from the fact that both of them were grounded upon the same feudal and mediæval ideas of government. The dissimilarity between them is mainly seen in two facts : The Scottish Parliament never, until 1690, obtained anything like the legislative authority which long before 1603 had been gained by the English Parliament, for except during revolutionary periods the Parliament of Scotland was, up to 1690, rather a body which registered the laws laid before it by the man or men who constituted the executive government of Scotland than a legislative body which legislated of its own authority. The Parliament of Scotland, again, failed during the whole of its existence to become the centre of Scottish public life in the sense in which the Parliament of England had, since at any rate the accession of Henry IV., become the centre of English public life.[1] These two are the main and most important results of a comparison between the Parliaments of the two countries.

---

[1] For the explanation of this failure, see Chap. II. p. 70, *post*.

PART I

THE PARLIAMENTARY GOVERNMENT OF SCOTLAND, 1603–1707

CHARACTER OF PART I

PART I. treats of the parliamentary government of Scotland as it existed from 1603 (the Union of Crowns) till May 1, 1707 [1] (the Union of Parliaments). We need, however, to consider the constitution of Scotland, in so far only as it is connected with the passing, the character, and the results of the Act of Union. But if a student of an immense constitutional change or reform carried through without violence and by strictly legal measures, may overlook many questions which most rightly must receive the attention of Scottish historians, he is bound to bring into prominence some facts which, rightly enough, are not much dwelt upon by historians whose business it is to describe the general course of events occurring in Scotland from the accession of James [2] to the English throne till the day when his great-granddaughter assented to the Act which united England and Scotland into the one State of Great Britain.

Three of such leading facts should be carefully borne in mind by any English student when reading Part I. of this essay.

[1] On this day the Act of Union between England and Scotland came into operation.

[2] Here, and in the following pages the name James, unless it is otherwise precisely stated, or is clearly apparent from the context, means James VI. of Scotland and I. of England.

First.—During the years 1603 to 1707 the inhabitants of Scotland lived under two different constitutions which, if it is allowable to make use of a modern but very convenient anachronism, may be termed respectively the Constitution of 1603 and the Constitution of 1690.[1] The first of these Constitutions was already in existence in 1603, and lasted, except for the period from 1638 to 1660, till 1690. The second of these Constitutions came into existence as a result of the Revolution Settlement, 1689–90, and lasted till the coming into force of the Act of Union in 1707.

Second.—The accession of James to the throne of England in 1603 took place without any dispute or disturbance on the part either of Englishmen or of Scotsmen. It was, we may presume, accepted with satisfaction in each of the countries of which James was thenceforward the King. But the essential difference between a union of Crowns and a union of Parliaments—that is of countries— should never be forgotten. James was from and after the death of Elizabeth the King of England as well as, what he had long been, the King of Scotland.

---

[1] Neither the term "Constitution of 1603" nor the term "Constitution of 1690" (see p. 59, *post*) is to be found in any Act of the Parliament, or in any History of Scotland; it is in each case an anachronism, for it involves the application of a modern expression to a bygone state of things. Such a use of modern language is (it is submitted) allowable when, as in the present instance, it affords the best way of making intelligible to the readers of the twentieth century the parliamentary Constitution of Scotland as it existed at the time of the accession of James to the throne of England in 1603, and as it in substance continued, if years of revolutionary violence be omitted, till 1690, when in consequence of the Revolution of 1689–90 William and Mary acceded to the Scottish throne, and there came into existence what in this treatise is called the Constitution of 1690, which lasted till the passing of the Act of Union in 1707.

But his power and his rights as King of Scotland were different from his power and his rights as King of England. His Parliament in Scotland had no power to pass any law affecting England, nor had his Parliament in England the least power to pass any law affecting Scotland. No English Court, such as, *e.g.*, the Court of King's Bench, could exercise any jurisdiction in Scotland, nor could any Court in Scotland, *e.g.*, the Court of Session, exercise the least jurisdiction in England. The Parliament of Scotland could not impose a penny of taxation upon the King's loyal subjects in England, nor could the Parliament of England impose a penny of taxation upon the King's equally loyal subjects in Scotland. James, to sum the matter up, was King of Scotland and had become also King of England. But his two characters ought not to be confused. A law passed in Scotland had no application to England ; a law passed in England had no application to Scotland. Some confusion in this connexion has been caused by the case of the *Post Nati*[1] in the Court of King's Bench, 1608. This case decided that Scotsmen born after the accession of James to the throne of England were not aliens in England. Of course this decision could of itself have no operation in Scotland, but the Scottish Parliament had already passed, in 1607, an Act allowing Englishmen to hold land in Scotland.

Third.—The accession of James to the throne of England greatly strengthened the power of the Crown

[1] See *Calvin's* case, 1608, 7 Rep. 5 A. and cf. State Trials ii. p. 607. The real name was Colvill. A test case was made by the purchase of land in England for an infant who was a grandson of Lord Colvill of Culross.

in Scotland.   Mr. Gardiner's statement that "it is
true indeed that James was now safe from personal
attack, but for any practical purposes his strength
was hardly greater than it had been before,"[1] is
characteristic of its author's intense desire to avoid
exaggeration, even in the shape of insistence upon
the effect of an important event, but its very caution
may easily mislead readers.   True it may be that
the chief advantage which the English Crown, and
residence in England, procured for the Scottish King
was safety from personal attack.   But, then, in the
conflict in Scotland, either with the Nobles or with
the Church of that country, the secured possession
of personal liberty might be, and probably was, to
James, decisive of victory.   The Ruthven Raid, the
Gowrie Conspiracy, the attack upon the King and
the Royal household at Edinburgh by the Earl of
Bothwell at the head of some 500 Border ruffians, the
submission of the King to the sacerdotal insolence
and almost pontifical power of Andrew Melville,
many incidents, in short, of James's life until he obtained the Crown of England are sufficient to prove that
to an ambitious King absolute personal safety from
violence might be the necessary condition of successful conflict with daring and unscrupulous opponents.
James, it may be remembered, obtained through
accession to the throne of England not only safety
but wealth.   The power to inflict punishment and also
to confer rewards certainly contributed to the noteworthy triumphs achieved by James during twenty
years of habitual warfare with the leaders of Scottish
Presbyterianism.   The development, further, in Scot-

---

[1] Gardiner, *History of England*, i. 301 (ed. 1883).

land of English methods of government by Council is the characteristic feature of the reigns of the three most powerful Scottish monarchs, James VI., Charles II., and James VII. The Privy Council became, in practice, both the Legislature and the Executive of the Kingdom. It is clear, from the history of his reign after 1603, that James as King of England held far greater power in Scotland than he did whilst merely King of Scotland. The fact may be pressed too far, but it deserves to be remembered constantly.

CHAPTER I

THE CONSTITUTION OF 1603—(THE NON-SOVEREIGN
PARLIAMENT [1])

Chapter
I.

*First Thought.—Under the Constitution of 1603
the Parliament of Scotland was the recognised organ
through which the King exercised his legislative
authority over all his Scottish subjects. The Parliament took, when acting together with the King, a
real part in legislation, but it was a non-sovereign
legislature, owing to its authority being limited by
the existence of two institutions, viz. (1) The Committee of the Articles; (2) the Conventions of Estates.*

AUTHORITY OF PARLIAMENT

FROM 1603, and indeed from a far earlier period, the
Scottish Parliament passed many laws, and often very
good laws, but the Scottish Parliament did not, before
the Revolution of 1689–90, in reality legislate for
Scotland, nor did it take a leading part in legislation; and still less did it govern Scotland. The
Parliament, however, is not to be considered as
entirely destitute of legislative power. It had the
right of rejecting proposed laws, or to use the English
term, Bills, and we may be pretty certain from the
very nature of the Committee of the Articles which

---

[1] As to the difference between a non-sovereign Parliament and a
sovereign Parliament, cf. Dicey, *Law of the Constitution*, chaps. i. ii.

we shall immediately examine, Bills would not often
be laid before Parliament to which the vast majority
of the Parliament gravely objected. The character,
however, of that Committee and its working had
the effect that under the Constitution of 1603 the
Parliament rather registered the laws laid before it
by the King than itself enacted them.

RESTRICTIONS PLACED ON AUTHORITY OF PARLIAMENT

The Committee of the Articles.—This Committee
constitutes by far the strangest and the most original
creation to be found in the whole Scottish constitution. The Parliament had from early times shown
a marked willingness to confer power and even legislative authority upon parliamentary committees.
This disposition to favour government by a body
selected from the Parliament itself reached its height
in the creation of the Lords of the Articles. The
special function of this Committee, which had a close
connexion with the King's Council,[1] was to prepare
the " Articles " which were to be submitted to the
Parliament for acceptance or rejection, and which, if
accepted by the Parliament and assented to by the
King, would become Acts of Parliament. The Committee was, during the period with which we are
concerned, regularly elected at the commencement
of each new Parliament, and had power to act until
that Parliament was dissolved.[2] The Committee
was carefully constructed so as to represent each class
of which the Parliament consisted, and generally

---

[1] R. S. Rait in *Scottish Historical Review*, October 1915.
[2] See Terry, p. 119.

contained somewhere about 40 members, ranging from 39 at the lowest, to 43 at the highest.[1] To understand the position of the Committee, it must be remembered that the Parliament was a One-House Parliament, and was never, as regards numbers, an unwieldy or an unmanageable body. Prior to the Restoration (1660) it never in number exceeded 183, and often consisted of only about 150 members. After the Restoration the Parliament only twice exceeded 190 members, and the Parliament of 1703–6 averaged only about 226 members.

Now, it is pretty certain that, on almost any mode of choice, the Lords of the Articles would bring to the work of legislation as much of official knowledge and of legislative ability as could be found among any 200 Scotsmen of the day.[2] If the Committee had merely prepared the Bills to be submitted to Parliament there would have been nothing very peculiar in its position. The extraordinary importance of the Committee arose from its exercising almost the whole legislative authority of the Parliament. Upon the election of the Lords of the Articles the action of the Parliament for the moment ceased. It did nothing, as a rule, by way of debate or otherwise, till it was summoned, say after a week or two, to meet again. The Bills prepared by the Committee were at such

[1] See particularly Terry, p. 108, and take as an example of the constitution and number of the Committee, the election thereof for 1612, in which the Peers number 8, the Bishops 8, the County members 8, the Burgh members 9, the Officers of State 7, making 40 in all. The Officers of State nominated to sit in Parliament formed part of the Committee. See p. 10, *ante.*

[2] Unless we had sought for them in the General Assembly of the Church of Scotland. But this Assembly was never looked upon with favour by any Stewart before 1690.

meeting submitted to the Parliament, and without debate or amendment accepted or rejected by the Parliament. If accepted and then assented to by the King, they became the enacted law of the land. And acceptance was far more usual than rejection.[1] Parliament, in short, had little voice in the matter of legislation beyond saying Aye or No to the Articles or Bills submitted to it. The person, or body of persons, who could control the Committee possessed for practical purposes the control of the Parliament.

The whole working of such a system depended upon the way in which the Committee was appointed; and from 1603 to 1690 — the revolutionary period (1638–60) of course excepted—the appointment lay in the hands of the King. James (in common with every man who had held executive power since the Committee had come into existence) had taken care, since the time when he held anything like real power, to secure for himself the nomination of the Lords of the Articles.

He achieved this end by a method singularly characteristic of his combined cleverness and unwisdom. In 1606, and probably in 1607 and 1609, he nominated the members who were elected. In 1612 he partially

---

[1] Opposition was not, however, unknown. When Parliament was invited in 1621 to ratify the Articles of Perth, there was opposition even among the Lords of the Articles, and the Act was passed with some difficulty. Of the burgess members, twenty voted for it, and twenty-four against it. The most notable instance of opposition occurred in 1686, when the Parliament did not adopt a suggestion of James VII. that they should pass a Catholic Relief Act, even though the King held out hopes of securing freedom of trade with England (A.P.S. viii. pp. 579-581; cf. Lauder of Fountainhall's *Historical Notices*, vol. ii. pp. 725-727). In 1625, a Convention refused to impose a Customs tax on coal. But there were no Lords of the Articles in Conventions.

revived and partially invented the following plan of appointment. The number of the prelates was small, and they were all the King's creatures. The peers, as he arranged it, were to choose the Lords spiritual who should form part of the Committee. Any bishop whom the peers chose would be, of necessity, not disagreeable to the King. The bishops were in turn to select the peers who should sit for the Committee. They were certain to choose men as obsequious to the King as themselves. These chosen representatives of the bishops and the nobles were to select the most suitable members of Parliament, whether burgh members or county members, to be Lords of the Articles. These again were sure to be persons pleasing to the King. He himself nominated the officials who had, as such, seats in Parliament to places on the Committee.[1] This royal scheme combined the nominal choice of the Lords of the Articles by and from the groups of which the Parliament consisted, with all but absolute security that no man should sit on this Committee of whose appointment the King disapproved.

The practical result of the power thus obtained by the Crown has been described in the following words :

" Except for the few years between the Revolution
" and the Union [1690–1707] the Parliament of
" Scotland was not a deliberative assembly like the
" House of Commons at Westminster. It could
" not be a deliberative assembly so long as the Com-
" mittee on the Articles existed, and when all that
" Parliament had to do was to accept or reject the

---

[1] See Rait, *Scottish Parliament*, pp. 53, 54.

" measures of the Committee.   'During all these Chapter
" ' centuries,' writes Innes, in describing the Scottish   I.
" Parliament from the fourteenth century to the
" seventeenth, 'I am not aware that an article, as
" ' we should say now a Bill, was brought in and dis-
" ' cussed, opposed, supported, and voted upon in Par-
" ' liament, I mean in open and plain Parliament.'"[1]

The language here used is slightly too strong.
After the Restoration, but before the Revolution of
1689–90, Bills presented to Parliament by the Lords
of the Articles were sometimes the subject of debate,
and the precedents of the years from 1640 to 1650
could not be at once forgotten, but instances of
opposition to the decisions of the Lords of the
Articles are very rare after 1663.   The words of
Innes appear to be substantially true ; they at any
rate come a good deal nearer to the truth than the
theory that the constitutional development of the
Parliament during the seventeenth century " may be
" expressed in the statement that, whereas at the
" beginning of the century the House was the servant
" of its Committee, a court of registration of public
" edicts, like the French *Parlements*, it had reduced
" the Committee to a subordinate and dependent
" place long before the century reached its close." [2]
This view, erroneous as it probably is, rests of course
on no ignorance of facts.   It is a misreading of
facts mainly based on the delusion that the progress

[1] Innes, *Lectures on Scotch Legal Antiquities*, p. 145, and see for
the whole passage here referred to, Porritt, ii. pp. 100, 101. Compare
Mackenzie, *Affairs of Scotland from the Restoration of Charles II.,
1660*, pp. 19, 20; Spottiswood's *History of the Church and State of
Scotland*, i. 33.
[2] Terry, p. 15.

towards civilisation must have been in the case of
Scotland, as in the case of England, closely connected
with the continuous development of the national
constitution and a development which, though slowly,
on the whole did tend towards democracy.[1]

It is admitted on all hands that, though to control
the Articles was to control the Parliament, yet "there is
" nothing to prove, indeed there is nothing to suggest,
" that before the middle of the seventeenth century
" the Committee which virtually reduced Parliament
" to the position of a court of registration was re-
" garded as incongruous or otherwise than with placid
" acquiescence."[2] This acquiescence is curious, but it
admits of explanation. Attendance in Parliament
was, before 1689, rather a burdensome duty than a
valuable right. Both to county members and to
burgh members it gave trouble and expense; and
both royal burghs and the King's freeholders in any
county, after they had obtained representation, had
to pay the expenses of their representatives. No want
of good sense can be inferred from the belief that
legislation would be improved by being left in the
hands of forty persons mainly elected by the members
of the Parliament, and constituting the most intelligent and most statesmanlike part of the House. The
submission of the Bills prepared by the Lords of the
Articles to the vote of the House seemed a guarantee

[1] " Constitutional progress was, for [Mr. Hill Burton] as for
" other writers on this subject, the only justification for a nation's
" existence. It did not seem possible that a people could advance
" worthily, except as England had advanced" (Rait, *Scottish Parliament*, p. 4). Scottish history will never be understood by any one
who does not realise that progress in Scotland was real, but at any
rate till 1690 did not follow the same path as progress in England.

[2] Terry, p. 107.

that no measure would pass into law which was
strongly opposed to any conviction or prejudice
shared by the majority of the Parliament.   Nor was
this guarantee in ordinary circumstances illusory.   It
is a modern delusion to suppose that an elaborate
system of representative government is the sole
method by which legislation which may grossly
misrepresent the real wishes of a people can be
averted.   Provided that a country is not ruled by
some foreign power, it is only when the citizens of
a State are divided among themselves by strong
differences of opinion that the need for representative
government is acutely felt.

It is therefore quite intelligible that, for many
years, the authority of the Lords of the Articles was
hardly felt to be a grievance.   The existence of the
Committee might be commended to men of sense
by strong though minor considerations.   It conferred
upon a One-House Parliament something like the
advantages which many political thinkers ascribe to
the existence of a Second Chamber.   It lessened the
evils arising from the absence in the Scottish Parliament of a Speaker.   Englishmen of to-day are not
in a position to blame with severity the ease with
which in early times the Parliamentarians of Scotland
allowed the legislative power of Parliament to slip
into the hands of a parliamentary committee.   Our
modern Cabinet performs most of the functions
discharged by the Lords of the Articles.   The Cabinet
determines in effect what are the Bills which shall
be brought before Parliament.   The Cabinet, if it be
a strong Government, decides which of these Bills
shall pass into law.   The House of Commons still

Chapter
I.

indeed tolerates debate, but the Cabinet can put an end to debate by various forms of closure. The Cabinet quite recently, amid general and possibly reasonable approval, received legislative authority more extensive in some respects than was ever acquired by the Lords of the Articles, for the Cabinet had power, acting in the name of His Majesty in Council, " during the continuance of the present war, " to issue regulations," or, in other words, to make any laws which approve themselves to the Cabinet, " for securing the public safety and the defence of " the realm." [1] The Cabinet, it will be objected, is more or less, though in a very indirect way, appointed by Parliament, and the Lords of the Articles were under the Stewarts practically appointed by the King. Does there live any prophet bold enough to predict that the Cabinet itself may not some day come to be appointed in fact by managers or bosses who may have got firm hold of the party machine ?

However this may be, the acquiescence of Scotsmen in the Committee of the Articles during part at any rate of the seventeenth century is explainable. It is worth notice that the revolutionary reformers of 1640 did not destroy the Committee, but only changed the mode of its appointment. The really noteworthy thing is not the acquiescence in a dangerous experiment of the Scottish Parliament, but the

---

[1] See the Defence of the Realm Consolidation Act, 1914 (5 Geo. 5, c. 8, s. 1), and compare *R.* v. *Sir F. L. Halliday, Times,* Feb. 10, 1916. It is worth noting that while the Cabinet is coming to exercise functions like those discharged by the Articles, the Parliament Act, 1911, goes near to converting our Two-House Parliament into a One-House Parliament.

astounding sagacity which, except on two occasions, forbade the English Parliament to transfer to any other hands than its own its supreme legislative authority. At the bidding of Richard in 1398 the suicidal Parliament of Shrewsbury delegated its legislative power to a parliamentary committee appointed in effect by the King; and it is possible that this instrument of tyranny may have been suggested by the precedent taken from Scotland of the power given some thirty years before to the Lords of the Articles.[1] This crime of the King was avenged and annulled by the dethronement and death of Richard. The Revolution of 1399 anticipated the more glorious and successful Revolution of 1689. In 1539 the dominating personality of Henry VIII. wrung from the Houses the Act which under considerable restrictions gave to royal Proclamations the authority of statutes. This Act was repealed in the next reign.

The English Parliament, except in the two cases already mentioned, held tenaciously to the principle that no Bill should become an Act of Parliament unless it had received both the real consideration and the assent of the two Houses of Parliament. This fundamental dogma of English constitutionalism was verbally recognised, but not in reality maintained, by the Scottish Parliament under the Constitution of 1603. For though in theory laws received the assent of Parliament, no law could be passed to which the Lords of the Articles refused their assent,

[1] But cf. *Acts of the Lords of Council in Civil Causes,* vol. ii., ed. George Neilson and Henry Paton, Introd. pp. xxxiii-xxxviii, H.M. Stationery Office, 1918.

and though the members of the Committee were elected by the Estates which made up the Parliament, their election under the last four Stewart Kings was in the main determined in accordance with the wish of the King.   The Parliament, further, hardly ever, if at all, discussed the laws presented to it by the Committee of the Articles, and as a rule did not reject such laws.   In 1633, laws, which made Charles I. unpopular in Scotland, and did not meet with the approval of his Scottish advisers, were sanctioned by the Committee of the Articles, and were then passed by Parliament in the presence of the King, at the actual meeting thereof.   It seems that some greater opportunity of discussing laws laid before Parliament by the Committee existed after the Restoration, 1660–1690.   But, up to 1690, the regular course of legislation was that no law should be laid before Parliament until it had received the approval of the Lords of the Articles, who were in effect themselves appointed by the King.[1]

Conventions of Estates.[2]—The King from 1603, and indeed from a much earlier period, had admitted authority to summon at any time (except during the meeting of Parliament[3]) a Convention of Estates, which possessed some executive and legislative powers.   A Convention of Estates seems to have been originally a strengthened or reinforced meeting

[1] The unwillingness of William III. to assent to the abolition of the Articles is extremely significant.   The Committee did no doubt avert disputes between the King and the Parliament of Scotland.

[2] See especially Rait, *Parliamentary Representation in Scotland,* iv. ; "Councils and Conventions," *Scot. Hist. Rev.,* April 1915.

[3] There is at least one instance of a Convention meeting simultaneously with a Parliament.   But this event took place in a period of disorder, and it also occurred before 1603.

of the Privy Council. It seems to have derived
additional authority from there being present at the
Convention some of the same persons from each of
the classes which, if a Parliament had been then
summoned, would have formed part of the Parliament. Thus from 1603 to 1690 a Convention might
contain Nobles, Bishops, Commissioners for shires,
and Commissioners for burghs. A Convention exercised three different functions :

(*a*) It gave recognition to a new ruler, and
strengthened the executive and judicial action of
the Privy Council.

(*b*) It passed temporary legislation, though such
legislation was held to need parliamentary recognition, and though a Convention could not strictly
repeal an Act of Parliament, it could explain an Act
of Parliament, *i.e.* it could declare authoritatively
the meaning of a parliamentary enactment.

(*c*) A Convention could grant taxes.

This power constitutes an essential difference
between the position of the Scottish and the English
Parliament. An English Parliament never sur-
rendered its exclusive right to impose taxes upon
England. It was in fact a right of which the House
of Commons was most jealous, and rightly, since it
was the arm by which the House of Commons has
made itself in reality supreme over both the King
and the House of Lords.

It was, however, never disputed that a Scottish
Convention acted in some sense in subordination to
the Parliament.

The fact that a Convention of Estates, though not
enjoying the full authority of a Parliament, could

make a grant of taxes to the King, suggests the following question :

Why did a King under the Constitution of 1603 prefer a Convention of Estates to a Parliament as an instrument of government ?

The answer seems to be that a Convention was at bottom only a Privy Council strengthened by the addition of a certain number of persons who would have had seats in a Parliament if then convoked;[1] and that they were fewer in number than would have been the body of elected members of the Parliament. If this be the case, government by Convention was simply one of several attempts made by Stewart Kings to substitute government by the Royal Council, or, as we should say, by the Privy Council, a body more or less selected by the Crown, for government by Parliament.

Second Thought.—The Constitutions both of 1603 and of 1690[2] *were governed by a principle which lay at the basis of the whole Scottish parliamentary system, namely, that no man who was not a King's freeholder (tenant in capite)*[3] *had a right to appear*

---

[1] The representatives of the burghs and the shires summoned to attend a Convention of Estates were persons elected at the moment to represent definite burghs or shires.

[2] For an explanation of this phrase see p. 28, *ante*.

[3] There was never passed in Scotland any Act like the Quia Emptores which arrested in England the process of subinfeudation. Hence the distinction between King's freeholders (tenants *in capite*) and freeholders holding land of subject-superiors continued to have in Scotland a political and electoral importance not only during the existence of the Scottish Parliament but even after the Act of Union, and an importance which it had apparently lost in England at the time of Henry VI. (1430) when 8 Hen. VI. c. 7 made the 40 shilling freeholders the electors of every county member. Compare Maitland,

in Parliament either personally or by his elected
representative (Commissioner).

The King's freeholders who were entitled to appear in Parliament were either:

(A) *King's freeholders who were entitled and under the obligation to appear in Parliament individually in virtue of their being individually summoned. They were—*

    (a) *Nobles, whatever their title, or*

    (b) *Bishops, when Episcopacy was legally recognised in Scotland.*[1]

(B) *King's freeholders who were not entitled to be individually summoned, but were entitled and*

Constitutional History, pp. 24, 25, especially pp. 86, 87 ; and Anson, *Parliament,* Part I., 4th ed., p. 105.

[1] The attendance of Bishops in Parliament had not ceased with the Reformation of 1560. There is continuous evidence of the presence of Bishops, or titular Bishops, in Parliament from 1560 to 1597, and, in the latter year, an Act was passed that "all ministers "provided to prelacies should have a vote in Parliament." In 1610 these titular prelates received episcopal consecration from the English Bishops. The presence of Bishops in Parliament was continuous from 1560 to 1639, but no Bishop sat in the Parliament of 1639, which abolished Episcopacy. The King assented to this Act in 1641, and, therefore, when the restored Scottish Parliament met in January 1661, no Bishop (even if any had been appointed by that date) could have sat in it. The General Act Rescissory, passed in March 1661, repealed the Act of 1641, and at the opening of the second session of the Restoration Parliament in May 1662 an Act was passed inviting the Archbishops and Bishops, who had been appointed in the preceding autumn, to take their seats. In the Convention Parliament of March 1689 the two Archbishops and seven Bishops were present, but they did not appear after the Convention had been made into a Parliament. It met in June 1689, and rescinded the Act of May 1662. The Episcopal government of the Church was legally abolished in 1690.

The attendance of the titular Abbots and Priors, or of the "Commendators" who received the revenues of the monasteries, also continued after 1560, but there are very few instances of their presence in Parliament after 1603, and these few belong to the years 1607–1617. As the custom was dying out in 1603, we have not included these commendators in our account of the composition of the Scottish Estates.

bound to appear in Parliament by their repre-
sentatives, on the King's summoning a meeting
of Parliament.   Such freeholders were—

    (a) *Royal Burghs, i.e. Burghs created or*
           legally supposed to have been created
           by the King, and

    (b) *Lairds, or, to use an English term, the*
           gentry, holding land as King's free-
           holders without being Nobles.

The Royal Burghs and the Lairds appeared in
Parliament by their elected representatives (Com-
missioners).

This Thought works out the fundamental idea of
Scottish constitutionalism, namely, that the Parliament
consisted of the King's freeholders, whose duty and
privilege it was to give him counsel and support.
This conception lay at the basis not only of Scottish
parliamentary government under the Constitutions
both of 1603 and of 1690, but also of the parliamentary representation of Scotland as it existed after
the Union (1707) until the passing of the Reform
Act of 1832.   The statement, moreover, that none
but King's freeholders could appear in the Parliament
of Scotland is (subject to the very narrowest exceptions) strictly true, but it must never be con-
founded with the totally different statement, which
is untrue, and never formed part of the theory of
Scottish parliamentary government, that every class
of the King's freeholders was represented in the Scottish
Parliament.   Take the following illustrations of cases
in which King's freeholders were not entitled to appear
in Parliament.   No King's freeholder was entitled to

appear by his representative unless he had land of the King of a certain value,[1] nor after 1707 was any Papist entitled so to appear.[2] The eldest son of a Scottish peer had no right to elect a representative or to be elected as a representative of a shire or a Royal Burgh in the Scottish Parliament.

As to the Nobles or Bishops who appeared personally in Parliament nothing more need be said than is contained in this Thought. We are here concerned only with the classes who appear by their representatives, *i.e.* with the Royal Burghs and the Lairds, or gentry. With regard to them, therefore, and with regard to them alone, is it necessary to consider the electoral system existing under the Scottish constitution. Here, however, it is convenient to remark that parliamentary representation grew up in Scotland later than in England, and in Scotland was applied first to the Royal Burghs and next to the Lairds or Gentry, or, to put the same thing in English terms, that the borough members came into existence before the county members. Hence we have to consider

THE ELECTORAL SYSTEM

As to the Royal Burghs.[3]—Subject to a very few exceptions,[4] no town which was not a Royal Burgh

---

[1] See pp. 52-56, *post.*

[2] 1707, c. 8; A.P.S. xi. 426. "The writers on the Election "Laws have been of opinion that the eldest son of a Scottish peer has "no right to elect or to be elected to represent the Commons in "Parliament" (Bell, *Election Laws*, pp. 341, 342).

[3] See as to the Royal Burghs, Rait, *Scottish Parliament*, pp. 26-33; Terry, pp. 47-63; A.P.S. ii. 95; Terry, *Scottish Parliament*, p. 168.

[4] These exceptions are Glasgow, Arbroath, St. Andrews, Brechin, and Dunfermline. Their representation was an exception to the

had during the existence of the Scottish Parliament a right to send representatives (or, to use the Scottish term, commissioners) to represent it in Parliament. The Parliament in 1326, and possibly at an earlier period, contained representatives of the Royal Burghs, and before 1690 it was settled that each Royal Burgh, except Edinburgh, was entitled to send to Parliament one representative or commissioner. Edinburgh, however, had the right to send two representatives.

It is probable, though not certain, that at an early date the commissioners representing a Royal Burgh in Parliament were elected by the Town Council.[1] An Act of Parliament, however, ordained in 1469 that upon the expiry of the term of office of existing magistrates and councils in Burghs, and thereafter, the new Town Council should be elected by their predecessors, and that both bodies should combine to elect the officers of the burgh.[2] This rule applied to commissioners who represented a Burgh

---

general theory of the constitution that Parliament was composed solely of tenants in chief, and their inferior status long delayed their admission to Parliament. That they were admitted at all is probably to be explained by their wealth, which made it desirable that they should pay the taxes levied on Royal Burghs. All of them became Royal Burghs—Arbroath in 1599, and the others in the course of the seventeenth century. Rait, *Scot. Hist. Rev.*, Jan. 1915, pp. 126, 128.

[1] See Rait, *Scot. Hist. Rev.*, April 1916, p. 314.

[2] Terry, p. 57. It is true that the Burghs had constitutions, or, as they were called, "sets," materially different from each other, and that here and there a Burgh, *e.g.* Stirling, did not follow the provisions of the Act of 1469. But on the whole the Act was obeyed. A Royal Burgh might be created by the King at any time before the Act of Union. Cromarty was created a Royal Burgh in 1700.

Note, further, that the burgesses of a Royal Burgh held on burgage tenure, and therefore were themselves King's freeholders. The number of Royal Burghs rose at the time of the Act of Union to 67. See Terry, pp. 48, 49.

in Parliament, since such commissioners seem to have been regarded as officers of the Burgh. Hence, under the Act of 1469, the Burgh Councils themselves, as a rule, were elected, as we should say, by co-optation. The members of these self-appointed Councils as a rule re-elected one another. Hence the commissioners for a Burgh were elected not by the citizens of a town, but by the Council thereof, which became more and more a close and narrow body. This point should be the more carefully borne in mind because the system of election of commissioners for the Royal Burghs was not ended by the Act of Union, but was made rather more close and was brought more under the influence of the Government[1] than before the passing of the Act, and continued in this condition up to the passing of the Reform Act, 1832.

Royal Burghs, it is important to recollect, were subject to certain burdens, and had some special advantages.

They were bound to pay their commissioners for attendance in Parliament; they also stood in a position as to financial liabilities quite different from that of an English borough. It is approximately true to say that the Royal Burghs bore the whole burden of the taxation imposed upon the estate of burgesses, and when, in 1693, an Act was passed legalising the extension of trade privileges to the non-royal Burghs of barony or regality, any burgh availing

[1] The grouping of the Burghs into districts under the Act of Union gave the election of the representatives of a Burgh into the hands of four or five electors, each of whom was elected by one of the four or five Burghs grouped into one district, and these four or five electors must have been easily influenced by the Government of the day.

itself of the Act had to " relieve the Royal Burghs of
" a just proportion" of the taxes imposed on them
by Parliament.

The privilege of the Royal Burghs was that they
enjoyed a practical monopoly of the trade of the
Kingdom.   This privilege, however, was, to some
extent, put an end to by Act of Parliament in 1672,
and though this abolition was modified by subsequent
Acts, the privileges of the Royal Burghs as to trading
gradually fell into desuetude though they were not
legally abolished until 1846.[1]   On the whole, it
would seem that, at all events down to 1672, the
privileges in point of trading exceeded in value the
special burdens imposed upon the Royal Burghs.

Royal Burghs were, in the seventeenth century,
legally restricted in their choice of commissioners to
" trafficking merchants and indwellers " of the burgh.
This restriction is probably to be traced to a jealousy
of interference by the barons of the shires in the affairs
of Royal Burghs, which is traceable from the end of
the fifteenth century.   Acts of Parliament passed in
1487 and 1535 ordered that all who held any jurisdiction in burghs must be resident indwellers.   This
regulation was extended by the Convention of Royal
Burghs, in 1574, to burghal commissioners to Parliament, and, in 1587, the decision of the Convention
of Royal Burghs received Parliamentary confirmation
in an Act prescribing that every member of Parliament
must " duly occupy the place of the self estate
" wherein he commonly professes to live and whereof
" he takes his style."   The Convention of Royal Burghs
had frequent reason to complain of the neglect of this

[1] Hume Brown, iii. 54.

rule and imposed fines upon the burghs concerned,
and it was not until 1681 that an elected member
was held to be disqualified because he was not "a
" residenter or trafficker in the burgh." This rule, for
the first time rigidly enforced, fell almost immediately
into desuetude, and it was, in fact, effective only
between 1678 and 1689.[1]

The Lairds or Gentry (Barons of the Shires).[2]—
The words Lairds or Gentry conveniently include all
the King's freeholders who were small landowners,
and were neither Nobles nor Bishops; they are often
called "Barons of the Shires." This term is employed ambiguously. It sometimes means the King's
freeholders in a shire, who elect commissioners (or, as
we should say, members) to represent them in Parliament, and this is the sense in which the term is
usually employed in this essay. But it sometimes, on
the other hand, means the commissioners elected by
such freeholders to sit in Parliament (or, as we should
say, county members). This confusion must have
arisen the more easily from the fact that originally
any commissioner elected to represent such King's
freeholders was required to be a King's freeholder,
though this requirement ceased to be insisted upon
after 1707. The title is in some respects a good one,
as it recalls the important fact that all the King's freeholders at one time formed part of the nobility. They
all had the right, and were under the duty, of attending, when summoned, the King's Parliament. The
attendance in practice was felt to be more of a burden
than a privilege. Various Acts of Parliament were

---

[1] Rait, in *Scot. Hist. Rev.*, Jan. 1915.
[2] See Terry, p. 19 *et seq.*

Chapter
I.

from time to time passed with a view to induce
attendance of King's freeholders in Parliament, and
to liberate the poorer of such freeholders from the
burden of attendance, or rather, from the penalties
for non-attendance. Such Acts are an Act of 1425 ;[1]
an Act of 1427 ;[2] an Act of 1503, 1504.[3] The effort,
however, to compel attendance failed, though there
was a large attendance of poorer King's freeholders or
smaller Barons in 1560,[4] who claimed a right to sit and
vote. The claim was admitted on that occasion, but it
continued to be extremely doubtful for the next
quarter of a century.[5] In 1587 the foundation was
laid by an Act of that year for a genuine representation
of the King's freeholders, not being Nobles or Bishops,
'in each shire or county.

The result of the legislation of 1587 was to create
a true representative system, and thereby to commute
the ancient right, or to discharge the obligation, of
personal attendance in Parliament on the part of the
King's freeholders below the degree of Lords of
Parliament, a right which had ceased to be exercised.
A similar attempt to create a representative system
had been made, unsuccessfully, in 1427, and the
provisions of the Act of 1427 were re-enacted in 1587,
with the addition of the limitation to 40 shilling
freeholders.[6] The number of commissioners for each

[1] See Rait, *Parliament*, p. 21.
[2] Terry, pp. 167, 168 ; A.P.S. ii. 15.
[3] A.P.S. ii. 244 ; Terry, p. 169.
[4] See Rait, *Parliament*, pp. 23-25.
[5] Rait, in *Scot. Hist. Rev.*, Jan. 1915, pp. 118-119.
[6] The Act of 1587 illustrates the carelessness with which Scottish
Acts were drawn. It only indirectly provides that the King's freeholders voting at any election for a shire shall be 40 shilling
freeholders of the King. The 40 shilling qualification for voting as
a King's freeholder was inserted in a petition of 1585 (A.P.S. iii.

shire—one each for Clackmannan and Kinross and two for each of the remaining shires—was determined by the Act of 1427. The restriction of the franchise to holders of land of the value of 40 shillings by the Old Extent introduces a term which is one of the puzzles of Scottish history. The Old Extent was a mysterious and still unexplained assessment of Scottish freeholders. Its date is unknown, and it is probable that it does not represent any single national assessment. In 1541 the value of the Old Extent was fixed by the Court of Session at one-fourth of the current or existing valuation,[1] but in

---

422 : None to have vote in the election of the commissioners of the shire, but "such as has fortyshilling land in free tenantry holden of the " King "). The petition of 1585 was not strictly an Act of Parliament: for it was merely remitted to the King for further consideration, but the preamble of the Act of 1587 recited it as if it were operative and so, constructively, created the limitation of the franchise. The Act of 1587, further, does not contain any reference to the Old Extent, or assessment, by reference to which the value of the estate, *i.e.* whether it was of the value of 40 shillings or not, was to be determined. It seems, however, to have been, from 1587, assumed that the value of the estate giving the vote was to be determined according to such Old Extent. The vote given to 40 shilling free-holders may possibly have been borrowed from England, but, oddly enough, the existence of 40 shilling freeholders as county electors in England, and the existence of 40 shilling freeholders as electors in Scotland, had a quite different effect in each of the two countries. The 40 shilling freeholder in England was a man who at a time when an election took place owned land valued at an annual rent of 40 shillings. Through the gradual decrease in the value of money the 40 shilling freeholder became a person who held land at a lower and lower rent. The 40 shilling freeholder in Scotland meant a man who held land which had been three or four centuries earlier valued at a rent of 40 shillings, *i.e.* land which, *e.g.* in 1800, was of far greater worth than 40 shillings. Hence the votes of 40 shilling freeholders became in England a democratic part of the English consti-tution, whilst in Scotland the votes of such freeholders meant generally the votes of men whose land was, *e.g.* in 1800, worth far more than 40 shillings. See Mathieson, *Awakening of Scotland*, Introd. pp. 17, 18.

[1] Skene, *De Verborum Significatione*, sub voce " Extent."

actual practice it was often returned as low as one-tenth or as high as one-half. All that can be said with certainty is that, in the seventeenth century, the Old Extent represented a varying fraction of the rental as expressed in current money. The Old Extent was used for valuations for purposes of national taxation, and New Extents were made for valuations for the payment of reliefs and other feudal dues.

The effect of the limitation of the franchise to men holding from the King land of 40 shillings annual value Old Extent was to confine it to tenants by the ancient feudal holdings of ward and blench. Feuars (*i.e.* perpetual lease-holders) of Royal lands, although freeholders of the Crown in feu-holding, could not come within the scope of the Act, because (1) their lands were not assessed by the Old Extent, and (2) they attended, not the Sheriff Courts where the elections were to be held, but the Courts of the Bailiffs or stewards of the lordships in which their feu-holdings were situated. It was not until 1661 that an Act was passed which gave the franchise to feu-holders, both of old Crown lands and of ecclesiastical lands which had been annexed to the Crown, if their yearly rental amounted to £1000 Scots after the deduction of feu duties.[1] The dignity of the old tenancy-in-chief by ward-holding and blench-holding was maintained by the greatly higher qualification required from feu-holders. The restriction to men holding land directly from the Crown was, of course, strictly maintained outside the County of Sutherland.[2] In 1681 the qualification required from

---

[1] A.P.S. vii. 235.
[2] Cf. p. 56, *post.* Cf. also Porritt, ii. 80, and 16 Geo. II. c. 11.

feu-holders was reduced from £1000 to £400 Scots.
By that date the Old Extent had ceased to be a basis
of taxation, and the 40 shilling freehold might therefore
become difficult to prove. Forty shilling freeholders
were therefore allowed to claim the franchise on the
alternative qualification of £400 of annual rent.[1]
This arrangement provided for cases in which a return
on the basis of the Old Extent could not be produced,
but it did not meet the case in which lands which
in 1681, or later, were worth £400 of annual rent
or more, had been actually returned at some previous
date at under 40 shillings of Old Extent. This
defect was remedied by an Act of 1743 (16 Geo. II.
c. 11).

The 40 shilling franchise was held by "those
" publicly infeft in property or superiority and in
" possession of a 40 shilling land of Old Extent holden
" of the King." This did not mean actual corporeal
possession of the lands, nor did it necessarily imply
the enjoyment of any pecuniary return from them.
What was required by the law was the superiority
alone, and the superiority was sufficient, even if the
whole pecuniary profit arising from the land had
been alienated. The possession of a vassal was in
the eyes of the law possession by his superior. This
distinction led to many anomalies, and to the creation
of fictitious votes, especially in the eighteenth century.[2]

It should be noted further that the extension of
the franchise to feu-holders of the Crown in 1661 did
not at first make a feu-holder eligible for election
as a commissioner to Parliament, for, in 1678, an
election was declared void on the ground that the

[1] A.P.S. vii. 353.   [2] Cf. Appendix A.

commissioner was not a 40 shilling freeholder of the King.[1]

There was one exception to the rule which confined the county franchise to tenants-in-chief. In 1631 Charles I. granted a charter to the Earl of Sutherland, creating Sutherland (which had been part of Ross-shire) a separate county, with the Earls as hereditary sheriffs.[2] Almost the whole land in the shire belonged to the Earl, and the Charter gave power " to the free barons *and the other inhabitants* of the "county" to choose commissioners to Parliament. The grant thus made was ratified by Parliament in 1633,[3] and in 1641 and 1661 these " other inhabitants " were required by Parliament to contribute to the payment of the commissioners. No regulation about the qualification for a vote in Sutherlandshire was made until 1743 (16 Geo. II. c. 11), when it was enacted that the qualification should be £200 Scots of valued rent, *i.e.* one-half of the qualification demanded in the other counties.

Third Thought.—How far under the Constitution of 1603 were the people of Scotland represented in the Scottish Parliament ?[4]

From a modern and democratic point of view it might be said that they were hardly represented at all. The Nobles and the Bishops did not sit in Parliament as representatives of any class. The elected members of Parliament represented none but landowners, and

[1] A.P.S. viii. 217.
[2] Reg. Mag. Sig. viii. No. 1847 ; cf. also vi. No. 1170.
[3] A.P.S. v. 62.
[4] Cf. also Chap. VIII. *post.*

represented an important but a very limited class
even of landowners, namely, the King's freeholders,
who were neither Nobles nor Bishops, but were
either members of a Burgh Council or were tenants
in capite of land which at an early period in
Scottish history was worth 40 shillings. It is
manifest that the electoral body must under the
Constitution of 1603 have always been a very small
one. The members of the Burgh Council and the
40 shilling freeholders taken together must at all
times have made up a very limited part of the
inhabitants of Scotland. One result, and a very
important result, of the limited number of elected
members who sat in the Scottish Parliament, combined
with the circumstance that the Scottish Parliament consisted of one House only, was that the representatives
of the 40 shilling freeholders, or, to use an English
term, the county members, did not become united,
as they did in England, with the members for the
Royal Burghs, or, to use an English term, the borough
members. Hence in Scotland the representatives of
the Commons had nothing like the power of opposing
either Nobles or Kings which was possessed by the
county members and the borough members who made
up the English House of Commons. Between 1603
and 1690, the Scottish Parliament, as our readers
must remember, did little more than register the
proposals or Bills laid before it by the Committee of
the Articles, though after the Restoration (1660) it
did to a certain extent debate such proposals.

It would nevertheless be a mistake to suppose
that even under the Constitution of 1603 the wishes
of the Scottish people obtained no representation in

Parliament.[1] One must never forget that even a despotic ruler may represent, and has often represented, the feeling of the people whom he has governed ; and this is even more true of a Parliament which in any sense and to any degree is elective. There is no reason whatever to suppose that the Nobles, the King's freeholders, and the Royal Burghs did not often, we may almost say usually, share the feelings of the Scottish people. It would be the greatest historical mistake, though it is a blunder often committed, to assume that the Scottish Parliament, however constituted, did not often, and to a great extent, represent the feelings of the people of Scotland. But though this statement is true it must constantly be modified by the circumstance that the people of Scotland should in this connexion be taken to mean the Scottish Lowlanders. It has been again and again remarked that the Highland clansmen were far more interested in promoting or opposing the power of the Duke of Argyll than in concern for the maintenance or the overthrow of the Revolution Settlement.

[1] See Burton, viii. 187.

CHAPTER II

THE CONSTITUTION OF 1690 : (A) THE PARLIAMENT—
(B) THE GENERAL ASSEMBLY OF THE CHURCH
OF SCOTLAND—(C) THE PARLIAMENT AND THE
GENERAL ASSEMBLY

*First Thought.—The Revolution Settlement had
one character in England and another and essentially different character in Scotland.*

REVOLUTION SETTLEMENT IN ENGLAND AND IN SCOTLAND

THE Revolution Settlement, to use an old term of
1689, was in its nature a different movement and
produced different results on each side of the Tweed.

In England it was at bottom a conservative
movement. Charles II., and James II., his brother,
meant to restrict the authority of Parliament, and to
a considerable extent achieved that end. James II.,
further, attempted to bestow on Romanism in England an authority at least equal to the power of the
Protestant and Episcopalian Church of England ; in
all probability he desired, if possible, to bestow upon
Romanism the supremacy to which, as a sincere
Roman Catholic, he deemed that form of religion to
be entitled. In resistance to this tyranny, Englishmen, whether Churchmen or Dissenters, were united.

In 1688 the seven Bishops, Tories though most of them were, became for the moment popular heroes, and have nearly been enshrined by the genius of Macaulay in the political hagiology of the Whigs. Neither the Church of England nor its clergy were deprived by the Revolution of a pennyworth of property, or of any religious prestige. The Revolution freed the Church of England from the fear of subjection to the Pope, and from the dread of being compelled to share her rank, her emoluments, her bishoprics, and her livings, with the priests of the Church of Rome. True it is that the Revolution conferred, gradually and indirectly, complete religious toleration upon most English Dissenters. But it did not give them political equality with Churchmen, whilst it did secure to the Church her existing rights or privileges. This conservative aspect of the Revolution Settlement may be overrated, and has been exaggerated by Burke when denying to the Revolutionists of France any similarity to the Whigs who brought about the Revolution of 1688. Yet the doctrine laid down by Burke, in his Appeal to the old Whigs, contains a vast amount of truth. No true revolution can be wholly conservative ; but the "glorious revolution" for which Burke, and even George III., had nothing but praise, was one of the most conservative movements that have ever been styled revolutionary.[1]

In Scotland, on the other hand, the Revolution Settlement was in the strictest sense a revolutionary movement. It closed once and for all the conflict,

---

[1] " An Appeal from the New to the Old Whigs in consequence of
" some late discussions in Parliament relative to the Reflections on
" the French Revolution" (Burke, *Works*, vi. (ed. 1808), p. 69).

carried on with varying fortunes on each side for more than a century, between Kings determined to force Episcopalianism on the people of Scotland, and the Scottish people, who were equally determined that Presbyterianism should be the national and established religion of their country. From the Restoration till 1685 the triumph of the Crown seemed to become more and more complete. The Revolution gave a final victory to the Scottish people. It established, or re-established, Presbyterianism as the one national religion. As a visible sign and consequence of this triumph, the General Assembly of the Church, which had never been allowed to meet for between thirty and forty years, was reassembled, and has met year by year to the present day as the acknowledged representative of the National Church. Let an Englishman never forget that in 1690 Scotsmen still remembered the "killing time" (1679–80), when Claverhouse and "Bloody Mackenzie" made martyrs of Covenanters who commanded the veneration of Presbyterians. The Revolution Settlement in reality gave to Scotland a new constitution. Of this constitution the Scottish Parliament and the General Assembly of the Church of Scotland each formed an essential part; they each, in different spheres and in different degrees, exerted both governmental and even legislative power.[1]

[1] This statement is made in language which no one would have used in 1690, and is not employed by Scottish historians, but it states in modern terms what seems to have been an indubitable fact.

(A) The Parliament

Second Thought.—From 1690 to 1707 the Scottish Parliament did in fact exercise predominant authority in the making of laws and, more or less, in the administrative and executive government of Scotland.

This Parliament, which first met after the flight of James II. from London, assembled as a Convention of Estates, on March 14, 1689. On June 5, 1689, it was declared by Act of Parliament to be a Parliament, and its legislation as a Convention was ratified.[1] It is conveniently known as the Convention-Parliament, and it sat from session to session, though with long intervals, till 1702. From the time and mode in which it was elected it represented mainly the Whigs of Scotland, or more accurately the persons who in 1689–90 approved of the Revolution.[2]

From the moment that the Convention assembled in 1689 its members were determined to assert their right to an authority at least equal to the power exerted or claimed by the two Houses of the English Parliament. This intention is clearly shown by the language of the Claim of Rights.[3] The celebrated Claim in the first place enumerates the numerous offences and crimes whereby James II. did " invade " the fundamental constitution [of the Kingdom of " Scotland], and altered it from a legal limited " monarchy to an arbitrary despotic power; . . .

[1] A.P.S. ix. 98.   [2] Macaulay, *Hist.* iii. p. 246.
[3] 1689, c. 28, A.P.S. ix. 38, 39.

" whereby he hath forfeited the right to the Crown, " and the throne is become vacant."[1]   With this part of the Claim we need not for the moment trouble ourselves.   The Claim in the next place enumerates a large number of rights and liberties which have been and ought to be respected by every Scottish King, and it offers the Crown to William and Mary, and the heirs of their body, on their undertaking to maintain and respect such rights and liberties.

Now the matter to be noted is that the long list of these rights and liberties in effect is a demand for every power belonging to the Parliament of England. If it be said that the Scottish Parliament thereby demands authority far exceeding any power which it actually possessed and exercised before the Re- volution of 1689, the truth of the assertion cannot be denied.   But in this mode of action the Scottish Parliament had precisely followed in the steps of the English Parliament.   The authority of the English Parliament has again and again been extended, not under the form of a request for new powers, but under the nominal demand that an existing power which has not been fully respected should henceforth be treated as part of the known law of the land. The Scottish Parliament in short in the Claim of Rights adopted the astounding method of " retrogressive progress " which has greatly favoured the growth, but also has disguised from many historians and constitutionalists the true nature, of the power obtained by the Parliament of England.[2]

[1] 1689, c. 28, A.P.S. ix. 38, 39.

[2] As to this method of retrogressive progress see Dicey, *Law of the Constitution* (8th ed.), p. 17.

This imitation of English parliamentary practice shows that Scottish statesmen had, towards the end of the seventeenth century, come pretty well to understand the working of English constitutionalism. They pretty well knew that when the Claim of Rights had been duly accepted, as it was, by William III.[1] and his consort, it would be necessary to give some parts thereof a reality which they had never possessed, and by so doing to bring about considerable changes in the law, or the practice of Scottish parliamentary government. The immensely increased authority or, as it may fairly be called, the new life, conferred upon the Parliament by the Revolution, in so far as it depended upon definite changes of law or of legal custom, was due to two causes: the first cause, which is comparatively unimportant though very noticeable, is that no Convention of Estates[2] has ever again been held in Scotland. Hence was put an end to the attempt of the Stewart Kings from 1603 to 1689 to substitute for parliamentary government the government of the King, advised by the Secret Council,[3] or to use English expressions, by the Privy Council, chosen by the King. The other cause, which is by far the more important, is the abolition

[1] As King of Scotland, he was, and was always described as, William II.

[2] See as to Conventions of Estates, p. 42, *ante.*

[3] This was the ideal of government apparently cherished by James, who had no wish to dispense with the use of learned councillors. He appreciated the wisdom of Bacon, and probably the learned pedantry of Coke, when they fell in with his own political notions. See especially as to Bacon's enthusiasm for the Union between England and Scotland, p. 119, *post,* and as to Coke, *Calvin's Case* (1608), 7 Rep. 5a. Re *Stepney Election — Isaacson* v. *Durant* (1886), 7 Q.B.D. 54; *United States* v. *Wong Kim Ark* (1897), U.S. Rep. 649; Dicey, *Conflict of Laws* (2nd ed.), Rule 22, p. 166, and note 4.

by the Convention - Parliament of the famous Committee of the Articles.[1]

The newly acquired freedom of debate and independent legislative power was exercised at once freely and effectively. Numerous are the illustrations of legislative energy. No one of these is more striking than the Act which put an end to the Articles. The method by which this grievance was got rid of is as full of significance as its actual abolition. The Convention of 1689 even before it was turned into a Parliament denounced the Articles as a grievance.[2] The Parliament was apparently more eager to achieve its own freedom from the control of the King or his Government than even to re-establish the national and Presbyterian Church of Scotland, though, to ordinary Scotsmen outside the sphere of parliamentary conflict, the religious independence of the Church must, we may be sure, have seemed of greater importance than the abolition of checks on parliamentary legislation. King William himself, naturally, and perhaps wisely, wished to retain a committee the authority whereof would go far to ensure the harmonious action of the Crown and of the Parliament, and was the more necessary

[1] 1690, c. 3, A.P.S. ix. 113; App. 142b. Even the excited loyalty of the Restoration had not prevented the Parliament from wishing to diminish the power of the Articles. "The Act re-"establishing the Lords of the Articles provided that any petitions not "presented by this Committee might be brought directly before Parlia-"ment" (Mathieson, *Politics and Religion in Scotland*, ii. 182 ; A.P.S. vii. 10-87).

[2] See A.P.S. ix. 45a and Burton, vii. 329. "The Estates of the "Kingdom of Scotland do represent that the Committee of Parliament, "called the Articles, is a great grievance to the realm ; and there ought "to be no Committees of Parliament, but such as are freely chosen by "the Estates to prepare motions and overtures that are first made in "the House" (Burton, vi. 329, note 1).

because the King was bound, if he could, to pursue a course of action both at home and abroad which should not be condemned by the Parliament either of Scotland or of England. Yet though the Revolution Settlement was hardly as yet in any way really determined, and certainly reposed upon very shaky foundations, the Scottish Parliament would not meet in any way William's desire to maintain a valuable instrument of government. It is hardly an exaggeration to say that, from June 5, 1689 to May 8, 1690, the conflict between the King and the Parliament continued unsettled. The King was willing to offer more than one form of compromise; he was willing to allow that the Articles should be *bona fide* elected by the three Estates.[1] The House of Parliament would hear of no compromise. An adjournment, or, as we should say, prorogation, from August 2, 1689 to April 15, 1690, allowed the passions of partisanship to cool down, and intelligent Whigs perceived that the conflict between the King and his only genuine supporters imperilled the whole success of the Revolution. An agreement between the Crown and the Parliament was a necessity. On the subject of the Articles the King gave way entirely, subject to a merely nominal concession that might slightly save his dignity. On the 8th of May 1690, the Act abolishing the Committee of the Articles was touched with the sceptre, and that body vanished for ever from the history of Scotland.[2]

---

[1] The three Estates, after the Bishops ceased, under the Revolution Settlement, to sit in Parliament, came to mean, in Scotland, the Nobility, the Commissioners for Shires (county members), the Commissioners for burghs (borough members).

[2] A.P.S. ix. 113, App. 142.

The legislation, indeed, of the Scottish Parliament under the Constitution of 1690 was, from the day of the meeting of the Convention - Parliament to the passing of the Act of Union, effective. This is seen clearly in its dealing with the Church. An Act of 1689 had already abolished prelacy in the Church of Scotland,[1] and the Bishops were thereby expelled from the Parliament. An Act of 1690 provided for restoring Presbyterian ministers who had been thrust from their churches since January 1, 1661. An Act of the same year abolished Church Patronage.[2] A further Act of 1690 ratified the Confession of Faith and settled the Presbyterian Church government of the Church of Scotland.[3] Nor did this legislative authority of Parliament in any way diminish, but tended if anything to increase, during the whole seventeen years which ended with the passing of the Act of Union in 1707. An Act of the Scottish Parliament sanctioned the Darien scheme.[4] And here we may note that the whole series of events connected with that disastrous scheme show that the Parliament not only legislated but also substantially governed. The same lesson may be learned from the Act Anent Peace and War of 1703 [5] and the Act of Security of 1704,[6] and from all the steps taken by the Parliament of Scotland which were intended to make certain that Scotland should either obtain a union with England on terms which the Scottish people could accept, or should be able on the death of Anne to

[1] A.P.S. ix. 104.
[2] A.P.S. ix. c. 53, pp. 196, 197 ; see also Balfour of Burleigh, p. 114.
[3] A.P.S. ix. 133, *et seq.* App. 147b.
[4] See Chap. III. *post.*   [5] See Chap. IV. *post.*
[6] See Chap. IV. *post.*

reassert complete national independence. From 1690 to 1707 the Scottish Parliament was not only a dominant legislature, but also to a great extent the Government of Scotland. Another change, which is little else than the same fact looked at from a different side, is very noticeable. Under the Revolution Settlement the Parliament gained new vigour; it became the scene of public debate; it began to produce parliamentary statesmen. This is specially obvious to any one who studies with care the debates with reference to the Act, or, as we should say, the Bill, for the Union between England and Scotland. Lord Queensberry, though like all politicians he made some blunders, displayed the special gifts of an old parliamentary hand. The Duke of Hamilton, who led, or misled, the Jacobites in their opposition to the Union, betrayed a singular lack of parliamentary skill, and Lord Belhaven, with his celebrated speech, anticipated before its time the possession of that rhetorical talent which now and again has been used to excite popular sentiment or prejudice against elaborate, and sometimes well-considered plans of reform. Indeed, it must be admitted that the sudden development of the importance of parliamentary government in Scotland almost immediately produced the admitted defects of what is now known as party government. The celebrated Club created at Edinburgh immediately after the Revolution seems to have been little better than a body of Whigs who had formed a machine for obstructing the government of the day in order to promote the personal interests of the members of the Club. For this object it allied itself even with Jacobites, sank into discredit, and

lost all influence.[1]   And to this day it is a matter
of dispute whether the *Squadrone Volante*,[2] composed
of men who by obtaining a casting vote which might
be decisive in favour of or against the passing of
the Act of Union, was simply a faction bent on the
attainment of advantages for its members, or, as is
possible, a body of politicians who saw that the union
of England and Scotland was a necessity, and determined by skilful manœuvring to ensure the passing of
an Act which they knew hardly commanded popular
support.   However this may be, we come round, by
whatever line of thought we pursue, to the conclusion
that under the Constitution of 1690 the Parliament
of Scotland occupied a new position of hitherto
unobtained authority.

A reader should note especially that while under
the Constitution of 1690 the authority of the Parliament was immensely increased, the form and
constitution of the Parliament itself were very slightly
changed.   In this respect the Parliament remained,
speaking broadly, from 1690 to 1707 the same as the
Parliament held in 1686 under the Constitution of
1603.   The two exceptions or limitations to the
accuracy of this statement are—

(1) The Act Abolishing Prelacy 1689 put an end
to the appearance of Bishops in Parliament, with the
result that the Scottish Parliament ceased from that
date to contain any representatives of any Church or
ecclesiastical body whatever.   But to Scottish Presbyterians this arrangement was perfectly satisfactory,
owing to the recognition given to and the annual

---

[1] See Macaulay, iii. 298, 377, 378, 695.
[2] See Chap. IV. *post.*

meeting of the General Assembly of the national and Presbyterian Church of Scotland.

(2) An Act of 1690 gave additional representatives to the greater shires.[1]

Third Thought. — The Parliament of Scotland never during the whole of its existence became the centre of Scottish public life.[2]

This statement is by far the most important

---

[1] It is perhaps noteworthy that the next Act in the Statute Book gave some privileges to the royal burghs (1690, c. 15, A.P.S. ix. 152) but no additional representation.

[2] Almost every powerful and progressive State has, it is worth notice, been at some period of its history specially and predominantly influenced by some one institution or body. The greatness of the Roman Republic was, so to speak, typified by and summed up in its Senate, and the Senate held a position of eminence for years after the Republic had been succeeded by the Empire. The French monarchy, under the *ancien régime*, became the centre of the public life of France. The Revolution, which in one sense destroyed the royal dynasty, really bore witness to the tremendous influence among Frenchmen of monarchical tradition. Tocqueville's doctrine that Napoleonic Imperialism revived and strengthened the power and the governmental system of the *ancien régime*, may be pressed too far, but is no mere paradox. It is, after all, nothing but a different way of looking at the desire of Frenchmen for equality which is the fundamental dogma embodied both in Tocqueville's *Democracy in America* and in his *Ancien Régime*. It is clear enough that the centre of English public life was to be found in the Houses of Parliament. The Restoration, it has been well said, was the victory as much of the Parliament as of the King. Is it not again clear that in the United States the Presidency rather than the Houses of Congress has become almost unconsciously the true centre of the country's political existence? This fact is proved both by the way in which, in spite of the language of the Constitution, the President is now chosen not by elected electors but in reality by the vote of the whole people. It is also proved by the extent to which happily and rightly enough Washington in one age, and Lincoln in another has been made the popular hero, or even the Saint of the Republic. The truth is that it is rarely that an assembly such as the English Parliament enlists popular enthusiasm. It is rather to be wondered that the Parliament of England has succeeded than that the Parliament of Scotland has failed in becoming the centre

conclusion put forward in this essay with regard to
the character of the Parliament of Scotland. It
contains at least half the explanation of the success,
under apparently unfavourable circumstances, of the
Union between England and Scotland. The doctrine
here laid down is simply the reinforcement, from a
slightly different standpoint, of the view put forward
twenty years ago by one of the present writers[1] that,
while the progress of England is contained in the
progressive development of her Constitution, the
equally undoubted progress of Scotland depended
upon many circumstances and institutions which have
little to do with her parliamentary system; and that
Scottish history may thus " be useful as exemplify-
" ing the limitations of the doctrine that national
" progress can be measured by constitutional advance."
An Englishman who tries to write a constitutional
history of England finds it difficult to define the limits
of his subject; for he soon perceives that the growth
of the Constitution can hardly be separated from any
circumstance whatever which promotes the development of the English nation, and ultimately of the
British Empire. A Scottish historian, on the other
hand, such as Burton, is troubled, and occasionally
misled, by the impossibility of closely connecting the
progressive civilisation of Scotland with the improve-
ment of her parliamentary machinery, or with the
issue of grand constitutional conflicts. This contrast

---

of a country's political existence. If, however, any one explanation of
this want of success is necessary, it must mainly be found in the historical certainty that at a most critical period of Scottish history, the
General Assembly of the Church of Scotland far better than the Scottish Parliament represented the aspirations and convictions of Scottish
Presbyterians.

[1] Rait, *The Scottish Parliament before the Union of the Crowns.*

and the fact which gave rise to it—namely, that the Scottish Parliament never won for itself the heart of the Scottish people—are equally certain.

How then did it happen that the Parliament of Scotland never became the centre of the public life of Scotland in the sense in which the English Parliament became the centre of, or might almost be identified with, the public life of England? How, in short, did the Parliament fail to become the typical representative of Scottish nationalism? The enquiry, in whatever shape it is put, admits of a pretty clear answer. The Scottish Parliament, from its nature and constitution, never rendered to Scotland the immense service which England owes, in part at least, to her Two-House Parliament. This service was the formation of that union between the gentry and the people of England which lay at the bottom of the authority gained by the Commons of England, and enabled the Commonalty and the Parliament, of which the Commons became the most important part, again and again to come forward as defenders of the rights of the people.

The comparative powerlessness of the Scottish Kings might at first sight seem to have been favourable to the growth of parliamentary power. But in fact it was an all but fatal hindrance to the extension of parliamentary government, and this for two reasons. On the one hand, no King, until the Union of the Crowns (1603), was sufficiently powerful to compel an alliance between the people and the nobility for the purpose of resisting royal despotism; and on the other hand, so long as the power of the King could obviously be defied by powerful nobles

or chiefs, it was impossible for the Parliament to
increase its own power, as did the Parliament of
England, by transferring to itself the impressive, if
not unlimited, authority of the Crown.   Add to all
this that Scottish history produced at no time whatever anything like the premature and imperfect
yet real constitutionalism which existed under the
Lancastrian dynasty.   The mere tradition of this early
constitutionalism was, even under the Tudors, of
great value to the English Parliament.   At lowest, it
compelled these powerful and self-willed monarchs
to govern under and through parliamentary forms ; it
thus kept alive and gave importance to parliamentary
discussion.   But, as already pointed out, the Scottish
Parliament was, before the Revolution of 1689–90,
hardly, if at all, a field for parliamentary debate.
We can therefore to a great extent explain how it
happened that the Parliament knew little of great
constitutional conflicts, and produced no Henry the
Second, no Simon de Montfort, no Edward the First,
no Hampden, and no Sydney.   A silent Parliament
can hardly move the heart of any people.

This failure of Parliament to become the embodiment of Scottish nationalism is illustrated and proved
by the whole course of Scottish sentiment.   Fidelity
to the Stewarts has often risen to tragic passion,
though the Stewarts were men whom it was far
easier to adore or die for when they were exiles, than to
trust at home as kings.   The Highlanders, when they
blackmailed the industrious and peaceable farmers,
were detested by Lowlanders as ruffians and robbers.
But, within sixty years after the Rebellion of 1745,
the Highland chiefs and their clans were transformed

into the national heroes of Scottish romance. This transformation was so complete that when George IV. paid his one visit to Scotland (1822), he flattered the citizens of Edinburgh by showing himself there, as is recorded, in the costume of a Highlander, and also by giving the toast of "the Chieftains and Clans "of Scotland" as equivalent to that of the Scottish people.   The Church of Scotland has deservedly excited the enthusiastic devotion of thousands of Scotsmen.   The one Scottish institution which never, except possibly for a moment before the passing of the Act of Union, kindled the enthusiasm of the Scottish people, has been the Parliament of Scotland.

No man took a wider or a more generous interest in the annals of his country than did Walter Scott. His heart and his imagination, though scarcely his judgement, were devoted to the Jacobites. He created the romance of the Highlands.   But, if he liked the Cavaliers, he also understood and commemorated the zeal and fortitude of the Covenanters ; and, if he has kept alive a very dubiously deserved sympathy with the misfortunes and the tragedy of Queen Mary, he has left in *The Heart of Midlothian* an undying picture of the warm affection, the spirit of self-sacrifice, the energy and the truthfulness, nurtured by Presbyterianism among the noblest of the Scottish peasantry. But it would be difficult to find in the whole of his works a single picture of the Scottish Parliament, or a single tribute to its virtues.   No Scotsman less resembled Walter Scott than did Thomas Carlyle. He was at bottom a Scottish Calvinist born out of due season.   He would have been in his proper place among the sterner Covenanters of 1638, or among the dogmatic preachers who drove Leslie's army to defeat at Dunbar.   Now, Carlyle was absolutely blind to the best side of parliamentary government, and, though an undiscriminating eulogist of Cromwell, could never understand the reverence for the parliamentary tradition of England which was felt as strongly by the Protector as by Hampden or by Locke.   The explanation is clear.   Carlyle was a typical Scotsman.   He had never inherited the tradition of loyalty to Parliament handed down by each generation of Englishmen to its successor.[1]

Here it may be objected that, under the Constitution of 1690, the Parliament was not only the Government of Scotland but the field of free and vehement debate.   We might, therefore, have expected it to become, in this period, the centre of Scottish public life.   The reply to this objection lies also ready at hand.   The influence of the Parliament was balanced, if not over-balanced, by the influence of a rival assembly which had already gained and had long possessed the trust and affection of every Scottish Presbyterian.   This rival was the General Assembly of the Church of Scotland.   The Assembly was nominally indeed, like the Parliament itself, primarily a Court, but it was in reality something very like a legislature.   It was from 1690 to 1707 at least as powerful a body as Parliament.   It was admirably constituted so as to represent the Presbyterians of Scotland.   It debated in public, it was not, as its name

[1] Is it too fanciful to suggest that the Toryism of Hume's *History*, though originating in dislike to religious enthusiasm or intolerance, may be connected with the absence in Scotland of this parliamentary tradition?

might suggest to Englishmen, a body of clerics. The
Presbyterian minister was not a priest. If the minister
sometimes possessed more than priestly authority, the
General Assembly contained, as it now contains, almost
as many elders (laymen) as ministers. The Assembly,
both before and after the Union, was the school in
which a preacher of eminence might be turned into a
statesmanlike orator. Knox in one age, Melville in
another, Carstares at the time of the Union, Chalmers
at a day which some men still living can remember,
were the ministers and the statesmen of the Church
of Scotland. The existence of the General Assembly
is not the only cause, but it is a chief cause of the
Parliament during its last eighteen years of existence
failing to become the centre of the public life of
Scotland; and we may add that the Act of Union
which merged the Parliament of Scotland in the
Parliament of Great Britain secured the prolonged
existence and continued authority of the General
Assembly.

A critic may well object to this explanation of the
failure of the Scottish Parliament to gain the hearts
of the Scottish people, that there is a curious analogy
between the position of the Parliament of Ireland,
which existed from 1782 to 1800, under what is
popularly called Grattan's Constitution, and the
position of the Scottish Parliament under the Constitution of 1690, and that the Irish Parliament, in
spite of many unfavourable circumstances, did become
before the Union the centre of Irish public life. The
analogy is certainly curious. Under the Constitution
of 1690 the Scottish Parliament obtained complete
legislative independence and practically also the

power to govern Scotland, and at the end of seventeen years consented to the Union between Scotland
and England. Under Grattan's Constitution, which
may be well called the Constitution of 1782, the
Irish Parliament obtained by the repeal or modifica-
tion of Poynings' Law complete legislative independence, and at the end of eighteen years assented to the
legislative union of Ireland with Great Britain. But
the Irish Parliament was during those eighteen years
the centre of the public life of Ireland. Why, one asks,
did the Irish Parliament succeed where the Scottish
Parliament failed ?

The answer to this question is apparently the more
difficult to find because, on the face of the matter, the
Irish Parliament suffered under disadvantages from
which the Scottish Parliament was free. The Irish
Parliament was not, while the Scottish Parliament was,
an institution of really national growth. The Irish
Parliament was imported by invaders or settlers from
England. It could hardly at any time have been
considered to represent the whole people of Ireland.
From 1691 to 1800 it did not contain among its
members a single avowed Roman Catholic. From
1691 to 1793 no Roman Catholic could vote for
a Member of Parliament. The rebellion of 1798,
crushed in many cases with savage cruelty, greatly
embittered Irish Protestants against Irish Catholics,
and Irish Catholics against Irish Protestants. The
defects of the Irish Parliament were patent. Its
virtues, even as represented by the learning and
fairness of Lecky, are at best hypothetical. But the
Irish Parliament even before 1782 had become the
centre of Irish political life. What is the explanation

of this historical paradox ?   It is not in reality hard to find.   The Parliament of Ireland was no doubt the legislature of the colonists rather than of the native Irish.   It became after 1691 the Parliament of the Protestants, and not of the Roman Catholics. But it had several advantages denied to the Parliament of Scotland.   The Protestant settlers from England had more or less inherited parliamentary ideas brought from England.   Among other ideas they had succeeded to the Lancastrian tradition. The Irish asserters of parliamentary power fought mainly if not wholly for the rights of the Protestants. But before 1782 the Parliament had become the asserter of Irish Nationalism.   The names of Molyneux, of Lucas, of Swift, were known to every Irishman. The oratory of Flood and Grattan was famous throughout Ireland and Great Britain.   These men had, in or out of Parliament, by writing or by speech denounced real and grievous wrongs done to Ireland. And the Irish Parliament before 1782 was a Parliament of speakers.   All classes of Irishmen had been educated in the belief that, whatever its defects, their Parliament was the body by whose action the wrongs of Ireland would find redress.   Lastly, the Irish Parliament shared with the Parliament of England all the prestige which belongs to a legislature which has no rival.   There was in Ireland no General Assembly whose existence detracted from the authority of the Parliament.

(B) The General Assembly

Fourth Thought.—Presbyterianism at the end of the seventeenth and during a great part of the eighteenth century was among the mass of the Scottish people supported by two beliefs which were then common to most Protestants.

The one was the conviction[1] that every word in the Bible, from the first verse in Genesis to the last verse of the Revelation of St. John, was dictated by Divine inspiration. The next belief, or rather assumption, was that every honest reader of the Bible could find revealed therein a divinely appointed form of Church government which ought to be accepted by every true Christian; and from these premises Scottish Presbyterians then deduced the conclusion that Presbyterianism, as practised in Scotland, was of Divine origin. Each of these beliefs has now lost much of its hold on the Protestant world; they are not apparently shared by the authorised leaders of the Established Church of Scotland.

"The government of the Church by Kirk-Sessions, " Presbyteries, Synods, and the General Assembly, " stands midway between Episcopacy and Congre- " gationalism, and gives an organic unity to the " Church in all parts of the country. Each form of " government may have certain advantages over the " others, and sometimes may meet individual prefer- " ences, and in practice does advance the higher " religious life of the souls of men, though none can

[1] See *Rise and Development of Presbyterianism, etc.*, by Lord Balfour of Burleigh, p. 38. For suggested modifications of this statement see Lindsay, *History of the Reformation*, pp. 453-467.

" claim exclusively a Divine sanction or authority."
This is the language of the *Church of Scotland
Year Book*, 1917; it is the expression of common
sense and of Christian charity.   But it would have
provoked the stern denunciation of Andrew Melville.

A competent critic will not deny that these
two beliefs explain the position and influence of the
General Assembly of the Church of Scotland, and
that the history of the Assembly records a singular
and successful experiment in the working of representative government, and also an early attempt to
carry into practice a definite theory as to the right
relation between Church and State.

*Fifth Thought.—Under the Constitution of 1690
the General Assembly of the Church of Scotland
was, as it still is, one of the most representative and
popular forms of Church government.*

The Assembly was really representative, since it
from time to time gave expression to the predominant
opinion of Scottish Presbyterians; it was popular,
since it admitted all classes of Presbyterians to a
share in the government of the Church.

The truth of these two statements is best established, first, by a consideration of the electoral system
under which the General Assembly was chosen; and,
secondly, by the consideration of the evidence of
history as to the character of the Assembly.

As to the Electoral System.—The Presbyterian
plan of Church government under the constitution
of 1690 depended on the existence of certain Courts [1]

---

[1] The Provincial Synod is purposely omitted since it had no
connexion with the election of the General Assembly.

or Assemblies, which each, though in different
degrees, combined governmental, legislative, and
even executive action,[1] and in 1690 and long before
that date Scotland was divided for ecclesiastical
purposes into districts which may conveniently be
called presbytery districts, and each such district consisted of parishes. The Courts with which we are concerned were (going from the lowest to the highest):

(i.) *The Kirk-Session.*—It consisted of the parish
minister, or, to use English terms, the parish clergy-
man or parson, who was *ex officio* the moderator or
chairman thereof, and of elders. These, be it remarked,
were not elected in the ordinary sense of that word.
They were rather selected by the existing Kirk-
session; the Kirk-sessions were, in other words, filled
up by co-optation, and it lay in the power of each
Kirk-session to fix its own number, nor was it obliged
to fill up vacancies when they occurred. The elder
chosen was always a man—no woman could be an
elder—and a communicant; before acting as an elder he
was set aside for the office by the minister. He held
office as long as he fulfilled the conditions thereof.

(ii.) *The Presbytery.* — It consisted of (*a*) the
ministers of the several parishes in each presbytery
district over which the Presbytery had jurisdiction,
and of the Professors of Divinity of every royal
university, if any, within such district, and (*b*) one
elder for each Kirk-session within such district, elected
annually by the Kirk-session.

(iii.) *The General Assembly.*—It was annually

---

[1] Compare Rait, *Scottish Parliament*, pp. 95, 96, and Balfour, pp.
47, 48, 64-67, and see also *Report of Archbishops' Committee*, pp.
192-197.

elected, and at the end of its sittings annually dissolved.   It consisted of (*a*) ministers and elders elected by each of the several presbyteries in Scotland; (*b*) two elders annually elected by the Town Council of Edinburgh, and one elected by the Town Council of each of the other 69 royal burghs; (*c*) a minister or an elder elected annually by the four royal universities.

Every member of the General Assembly sat there by virtue of election.   No one of them owed his seat to his holding any office, whether ecclesiastical or civil, whilst, on the other hand, no man who was a Presbyterian was ineligible to the Assembly by reason of his rank or of his holding any office.   A Duke, a Judge of the Court of Session, a lawyer, could be, and often has been, a member of the General Assembly, and so might be the poorest of parish clergymen, a laird possessed of a small estate, or a gardener who was not a landowner at all.   The General Assembly again was no mere clerical body.[1] It has generally, though not invariably, contained a majority of parish clergymen, but it has always contained a large body of laymen.   Herein it has differed entirely from the English Houses of Convocation, which have never represented any class of Englishmen except the clergy.

This bare outline of the manner in which the General Assembly was elected under the Constitution of 1690 suggests the likelihood that the Assembly would in fact represent the dominant opinions of

---

[1] "The first General Assembly of the Kirk of Scotland met at "Edinburgh, constituted of six ministers and thirty-five laymen" (Balfour of Burleigh, p. 23).

Scotland, in so far, at any rate, as Scotland was a
Presbyterian country. The Assembly was, on the
face of it, a body far more fitted to represent the
dominant national opinion than was the Parliament
of Scotland, for the Parliament, though it did in a
rough way, under the Constitution of 1690, give
better expression to Scottish feeling and opinion
than many critics have supposed it to have given,
did technically represent nothing but the opinion
of the King's freeholders and of the close and non-
representative councils of the Royal Burghs. And
the same outline also shows that the Assembly
admitted, though in unequal degrees, Presbyterians
of all classes to a share in the government of the
Church.

As to the Evidence of History.—The action of
the Assembly has in general harmonised with the
course of Presbyterian opinion. The Assembly was
active in promoting the education of the people; the
Assembly saw to the distribution of poor relief; the
Assembly took in hand the provision of religious
instruction for the Highlands, and effectively converted to Presbyterianism the large number of
Roman Catholics to be found there in 1690; add
to this that on secular topics, not falling wholly
within spiritual matters to which alone the authority
of the Assembly extended, parliamentary legislation
was often clearly carried at the instigation of the
Assembly. In 1697 the Barrier Act[1] passed by the
General Assembly anticipated the principle of the

[1] The laws enacted by the Assembly were, under the Constitution
of 1690 and still are, called Acts. The word "Act" in England is
confined to laws passed by Parliament.

Chapter
II.
Referendum, and in effect provided that no law passed by the General Assembly which permanently affected the rules or the constitution of the Church could become a law until the Act, or, as we should say, the "Bill," having first been passed by the Assembly, had been ratified by the majority of the presbyteries, and had then been passed again by the Assembly which met in the next year. No provision could be more obviously popular than a law which thus makes the sanction of the presbyteries necessary for the enactment of any important piece of ecclesiastical legislation. The representativeness of the Assembly under the Constitution of 1690 is visible even in its errors. The Church of Scotland shared the universal enthusiasm in favour of the calamitous Darien scheme. The General Assembly did not protest against the intolerance, the cruelty, and the gross straining of the law which caused the execution of Aikenhead for the alleged but unproved crime of reviling or cursing the Supreme Being or some Person of the Trinity. The case disgraced every man connected directly or indirectly with the government of Scotland in 1696, and any one must painfully regret to find no record of a protest by William Carstares against this act of iniquity; but who can doubt that whatever intolerance was to be found in the General Assembly represented (in so far as it did not fall short of) the intolerant spirit prevalent among the mass of Scottish Presbyterians? One effect of the Act of Union was that the Scottish National Church outlasted the Parliament and remained substantially unchanged until the present day. But it is worth noting that, if we allow for

the indirect effect of the Disruption in 1843, the
General Assembly has continued to display its representative character for the two hundred and more
years elapsing since 1707. The ill-fated restoration
of Church Patronage by an Act of the British Parliament in 1712 gives, curiously enough, an opportunity
of tracing the extent to which the General Assembly
inevitably represented the course of public opinion,
or, in other words, the precision with which the
feeling of the Assembly on the whole corresponded
with the feeling of the nation. The Assembly at
first protested year after year against the restoration
of Church Patronage by the British Parliament in
1712. But the gradual predominance of secular
interests told after a time no less upon the Assembly
than upon the people of Scotland. The rule of
Robertson and the Moderates, which was in many
ways of benefit for the country, for it discouraged
intolerance and encouraged the cultivation of literature and science, checked the growth of religious
fervour, so that in 1783, when the power of the
Moderates reached its utmost strength, the Church
Parliament refused any longer to treat patronage
as a grievance, or, in other words, the General
Assembly reflected the prevalent sentiment of the
day. The gradual rise of the High-flyers or Evangelicals, which from about the end of the eighteenth
century till 1843 became more and more visible in
the Assembly, represented a change of religious
sentiment or conviction, both in the Assembly and
in the country. Even the Disruption of 1843, more
accurately than was then perceived, either by the
Free Churchmen who conscientiously left, or by their

opponents who with equal conscientiousness remained within, the Established Church, represented a deep-rooted difference of opinion which inevitably split the Scottish nation into two parties.[1] That the Constitution of 1690 in regard to the Scottish Church had succeeded both in representing the Scottish people and in giving each class thereof an active interest in the management of their own Church is proved by one consideration. The Reform Act of 1832 swept away almost the last relics of the Scottish Parliament. The Act was passed amid much excitement and discord, but, even at a time of almost revolutionary passion, hardly a single eminent Scotsman, and certainly no Scottish party, demanded a change in the constitution of the National Church.

Why, it may be asked, is not this fifth Thought summed up in the statement that the General Assembly was one of the most democratic forms of Church government? The avoidance of the ambiguous word "democratic"[2] is, however, intentional. The term democracy is connected with ideas foreign

---

[1] "The whole commotion ... arose from the spirit of the eighteenth "century attempting to crush the worn-out spirit of the seventeenth, "and the spirit of the seventeenth lifting up its head and leaving its "sting before it died. It was the battle of progression and retro-"gression" (Mathieson, *The Awakening of Scotland*, p. 147, citing Cunningham's *Church History of Scotland*, ii. 446).

[2] Compare Cromwell's address to the Short Parliament (Stainer, *Speeches of O. Cromwell*, pp. 105, 106): "Truly God hath called you to "this work by, I think, as wonderful providences as ever passed upon "the sons of men in so short a time; and truly I think, taking the "argument of necessity, for the Government must not fall, [taking] the "appearances of the will of God in this thing, I am sure you would "have been loathe it should have been resigned into the hands of wicked "men and enemies; I am sure God would not have it so. It comes "therefore to you by way of necessity, it comes to you by the way "of the wise providence of God, though through weak hands."

alike to the spirit and to the working of Scottish Presbyterianism. Calvinism indeed, in Scotland and elsewhere, has inspired resistance to political and religious oppression. But it is in its essence as much an aristocratic as a democratic creed.[1] The conviction that the blessing of Heaven is reserved for the Elect points to the conclusion that the Elect, that is, the good and the wise, are the rightful rulers of a Christian State. This belief condemns off-hand the *vox populi vox Dei* which is latent in modern democratic sentiment. The constitution again of which the General Assembly is the final outcome rests at bottom on the self-elected Kirk-sessions, *i.e.* bodies not depending on popular election. And that constitution, be it observed, attained two objects rarely if ever achieved under modern forms of popular government. The one is that both the members and the electors of the General Assembly were men all of whom could read, and many of whom had received a good substantial education and had felt the stimulus of ardent theological controversy based on Biblical knowledge ; the second object was that the Scottish peasantry should be accustomed to active participation in matters concerning the Church, under which term were included the education of the people and the management of poor relief.

[1] Protestantism in France was accepted rather by the nobility or the gentry than by the common people. The populace of Paris during the massacre of St. Bartholomew (1672) and during the siege by Henry IV., as in later days during the massacres of September 1792, exhibited the worst features of democratic passion.

Sixth Thought.—Under the Constitution of 1690 the General Assembly possessed, both legally and morally, high authority.

An Englishman of the twentieth century finds it difficult to realise how extensive was this influence. The General Assembly possessed wide and indisputable legal powers. On all matters of religious doctrine the General Assembly had, as the supreme and final court of appeal from every lower Church Court, final and absolute jurisdiction. The Assembly, again, possessed on all religious matters and on all matters purely concerning the Church a very large amount of legislative authority. The Barrier Act, as already pointed out, showed its indisputable power to regulate the government of the Church. The Assembly had in its hands every matter connected with either popular or university education throughout the country. The Assembly could direct inferior Courts to give effect to its own powers, and it was certain that its directions would be obeyed. The Assembly, unlike the Parliament, was elected and met every year. Each Assembly, in this, too, unlike the Parliament, before its dissolution appointed a Commission chosen from its members which, until the meeting of the next Assembly, could exercise many of the powers of the Assembly, and was bound generally to provide for preserving and maintaining all the rights and privileges of the Church. This Commission perpetuated to a great extent the governmental power of the General Assembly during the time which elapsed between its annual meetings. But the moral power of the

General Assembly transcended its extensive legal
powers. Around the Church and the Assembly as
its representative had collected all the romance of
Presbyterianism and its martyrs. Formal excom-
munication by the Church Courts was, it is said,
little used after 1690, and after 1712 the Civil Courts
completely ceased to enforce civil penalties upon
excommunicated persons. But through the exclusion
of a parishioner from the Communion, and by other
means, the Church Courts could impose very severe
punishment upon a man deemed open to the censure
of the Church. We all now know by recent experience the true meaning of a boycott. The victim who
" was left severely alone " underwent a more agonising
punishment than could be inflicted by any Court
known to the law of the land. Imagine a boycott
in the South of Ireland backed by the authority
of every Roman Catholic parish priest. One can
thereby form some idea of the position of an offender
who during the seventeenth and a great part of the
eighteenth century was repelled by the Kirk-session
from communion with and was proclaimed unworthy
of associating with his fellow-Christians. Add to all
this that under the Constitution of 1690, and indeed
for many years after the Union, the Presbyterian
pulpit influenced Presbyterian opinion at least as
strongly as does the press of Great Britain now
influence the opinion of the electors, and the Presbyterian pulpits were under the control of the
General Assembly.

(C) THE PARLIAMENT AND THE GENERAL ASSEMBLY

Seventh Thought.—Under the Constitution of 1690 the Parliament and the General Assembly of the Church of Scotland each gave effect to the doctrine of Scottish Presbyterianism with regard to the relation of Church and State.

"The [Scottish] State indeed was a Christian "State, and had duties as such, in co-operation with "the Church. But already the Reformed Church in "Scotland was beginning to develop its characteristic "view of their relations as independent, co-ordinate, "and correlated powers. No churchman was to haunt "courts or to accept civil office ; the civil magistrate "had his own place divinely appointed ; but so had "the Church ; and in its own place it must be free.

"Yet when two divinely appointed institutions are "working in the same country towards the same end, "human frailty and corruption inevitably produce "friction. The attempt to establish a line of de-"marcation between their respective jurisdictions, "and the settlement of disputes arising from alleged "transgressions of that line by one side or the other, "form a large part of Scottish history, both political "and ecclesiastical." [1]

[1] Balfour, *Rise of Presbyterianism*, p. 41. This doctrine of "the "separation of powers" in the relation between Church and State, as understood in 1690, may roughly but logically be thus summed up :

1st. There has from an early date in the Reformation existed, and there ought always to exist, in Scotland a national and Presbyterian Church of Scotland maintained by, and existing in alliance with, the State.

2nd. Such Church and State ought each to be, the one in the spiritual sphere, and the other in the temporal sphere, supreme ; the

These words describe, from an historical rather than
from a logical point of view, the doctrine entertained
in 1690 by the Scottish Church as to the relation
which, in Scotland at any rate, ought to exist between
Church and State : they are in a very special sense
applicable to the opinion on this matter held between
1690 and 1707 by the best and wisest of Presbyterians either in the Parliament or in the General
Assembly.

The following points deserve notice :

(1) In 1690 the history of Scotland singularly
facilitated the attempt, which on the face of it was
difficult of achievement, to maintain at the same
time in one and the same country a national Church
and a national Legislature which should possess, each
in its own sphere, supreme and co-ordinate authority.
For the success of such an experiment it was a great
advantage that for a century and more the Scottish
people should have been accustomed to the co-existence
of two representative bodies, whereof the one (the
General Assembly) was concerned with the religious
interests, and the other (the Parliament) was mainly
concerned with the political interests of Scotland.
But Scottish history proved also that these two
bodies might easily come into hostile collision with
each other.   The peculiarity of the situation is that
in 1690 the General Assembly (which for our present
purpose may be identified with the Scottish Church)
and the Parliament each stood in mutual need of the

Church being ultimately represented by the General Assembly
thereof, and the State by the Parliament of Scotland.

3rd. Such Church and State ought each to support the other
within its proper sphere.

other, and were each inclined not to press too far the
claim to supremacy. The General Assembly had for
a century and more been a far truer representative of
popular feeling than the Parliament which usually
had registered the decrees of the King. But the days
when the Assembly could nullify an Act of Parliament
and prohibit all persons from obeying it "as they
" would not incur the wrath of God and the censures
" of the Kirk" [1] were past and gone. The guidance of
the Church had led to disaster. The defeat of Dunbar
was due to the influence of the Church and its
ministers. The credit of the Assembly was injured
by the lasting feud between Resolutioners and Pro-
testers. The attempt, first to enforce Presbyterianism
upon England, where it was almost equally hateful
to Cavaliers, to Independents, and to the mass of the
English people, the fighting for Charles II. as a
Covenanted king, and the childish faith which at
the Restoration leading Presbyterians placed in
the most untrustworthy of kings, and their con-
sequent failure to obtain any security whatever,
either for the maintenance of the Presbyterian Church
in Scotland or for the toleration of Presbyterian
dissenters in England, had hopelessly shaken confidence in the political wisdom of the Church.

Sincere Presbyterians, moreover, must have felt
that the interference of the Assembly in merely secular
politics was as much opposed to Presbyterian doctrine
as was the interference of the Parliament or of the
ordinary law courts with the spiritual or religious

[1] Act of the General Assembly, July 28, 1648, in *Acts of the
General Assemblies of the Church of Scotland, 1638–1842*, p. 170. Cf.
Mathieson, *Awakening of Scotland*, p. 8.

concerns of the nation.   To every Scottish Presbyterian, however, the Revolution would have been
worthless had it not re-established the national
Church and re-assembled the General Assembly.   The
Parliament had, on the other hand, through the
abolition of the Lords of the Articles, for the first
time become, from a legislative point of view, a
supreme legislature; but the Scottish Parliament
had not behind it, as had the Parliament of England,
an immemorial tradition of legislative sovereignty;
nor had it the popular authority which belonged
to the General Assembly as the defender of national
Presbyterianism against royal aggressions, which were
supported by the wealth of England.   Parliament
had indeed joined in the expulsion of James, but this
tardy patriotism could not obliterate from any one's
memory recent displays of parliamentary and judicial
subserviency to the will of despotic kings.   The
authors, too, of the Revolution, whether in the Parliament or in the Assembly, had everything to fear from
the not improbable restoration of the Stewarts.   Hence
every Whig and Presbyterian felt that the Assembly
and the Parliament must act in harmony with one
another.

(2) It was a time for compromise, and both the
Assembly and the Parliament wished to obviate any
conflict between Church and State.   They were each
prepared to make concessions.   It is often assumed
that the clergy were constantly bent on the increase
of their own authority.   But this idea is opposed to
plain facts.   The Assembly acquiesced in restrictions
imposed by Presbyterian doctrine on the power of
ministers of religion.   No Presbyterian minister after

1690 ever took a direct part in parliamentary or official life. Even during the utmost heat of the controversy over Church Patronage it was admitted that, while the induction of a minister might concern the Church and the Church Courts, the due payment of his salary was a matter within the jurisdiction of the civil Courts, and subject to the control of Parliament; yet the parish clergymen in Scotland certainly were and remained for many years miserably underpaid.

In 1693 Scotland was threatened with a direct conflict between Church and State. The once terrible question whether the General Assembly could of its own authority determine its meeting and its dissolution, or could be summoned and dissolved only by the Crown, called for decision. A compromise was arrived at which suited either view, and thenceforth has been followed. When the session comes to an end the Moderator fixes a date at which the next Assembly should meet, but he does this without reference to the Royal Commissioner who represents the Crown. The Royal Commissioner immediately afterwards also announces the date, being the same as that already fixed by the Moderator, at which the next Assembly will meet, and makes no reference to the Moderator. The General Assembly under these proceedings is dissolved and the next General Assembly is summoned to meet. The rights, whatever they may be, of Church and State are treated with due respect. The acceptance by the General Assembly of this pleasant fiction of constitutionalism is a visible sign of the spirit of compromise. Parliament, on its part, went far to meet the wishes of the Presbyterians.

In 1690 the General Assembly was assembled or re-　
assembled after having been in abeyance for well-　
nigh forty years, and has met yearly ever since.　In
1693 Parliament passed an Act establishing or re-
establishing Presbyterianism as the national religion
of Scotland.　In 1690 it abolished Church Patronage.
In 1697 it passed an Act for the settling of schools
which permanently regulated the education of the
country in accordance with the wishes of the Church.
No attempt was made accurately to define the limits
which divided the authority of the Church in spiritual
matters from the authority of the State in secular
matters.　But it was clearly understood by all Presbyterians that in all matters purely spiritual, *e.g.*
matters of religious doctrine, the General Assembly
had supreme power, and that in all matters purely
secular, *e.g.* questions of property, the Parliament had
supreme power, and further that the Assembly and
the Parliament, or, in other words, the Church and
the State, should co-operate for the benefit of the
nation.

We reach therefore the following conclusions : The
Constitution of 1690 gave practical effect to the
Presbyterian doctrine of the proper division of powers
between Church and State ; and this result was
achieved because it was favoured by the historical
position both of the General Assembly and of the
Parliament.

Eighth Thought.— Under the Constitution of 1690,
the position and the character of both (1) *the Par-*
liament, and (2) *the General Assembly of the Church*
of Scotland, facilitated the passing of the Act of
Union.

As to the Parliament.—Under the Constitution of
1603 the Parliament, controlled as it was by the
King, would not have possessed anything like the
national or moral authority needed by a body called
upon to take part in the first great achievement of
really British statesmanship, namely, the Treaty
between the Parliament of Scotland and the Parliament of England which merged them both in the one
common British Parliament, and thereby constituted
the truly united state of Great Britain. If the Constitution of 1603 had lasted unchanged till 1707 it is
more than doubtful whether a Parliament controlled
and manipulated by Anne through the Committee of
the Articles could finally have transformed the two
kingdoms of Scotland and England into the one
Kingdom of Great Britain, for a Parliament controlled
by the Queen could hardly have been felt by Scotsmen to be capable of expressing the will of the Scottish
nation. It was a happy circumstance, therefore, that
in 1707 the Parliament had come without any great
change in its constitution—except the abolition of the
Lords of the Articles—to represent roughly but truly
the sense, if not exactly the sentiment, of the Scottish
people.

It was also a fortunate circumstance that the
Scottish Parliament with this increased authority
was, owing to the Act of Union, not suffered to exist

for fifty or sixty years longer, or even say till 1745.
It is quite possible that a Parliament, which might
have at last become the real centre of Scottish public
life, would have hesitated at building up the common
Parliament of Great Britain.   The personal ambition
of Scottish statesmen might in that case well have
seemed to point in the same direction as patriotism,
for it must never be forgotten that to many Scotsmen,
living at the time of the Union, the Treaty of Union
seemed, though the appearance was delusive, to con-
tradict the traditions of Scottish history.   It was,
moreover, a happy circumstance that between 1705
and 1707 the Parliament, not only of Scotland but
also of England, was to an unparalleled degree led by
sagacious statesmen.   The wisest politicians of both
countries knew that the Union would create a State
infinitely more powerful than the two countries which
it brought permanently under the rule of one Parliament and of one King.   We may be sure, to speak
plainly, that the wisdom of Somers, supported by
Marlborough, and the sagacity of Queensberry, guided
by the good sense of Carstares, could far more easily
discover the path both of safety and of prosperity for
the whole inhabitants of Great Britain than what is
sometimes called " the great heart of the people."
It is indeed more than possible that if, in 1707,
the electors either of Scotland or of England had
been polled man for man and had been called upon
to decide whether the Treaty of Union should
become an Act of Parliament, there would have
been obtained in each country a majority against
the most beneficial statute which the Parliament
of either country has ever passed.   But it should

be remarked that so disastrous a vote would in each country have been caused by a combination of parties who disliked the Union on totally different grounds. Every Jacobite would have voted against it because he detested the Revolution Settlement. Many Whigs might have voted against it because they disliked something in the Union itself, and could not be made to see that it was the one certain security against a restoration which both in England and in Scotland would overset the Revolution Settlement. It is certainly fortunate for the whole of Great Britain that the union of Crowns, without the union of Parliaments, was not suffered to exist long enough for the Parliament of Scotland to acquire the hold over the patriotic imagination of Scotsmen which the Protestant Parliament of Ireland had in 1800 acquired over the imagination of Irish Roman Catholics to whom it had never conceded the right to sit in the Parliament at Dublin.

As to the General Assembly.—The Act of Union was unpopular in Scotland in 1706–7. At that date the opinion prevailed among Tories, and also among many Whigs, that the policy of Union was a ministerial chimera, for it was certain that a coalition of extreme Presbyterians with Jacobites might at any moment cause the Scottish Parliament to throw out the Act of Union; and both Jacobites and Presbyterians had solid grounds for disliking the Act. The Jacobites saw in it a bar to the possible restoration of the Stewart kings. To Presbyterians the creation, by the Act, of a British Parliament, in which the representatives of Scotland would form an insignificant minority, inspired the not unreasonable dread

of an attempt by that Parliament to force Episcopalianism upon the Scottish people.   In this state
of things it depended upon the action of the
General Assembly whether the Bill for creating the
Union should become the law of the land.   The
Jacobites were only too ready to form a coalition
with the Church, but the General Assembly was in
reality alarmed by the ominous enthusiasm of
Jacobites for the rights and privileges of the Presbyterian Church.   The General Assembly realised
that union with England constituted, in fact, the
best safeguard of Scottish Presbyterianism, and acted
with consummate foresight and prudence.   It secured
the passing of an Act by the Scottish Parliament for
securing all the rights and privileges of the national
and Presbyterian Church of Scotland.   Having
obtained for that Church every safeguard which an
Act of Parliament could possibly give for the security
of the Church, the General Assembly in fact, if not
in form, gave its support to the Act of Union.   To
the Whigs of England and of Scotland and to the
General Assembly is due the creation of the United
Kingdom of Great Britain.

*Ninth Thought.—How far has the Presbyterian
doctrine as to the relation between Church and State,
established and worked out under the Constitution
of 1690, been beneficial to Scotland?*

It is, in the first place, objected by some modern
jurists that it is impossible at one and the same time
to maintain the sovereignty and the independence
of the Church, and also the sovereignty and inde-

pendence of the State.   The best reply to this objection is afforded by history.   During the existence
of the Constitution of 1690 (1690–1707) Church
and State in Scotland did in reality keep within
their respective spheres as understood by Presbyterians.   True of course it is that if in one State two
persons, or two bodies, each are considered to be
in the strict sense sovereign, *i.e.* each to have power
of legislating on every topic whatever, a logical contradiction may lead to constant conflict.   But the
further dogma of Austinian jurists that in every
State there must of necessity exist some absolutely
sovereign power is not in fact true.   If, as may
often happen, the citizens of one State habitually
obey one sovereign (*e.g.* the Pope) on one class
of matters, *e.g.* matters of religious doctrine, but
also habitually obey another person (*e.g.* the King)
on another class of matters, *e.g.* political matters,
there may well exist for an indefinite time a system
which may properly be called one of divided sovereignty.   Such was in fact the state of things in
Scotland under the Constitution of 1690 ; the vast
majority of Presbyterians were prepared to obey
the General Assembly on matters, *e.g.* of religious
doctrine, which such Presbyterians deemed spiritual,
and were prepared to obey the Parliament, including
in that term the King, in regard to matters which
such Presbyterians deemed temporal.   Whether this
condition of things may or may not be called a
condition of divided sovereignty is a question of
words and of no great importance.   That the verbal
or logical difficulty of determining the different
spheres within which Church and Parliament had

respectively supreme authority was perceived in the Chapter seventeenth century both by Parliamentarians and by II. Divines is shown by a curious fact. The Act of Parliament of 1690, intended to settle the government of Christ's Church in Scotland, uses language which clearly intimates or hints that the establishment of Presbyterian Church government was originally settled by, and still depended upon, an Act of Parliament. In 1698 there was published under the authority of the General Assembly "for the " satisfaction of uneasy members of the Church a " Seasonable Admonition," and this Seasonable Admonition uses language which implies that Presbyterian Church government was instituted by Christ, and therefore not by the authority of any mere Act of Parliament, and suggests that what Parliament did not create Parliament could not alter.[1] In other words, the Parliament and the Assembly each declared its own belief in its own supreme authority, but were each determined that verbal controversies should not give rise to real conflict.

It is urged in the second place that Presbyterianism led in Scotland to gross religious intolerance, combined, in many cases, with constant inroads upon personal freedom of action, and with that most desirable freedom of opinion, which, by the way, should always be called, if we are to avoid confusion of ideas, freedom of discussion.

This charge contains within it a considerable amount of truth. Religious toleration was, in the sixteenth and seventeenth centuries, no part of the

[1] See Balfour, *Rise and Development of Presbyterianism in Scotland,* p. 114.

Presbyterian creed.   The execution in 1697 of
Aikenhead for the unproved crime of reviling the
Trinity was a brutal act of intolerance which was the
disgrace of the Scottish Courts, and indirectly of the
Scottish clergy, whilst in 1831 the deposition of
Macleod Campbell of Row, in which Moderates and
Evangelicals united to expel from the Church a man
of great spiritual activity and devoted Christian
character, for alleged heresy in regard to the
Atonement,[1] suggests that Scottish Presbyterianism,
if it had given up the ferocity which prevailed to
the very end of the seventeenth century, retained,
even in the nineteenth century, the moral intolerance of the seventeenth century.   It is indeed
the conviction that neither the dogmas nor the
sentiment of Presbyterianism in Scotland promoted
the growth of toleration, which has hindered critics
devoted to freedom of thought[2] from judging the
faults of the Scottish Church with fairness, or doing
justice to the services which that Church has rendered
to the world.   It was this sense of Presbyterian
intolerance which made Englishmen, who agreed in
nothing else, offer, even in the seventeenth century,
vehement opposition to the attempt to introduce
Presbyterian Church government into England.   That
a Church which detested Episcopacy should be hated
by James, by Charles I., or by Laud, was inevitable,
but it was Cromwell who addressed to the Scottish
divines the remonstrance, "I beseech you, in the
" bowels of Christ, think it possible that you may

[1] Balfour, p. 158.
[2] See Buckle, *History of Civilisation in England*, iii. chaps. ii.
and iii.

" be mistaken."[1] It was Milton who declared that "*New Presbyter* is but *Old Priest* writ large."[2] It was, we may say, the whole English people who looked askance, even though strong Protestants, on anything like the establishment of Presbyterianism in England. Yet all that can fairly be alleged against the Presbyterian statesmen or the Presbyterian clergy who lived under the Constitution of 1690 is that they were, in the matter of toleration and in their ideas of the respect due to liberty of opinion or discussion, a good deal behind some of the best and most enlightened of English or Continental moralists or thinkers; but on the whole they did not in these respects fall much below either the humanity or the toleration generally practised in other Protestant countries.

The third, and by far the strongest, objection to the Scottish doctrine of the separation of powers lies in the attempt then made in almost every Protestant country to combine two convictions, namely, that every country, and especially Scotland, ought to have a national religion, that is, a religion professed and believed in by the whole of the nation, or at any rate by the rulers of the nation, and by the vast majority of their subjects, and also that every individual is responsible for his own religious belief. The perplexities caused by the effort to give effect to these two beliefs are by no means peculiar to Scotland. They equally apply to any country where

[1] Cromwell to the General Assembly, August 3, 1650, in *Cromwell's Letters and Speeches*, Carlyle's edition, edited by S. C. Lomas, Letter cxxxvi., vol. ii. p. 77.

[2] Sonnet " on the new forcers of Conscience under the Long " Parliament."

there exists an established or national Church, *e.g.*
to England.   In each case they have almost inevitably led to the result that the national Church has
gradually ceased to be the Church of the whole or
of anything like the whole of the nation.

At the end, however, of the seventeenth century
it seemed quite conceivable that Scotland might
become a land where, if not the whole, yet the vast
majority, of its inhabitants should be Presbyterians.
And the Established Church of Scotland did certainly,
with great energy and with very considerable success,
labour to attain this end by bringing over to Protestantism the Roman Catholics of the Highlands.   But
in recent times an eminent Scottish lawyer has laid
down that "Knox's descendants have found, what
" that great man strove not to see, that a Church with
" both independence and nationality, to him the most
" beautiful of all things, may at any moment be found
" to be practically impossible.   The shining of that
" devout 'Imagination' has fascinated the eyes of
" many generations in Scotland, but will do so no
" more."[1]   It is possible, without either affirming
or denying the truth of this assertion, to insist upon
two facts.   There exists, in the first place, a marked
current of opinion in Scotland towards the reunion
of all Presbyterian bodies into one national Church,
and such a reunion might go far enough for practical
purposes towards identifying the Established Church
of Scotland with the Scottish people or nation.   It
is in the next place highly probable that if such
reunion cannot be achieved this failure must lead
to every Church throughout the country becoming

[1] Innes, p. 90.

by law a voluntary association, deriving its existence from an actual or implied contract between the members thereof. No doubt the success of religious Voluntaryism throughout the United States points to the probability or possibility of such a solution of the relation between Church and State.[1] Yet an impartial judge will observe that Voluntaryism denies the existence of a problem rather than solves it, and that the marked tendency by the statesmen, the thinkers, and the people of Great Britain to extend the control of the State over matters really belonging to the sphere of morality and sometimes of religion, suggests that before the end of the twentieth century the ideas which identify Church and State in the mind of Knox, in the mind of Chalmers, and in the mind of Dr. Arnold, may revive in a new form.

Turn now from the criticism to which the Presbyterianism of Scotland is open, and consider the benefits which the Church of Scotland has all but admittedly conferred on her people. We may call as witnesses to the reality of some of these blessings four men, each from different points of view, acquainted with Scottish history, of whom two have been the critics and two the appreciative judges of Scotland and her Church.

The Scottish clergy, we are told by Buckle, covered the great ones of the earth with contempt, and thus discountenanced "that pernicious and degrading " respect which men are too apt to pay to those whom " accident and not merit has raised above them," and

---

[1] The fairest statement of the success of Voluntaryism in the United States is given in Bryce's *American Commonwealth*, ii. (3rd ed.) 601-712 and 812.

that " herein they did a deed which should compensate
" for all their offences, even were their offences ten
" times as great,"[1] for they facilitated the growth of
proud and sturdy independence.

Macaulay insists in the most emphatic language
that the prosperity of Scotland is to be attributed,
not indeed solely, but principally, to the national
system of education, and that this national system
depended at bottom on an Act of Parliament passed
in 1697 whereby Scotland, " in spite of the barrenness
" of her soil and the severity of her climate, made such
" progress in agriculture, in manufactures, in commerce,
" in letters, in science, in all that constitutes civilisa-
" tion, as the Old World had never seen equalled, and
" as even the New World had scarcely seen surpassed."[2]
And this scheme of education was, as is well known,
favoured by and due to the Church of Scotland.   Nor
can any one doubt that the high standard of
education attained by the poorer classes in Scotland,
combined with the popular discussion of theological
problems in connection with the management of
Church business, kept alive among Scottish farmers,
labourers, and workmen, an aptitude for political
affairs which was little, if at all, cultivated, at any
rate before the Reform Act of 1832, among the rural
labourers of English parishes or the artisans of English
cities.

Consider next the judgement of one of the latest
and one of the most authoritative of writers on the
history of Scottish Presbyterianism :

[1] See Buckle, *History of Civilisation in England,* iii. (new ed.
1878) p. 113
[2] Macaulay, *Hist of Eng.* iv. 780-781.

" Beyond doubt, the principal services of the
" Scottish theological schools "—or we may say of the
Scottish school system generally—"have been in the
" formation of a thoughtful and reverent people,
" accustomed to great themes and serious reflection
" upon them, by the ministrations of an educated
" clergy, whose first vocation has always been held to
" be the preaching of the Gospel in its fulness, and
" the elucidation of the mind of the Spirit in the Word
" of God." [1]

Listen, lastly, to the most ardent and the most
famous of Scottish nationalists—Sir Walter Scott.
He was a member and had been an elder of the
Scottish church, though in later life he preferred the
Episcopalian form of worship.   He entertained an
imaginative interest in Jacobitism, though thoroughly
loyal to the Union, which he was sensible to have
been a wise scheme.[2]   He realised to the full the
weaknesses of Presbyterian government.   He was a
Tory who hated any change even in the institutions
and even in the minor habits of Scotland, but he
appreciated to the full the virtues of the Scottish
peasantry, which without doubt suggested to him the
following words :

" I have read books enough, and observed and
" conversed with enough of eminent and splendidly
" cultivated minds, too, in my time ; but, I assure you,
" I have heard higher sentiments from the lips of
" poor *uneducated* men and women, when exert-
" ing the spirit of severe yet gentle heroism under

[1] Balfour of Burleigh, *Rise of Presbyterianism*, pp. 163-164.
[2] See letter to Miss Edgeworth, July 16, 1825 ; Scott's *Familiar Letters*, ii. 312, and Lockhart, chap. lxxxiv.

" difficulties and afflictions, or speaking their simple
" thoughts as to circumstances in the lot of friends
" and neighbours, than I ever yet met with out
" of the pages of the Bible.   We shall never learn
" to feel and respect our real calling and destiny,
" unless we have taught ourselves to consider every-
" thing as moonshine, compared with the education
" of the heart." [1]

[1] Sir Walter Scott, in conversation with Lockhart, when Miss
Edgeworth was present (1825): Lockhart's *Life*, iii. 282.

PART II

THE PASSING OF THE ACT OF UNION

CHARACTER OF PART II

Part II. deals with the following topics:

First, the state of opinion with regard to the Union on the eve of the passing of the Act of Union.[1]

Second, the conflict between the Parliaments of Scotland and of England.[2]

Third, the appointment of the Commissioners to draft the Treaty of Union, the character of the Commissioners and of their work,[3] and

Fourth, the steps by which the Treaty of Union was ratified, and the Act of Union was passed, first by the Parliament of Scotland, and next by the Parliament of England.[4]

[1] See Chap. III. *post.*
[3] See Chap. V. *post.*

[2] See Chap. IV. *post.*
[4] See Chap. VI. *post.*

CHAPTER III

THE STATE OF OPINION ON THE EVE OF THE UNION [1]

First Thought.—The Union did not originate in the sort of feeling which is now called " National-ism," though it resulted in creating a new State of Great Britain.

A CRITIC employed in examining the work of the Whigs who at the beginning of the eighteenth century created the new State of Great Britain may naturally imagine that the Act of Union was the product of something very like the nationalism which in our own day produced the unity of Italy. This idea contains a slight element of truth, but is not, in the main, justified by the facts of history.

At the beginning of the eighteenth century, say in 1703, Englishmen had no enthusiastic desire for union with Scotland. The mass of Scotsmen certainly felt that the union of Crowns had turned out of no benefit to their country. Under the rule of the Stewarts, it had not given prosperity to Scotland. The failure of the Darien scheme under William III. had proved that a union of crowns, which in fact transferred the

---

[1] Cf. Hume Brown, iii. chaps. i. ii.; Burton, viii. chaps. lxxxv., lxxxvi.; Mackinnon, chaps. i., vii.

government of Scotland to London, made England Chapter III.
not the promoter, but the enemy, of any attempt
to create a Scottish colony in the New World.[1] Never
did there exist since the accession of James to the
throne of England in 1603 more bitter hostility
between Scotland and England than at the meeting of
the Parliament of Scotland convened in 1703 which
nevertheless passed the Act of Union in 1707. The
nationalism of Scotland was not the cause of, but the
obstacle to, the parliamentary union of the two parts
of Great Britain. It is essential therefore to ascertain
what were the circumstances which, broadly speaking,
from the beginning of the eighteenth century onwards,
told in favour, and what were the circumstances
which, from the same time, told against the legislative
union of England and Scotland.

Second Thought.—*The circumstances which told
in favour of Union, may be summed up under*—

(1) *The tradition of statesmanship.*

(2) *The interest of Protestantism (and especially
of the National Church of Scotland).*

(3) *The pressing need of Scotland for material
prosperity.*

(1) *The Tradition of Statesmanship.*—In England,
and in some cases in Scotland, the most statesmanlike
of the leaders of the country had for a century and
more felt that the political unity of the whole island
of Great Britain was something like a necessity.

*Attempted Union of the Crowns through Marriage
(from Edward I. to James).*—This feeling, indeed,
may be traced as far back as the original proposal of

[1] See pp. 145-151, *post.*

Edward I. to unite the two kingdoms by the marriage of his son, afterwards Edward II., to the little heiress of the Scottish Crown, and it should not be forgotten that this project was welcomed by the Scots. They were faced by the dangers of a disputed succession, from which the marriage treaty promised to save them, and almost a hundred years of peace had created in thirteenth-century Scotland a tradition of friendship with England. That tradition was rudely broken by Edward I.'s attempt at conquest, and, from the year 1296, England became "the auld enemy." The Scots rejected, with contumely, a tactless attempt of Edward III. to bring about a union by the succession of one of his sons to the throne of the impoverished and childless David II., and it was not until the early years of the sixteenth century that any advocate of union appeared on the Scottish side of the Border. Oddly enough, the first Scottish writer to urge the unity of the two countries was himself the very type and flower of the Franco-Scottish tradition which had grown up since the War of Independence. Of all Scottish scholars, with the exception of George Buchanan, John Mair or Major (1469–1550) was the greatest and the most closely associated with France, and the book in which he advocated a union was printed in Paris in 1521. Its title, *Historia Majoris Britanniae*, was a pun upon his own name; its thesis was the creation of a Kingdom of Britain, greater than the Brittany which had just been absorbed into the Kingdom of France, greater than the half-legendary Britain of King Arthur. Greater Britain was to be England and Scotland not merely friendly, but united :—

" This, in my judgment, is the course that should
" ever be followed : that the Scots King should marry
" with the daughters of the English Kings, and con-
" trariwise : and thus, some day shall one of them
" come to have a lawful right to all Britain; for with-
" out such lawful right I see not how the Scots shall
" ever master the English, nor yet the English the
" Scots. . . . And any man, be he Englishman or
" Scot, who will here say the contrary, he, I say,
" has no eye to the welfare of his country and the
" common good." [1]

An opportunity for carrying out Major's policy
occurred twenty years after the publication of his
book, when, in 1542, there was again a baby heiress
to the Scottish Crown. The chance was taken and a
treaty was negotiated for a marriage between the
infant Queen Mary of Scotland and the boy who became Edward VI., but the impatience of Henry VIII.
forced the Scots into a renewal of the league with
France. The merciless invasion which followed,
known in Scotland as the " English Wooing," was
conducted by the Earl of Hertford, who, a few years
later, as Protector Somerset, made an effort—hopeless in the circumstances—to persuade the Scots to
agree to a marriage treaty which would unite the
nations and the kingdoms on something like equal
terms :—

" We intend not to disinherit your Queen, but to
" make her heirs inheritors also to England. . . . If
" we two being made one by amity be most able to
" defend us against all nations, and having the sea for
" wall, mutual love for garrison, and God for defence,

[1] Major's *History*, trans. Scottish History Society, pp. 218, 289.

" should make so noble and well agreeing a monarchy,
" neither in peace may we be ashamed nor in war
" afraid of any worldly or foreign power, why should
" not you be as desirous of the same, and have as
" much cause to rejoice at it as we ? " [1]

As the Reformed Faith won fresh converts in
Scotland, the sympathies of Scotsmen were transferred
from France to England—not the England of Henry
VIII., but the England of Cranmer and Ridley and
Latimer. After the death of Henry VIII., Scottish
Protestants who wished to escape the danger of the
fiery death were welcomed to England by Edward
VI. and his guardians. Thus there grew up, for the
first time in two centuries and a half, a real bond of
union between Scotland and England, and the English
cause in Scotland ceased to be championed only
by traitorous nobles. The reign of Mary Tudor
strengthened this bond, for its effect upon Scotland
was to blot out the memory of the past, and to con-
centrate attention and sympathy upon the suffering
English Protestants. The reliance of the Scottish
Queen-Regent, Mary of Guise, upon her native land
made the French Alliance not less unpopular than
the Roman obedience. In the early days of the Protestant revolution, the cry which was raised by the
Lords of the Congregation was a protest against the
policy which made Scotland a province of France,
and it was on the plea of resenting French aggression
that they commended their cause to the princes of
Europe. In the crisis of the revolt, they went so far

[1] Somerset's *Epistle to the Nobility of Scotland, 1548*, ed. Murray,
Early English Text Society, 1872. Somerset contemplated a real
union under the name of the Kingdom of Britain.

as to invite Queen Elizabeth to " accept the realm of
" Scotland into her protection and maintenance for
" preservation of them in their old freedoms and
" liberties, during the time the marriage shall continue
" between the Queen of Scots and the French King,
" and one year after." [1] They were even prepared to
bring about a union at once by deposing Queen Mary
and placing on the throne the next heir, the Earl of
Àrran, on condition of the English Queen's consenting
to marry him—a stipulation which, for many reasons,
was distasteful to Elizabeth.

Mary, on her return to Scotland, acting by the
advice of her able and acute Secretary of State,
William Maitland of Lethington, adopted a policy
of friendship with England. Her position as
Elizabeth's heir-presumptive rendered this attitude
necessary if she was to aim at the English succession.
She made the succession the pivot of her foreign
policy during her few years of power, and the correspondence of Lethington with Cecil shows how
earnestly the Scottish Secretary worked for a Union
of the Crowns in the person of his mistress, after
the death of her cousin. Elizabeth, who, ultimately,
took the precaution of outliving Mary, declined to
commit herself. " As long as I live, I shall be
Queen of England," she said ; " when I am dead, they
shall succeed that have most right." [2] James, except
for some serious aberrations into which he was led
by his natural impatience, followed his mother's
example, and, during the last half of the sixteenth

[1] Rymer's *Foedera*, xv. pp. 569-571.
[2] " Lethington's Account of Negotiations with Elizabeth, 1561,"
printed in Appendix to *Mary's Letter to Guise* (Scottish History Society).

century, Scottish statesmen looked forward to a coming union of some description.

Attempt to effect Union of the Countries [Parliaments] from James (1603) to Anne (1707).—
When King James ascended the English throne he hoped to bring about a complete incorporating Union of the two kingdoms, and to leave at his death "one "worship of God, one kingdom entirely governed, one "uniformity of law." He recommended the project in his first speech to his English Parliament, on March 19, 1603-4. The conception, like many of James's ideas, was statesmanlike, but the grotesque rhetoric in which he clothed his advice was not likely to impress his audience :—

"What God hath conjoined, let no man separate. "I am the Husband and all the whole Isle is my "lawful wife; I am the Head, and it is my Body; "I am the Shepherd, and it is my flock; I hope "therefore no man will be so unreasonable as to "think that I that am a Christian King under the "Gospel, should be a Polygamist and husband to "two wives; that I, being the Head, should have a "divided and monstrous Body : or that being the "Shepherd to so fair a flock (whose fold hath no "wall to hedge it but the four seas) should have my "flock parted in two. . . . And as God hath made "Scotland the one half of this Isle to enjoy my "Birth, and the first and most imperfect half of my "life, and you here to enjoy the perfect and the "last half thereof, so can I not think that any would "be so injurious to me . . . as to cut asunder the "one half of me from the other." [1]

------

[1] Printed in King James's *Collected Works*, 1616.

More persuasive arguments were put forward by two members of the Joint Commission appointed by the Parliaments of England and Scotland to consider the royal proposal, or, rather, the portions of it which James wished to carry into immediate execution—commercial equality and the naturalisation of subjects of either country in the other. Bacon urged the House of Commons to knit "the knot " surer and straiter between the two kingdoms by " the communication of naturalisation "; and in a memorandum prepared for the King, he insisted that this was the true path to security and greatness. Bacon accepted the King's proposals for the unification of the laws of the two kingdoms, and prepared a memorandum on the subject.[1] His fellow-commissioner, Sir Thomas Craig, the distinguished Scottish feudalist, did not go so far. In his *De Unione Regnorum Britanniae*, written in 1605, but not printed until 1909, he urged the necessity of uniformity in religion, with regard to which he considered "the situation conspicuously favourable " to close and complete union."[2] But it was, he thought, "by no means imperative that the two " kingdoms should submit to identical laws "; each of the two nations should continue to be governed " in accordance with its own laws and customs."[2] Craig also believed that "the Parliaments of the " two nations must retain their own status and " authority," and he does not seem to have contemplated the emergence of any practical difficulty

[1] Bacon's *Works*, ed. Spedding, vi. 39, 371.
[2] Craig, *De Unione* (Scot. Hist. Soc.), ed. and trans. Terry, pp. 286, 303, 465.

from his rule that " war must not be declared without
" the assent of either Parliament." But, indeed, King
James's proposals never got so far as the discussion
of a union of the Parliaments. There was vehement
opposition in England.

"When I was in London as one of the Com-
" missioners at the recent Conference," wrote Craig,[1]
" I had a good deal of conversation with Englishmen
" on the association or incorporation of the two
" peoples in a single state. They frequently ex-
" pressed themselves in a manner depreciatory of
" Scotland, and were frankly indignant that our
" countrymen should have equality in honours and
" employment, their own reputation and resources
" being so much the greater."

The Scottish Parliament accepted the report of
the Commission, which recommended an incomplete
commercial union, but made its decision dependent
upon the adoption of a reciprocal scheme by the
English Parliament. There is no indication that the
Scots wished to go further than this in the direction
of union, and the English Parliament declined to go
so far. They rejected the commercial scheme and
consented only to the repeal of laws which treated
Scotland as a hostile country. The discussion, in
England, became involved in disputes about the royal
prerogative, and the most important advance was,
in fact, made along this line. The judicial decision
about the rights of the *post-nati*, to which we have
already referred,[2] was based upon a recognition of
rights inherent in the Crown, and the King used his

[1] Craig, *De Unione* (Scot. Hist. Soc.), ed. and trans. Terry, pp.
466, 354.   [2] See p. 29, *ante.*

prerogative to bring about an important change of
nomenclature.   James proposed that England and
Scotland, after the passing of what would have been
no more than a commercial union, should be known
as Great Britain.   This suggestion evoked vehement
opposition in the House of Commons, partly on the
constitutional ground that " the alteration of the
" name of the Kingdom doth inevitably and infallibly
" draw on an erection of a new kingdom or state,
" and a dissolution or extinguishment of the old, and
" that no declaration, limitation, or reservation can
" clear or avoid that inconvenience," and partly on the
less practical, but not less popular, plea that "no
" worldly thing is more dear to men than the
" name . . . that the contracted name of Britanny
" will bring in oblivion the names of England and
" Scotland " and that " whereas England, in the
" style, is now placed before Scotland, in the name
" of Britannie that degree of priority or precedency
" will be lost." [1]   Without waiting for the report
of the Commission, James, by a Proclamation dated
November 15, 1604, informed his subjects that
" by the force of our royal prerogative, we assume
" to ourselves the style and title of King of Great
" Britain, France, and Ireland, Defender of the Faith,
" . . . . discharging and discontinuing the several
" names of England and Scotland to be expressed
" in our titles, except in legal proceedings, instru-
" ments, and assurances of particular parties who, by
" the said alteration, may be prejudiced." [2]
   Like many of James's projects, the scheme for

[1] Bruce, *Report on the Union*, ii. App. VI.
[2] Bruce, ii. App. XIV.

union revealed a statesmanlike conception, marred by an impatient recourse to the prerogative to accomplish what could only be done by persuasion. But a sentence from the speech with which he closed the first session of his English Parliament stands to the credit of his prescience. "Those two kingdoms," he said, "are so conjoined that if we should sleep in our "beds, the union should be, though we would not."[1]

The Cromwellian Union, though forced upon Scotland by England, was a settlement remarkably generous in the circumstances. Scotland formed part of the "Commonwealth of England, Scotland, and Ireland," and was represented in the Parliament which met at Westminster, and the arrangements made at the Cromwellian Ordinance formed a precedent which was followed in 1707. The reduction of the number of commissioners to a total of thirty was brought about by creating groups of the less important shires and burghs, and the Cromwellian arrangements formed a model which influenced the representation of Scottish burghs down to 1918. The legal and judicial system was remodelled, but Scots Law was not abolished. Free Trade was established between Scotland and England. The country was too deeply impoverished by the civil war and by heavy taxation to reap the full benefit of the commercial union, but after the Cromwellian legislation had been rescinded at the Restoration, the Scots suffered greatly from English restrictions upon trade. Negotiations for a new commercial treaty were conducted in 1667 by a body of Commissioners representing the two countries, but they broke down owing to the

[1] Bruce, ii. App. XI.

refusal of the English Commissioners to agree to
exempt Scotland from the operation of the Navigation
Act.

The proposal for a union which followed the
failure of the Commercial Treaty seems to have
originated with Charles II., who "had found some
" instructions left by King James wherein he recom-
" mended . . . to his successors . . . that they should
" endeavour to establish a firm Union at home be-
" twixt Scotland and England."[1] The suggestion
was, according to the contemporary, but, possibly,
not unbiassed, evidence of Sir George Mackenzie, the
King's Advocate, very unpopular in Scotland, but
both Parliaments agreed to appoint Commissioners.
The most interesting suggestion made in the course of
their discussions was a scheme recommended by the
Scottish Commissioners for the continuance of separate
Parliaments "so as that there might be a certain
" number of Englishmen appointed to sit in the Scottish
" Parliament, and upon great emergents concerning the
" monarchy, and his Majesty's interest, his Majesty
" might call both Parliaments together at Westminster,
" or where he pleased, to meet and consult concerning
" the public affairs of the monarchy."[2] In the end, the
Scots adopted the policy of a union of the Parliaments
on the condition that "none of the constituent mem-
" bers of Parliament were to be excluded from the
" Parliament of Great Britain." The English Commis-

[1] Sir George Mackenzie's *History of Scotland*, 1821 ed. p. 138.
By far the best account of the discussion in 1669–70 is given in Sir
George Mackenzie's *History*, from notes made by Sir John Baird of
Newbyth, one of the Commissioners. The official journal is printed
by Professor Terry as an Appendix to his *Cromwellian Union*
(Scottish History Society).

[2] Mackenzie, pp. 207, 208-9.

sioners also agreed to a union of the Parliaments, but insisted that only a proportion of the members of the Parliament of Scotland should have seats in the United Parliament.[1]   On this issue, the Commission was unable to come to any agreement, and the negotiations came to an end.   Mackenzie's comment upon the termination of the discussion is interesting as showing the existence of a feeling that the proposal had something to recommend it from the point of view of statesmanship.

" This event had that grand design, which had
" so long exercised the thoughts, and entertained the
" expectations of two kingdoms : and thus it stopt,
" rather to the wonder than dissatisfaction of both
" nations, who expected that the wise statesmen of
" both sides had adjusted all the differences that could
" have intervened before they brought it in public." [2]

This tradition of statesmanship led, after the Revolution, to a proposal,, originating in the Scottish Convention, for a Union of the Kingdoms.   No sooner had the Estates proclaimed William and Mary than they sent a letter to the King, informing him that they had nominated Commissioners " to treat the
" terms of an entire and perpetual union betwixt the
" two Kingdoms, with reservation to us of our Church
" government, as it shall be established at the time of
" the union."   They even went so far as to make an offer which might have been of the first importance :
" If any difficulty shall arise in the Treaty, we do
" upon our part refer the determination thereof to
" your   Majesty." [3]   William   duly   recommended

---

[1] Mackenzie, pp. 207-209.   [2] *Ibid.* pp. 212-13.
[3] A.S.P. ix. 60.

the proposal to his English Parliament, and asked Chapter III.
for the appointment of English Commissioners,
but no action was taken. He soon became very
unpopular in Scotland, and at no other period of his
rule was the Scottish Parliament likely to place the
fate of the Kingdom in his hands. A great opportunity had been lost. William was personally in favour
of Union throughout his reign. " I have done all I
" can in that affair," he once said to Defoe, " but I do
" not see a temper in either nation that looks like it.
" . . . It may be done, but not yet." [1]

It is a proof of William's wisdom that he recognised
in the bitter temper of both nations after the failure
of the Darien scheme, a reason not for postponing
but for accelerating a union. In February 1700, he
reminded his English Parliament of the recommendation which he had made shortly after his accession,
and expressed the hope that the centenary of the
Union of the Crowns would witness a Union of the
Kingdoms.[2] The House of Lords responded by
passing a Bill for the appointment of Commissioners,
but it was rejected by the Commons. The subject
was again discussed in the Lords in the summer
of 1701, but without any practical result. In the
beginning of the following year, William, then on
his deathbed, sent to his Parliament a Royal message,
in which he urged that " nothing can contribute more
" to the present and future peace, security, and
" happiness of England and Scotland than a firm
" and entire union between them." [3]

In accordance with this recommendation, Queen

[1] Defoe, *History of the Union*, ed. of 1786, p. 64.
[2] Lords' Journals, xvi. p. 514.   [3] *Ibid.* xxii. p. 57.

Anne, on her accession, invited the Parliaments of
England and Scotland to appoint Commissioners to
draw up a Treaty of Union.   A Joint Commission
sat from November 1702 to February 1703, when the
Queen, in view of their dissensions, adjourned their
meeting till October.   In September, the Scottish
Parliament passed a resolution rescinding the powers
given to its Commissioners.   The questions raised and
discussed in 1702-3 were precisely similar to those
which we shall have to consider in connexion with
the Treaty of 1707.   The Scots were willing to accept
the Hanoverian Succession and a Union of the
Parliaments on condition of the extension to them of
the trading privileges possessed by English subjects.
John Bruce, who, in view of the approaching Union
with Ireland, drew up, in 1799, at the request of the
Duke of Portland, a "Report on the Events and
" Circumstances which produced the Union of the
" Kingdoms of England and Scotland," attributes the
failure of the negotiations of 1702-3 to " the resolution
" of England to retain an exclusive commerce.   The
" English Commissioners," he says, " notwithstanding
" the progress of trade for a century, still entertained
" the narrow maxim that the profits of this trade would
" be abridged by introducing the industry of the Scots."
He adds that, "in Scotland, where, reflecting on the
" advances which had been made by the reiterated
" appointment of Commissioners to treat of an union
" during a century, and on the uniform refusal by
" England to admit the Scots to commercial privileges,
" both the Parliament and the people felt the highest
" resentment." [1]

[1] Bruce, *Report on the Union*, i. 268-9.

It is thus evident that, at any rate, since 1603, statesmen endowed with political foresight had seen that the political unity of England and of Scotland promised immense advantage to the inhabitants of each country, and that a union ought to be brought about not by force of arms but by legislative agreement.[1] Bacon's opinion no one will treat with contempt, and James, it must be remembered, though his demeanour was seemingly undignified, his pedantry noticeable, and his moral deficiencies undeniable, was a man of considerable sagacity. He was far better acquainted with Scotland than were most English politicians; he had meditated far more deeply on the condition of England than had most Scottish politicians. Many circumstances bear witness to his shrewdness. From his accession to the English throne he laboured systematically to inaugurate the rule of peace throughout the Border counties. The determination wrung by him from the Law Courts that no Scotsman born after James's accession could be an alien in England, was a true step towards national unity.[2] He constantly made efforts to favour, in practice, free trade between England and Scotland.[3] His colonisation of Ulster by Scottish Borderers at once contributed to the peacefulness of the Borders, and to

Chapter III.

[1] Bacon "was perhaps the only man in England besides the King "who was enthusiastic in support of the Union" (Gardiner, *Hist.* i. 352). See further as to Bacon, "A Brief Discourse of the Happy "Union, &c.; Certain Articles or Considerations touching the Union"; *Letters and Life*, iii. 90, 218.

[2] See p. 29, *ante*.

[3] Bruce's Report, App. No. XXXI.; Sir George Mackenzie's *History of Scotland*, p. 137 *et seq.*
Note the statement that Scotsmen had enjoyed free trade in England for more than fifty-six years, and see notes in Burton, vii. 185, 186.

the prosperity of Irish Protestantism.   James further, whether one sympathises with his policy or not, did with extraordinary skill gain a victory over the Church of Scotland which, had Charles I. possessed half the sagacity of his father, might probably have established a moderate form of Episcopalianism in Scotland, whilst the King's obtaining a decision from the English Law Courts in favour of the royal prerogative to lay duties on foreign imports, shows a perception of the truth, now recognised wherever a federal government exists, that the least unpopular form of taxation is the imposition of duties on goods imported from foreign countries.   One doubts indeed whether in the seventeenth century to the mass of Englishmen such duties did not appear to be payments in reality as in form exacted from foreign traders.   However this may be, James's policy, if carefully examined, is from many points of view the policy of a ruler whose sagacity cannot be denied, though his moral defects often rendered his intellectual power useless to himself and to his subjects.   On the matter of the Union of the two countries Cromwell, as we have seen, followed, as far as he could, the policy of James.   He, like the King, and even more completely than James, put an end to the meetings of the General Assembly of the Church of Scotland, and, like James, he left the action of the subordinate Church Courts undisturbed. He, like James, believed that free trade would make the Union with England popular, and he acted on this belief.   But the position of the Protector placed him at a disadvantage as compared with the King. The union with the Commonwealth offered to, or rather enforced upon, Scotsmen by the Puritan leader rested, conceal it as you might, on the conquest of Scotland Chapter
III. by England. The unity of Great Britain as designed by a Scottish King who had become by legal descent the King of England was to be based upon a real contract between the Parliaments of the two countries.

Anne's accession to the Crown in 1702 seemed at first sight a circumstance which was likely to facilitate the passing of an Act of Union. Anne was an un-doubted Stewart; she was attached to the Church of England, but displayed no inclination towards Roman Catholicism. Jacobites under her government de-scribed themselves as Cavaliers. A union carried out under her guidance might well appear to be the victory of the Scottish Crown. As already pointed out, both the Parliament and the General Assembly of the Church of Scotland had from the Revolution acquired a new authority, and the Parliament especially had become for the first time a real representative of the nation, and an assembly in which a treaty of union could receive full discussion. In 1702, the tradition of statesmanship in favour of a union, and of a union carried through not by force but by a Treaty, and an Act of Parliament, passed by the Parliament of each country, was supported by the experience of a century, though popular opinion at the time did not appreciate the full importance of this tradition.

(2) *The Interest of Protestantism.*—The interest of Protestantism had, from the beginning of the Reformation in England and in Scotland, tended to break up the Franco-Scottish alliance, and had told in favour of a permanent alliance, if not an actual union, between England and Scotland.

Scottish Protestantism began as a movement in

favour of friendship and connexion with England, and the intrigues of James VI. (before 1603) with France and Spain strengthened this side of it. The Solemn League and Covenant of 1643–44 was, to this extent, in direct continuity with the National Covenant of 1559, and though the failure of the Long Parliament to carry out its provisions produced a reaction, yet the personal association of English Puritans and Scottish Presbyterians created new bonds of sympathy which were strengthened by common sufferings during the persecutions of the reign of Charles II. and by the common fear of Papacy. Thus there had grown up, before the Revolution of 1689, a tradition of Protestantism as well as of statesmanship in favour of union with England. When, therefore, at the beginning of the eighteenth century a real effort was made to form a true and parliamentary union between England and Scotland, the General Assembly of the Church of Scotland was, in the main and finally, influenced by its regard for the maintenance of Protestantism which was identified in Scotland with the maintenance of Scottish Presbyterianism. Protestantism, in short, as represented by the General Assembly, did more than any other sentiment to counterbalance the tradition of Nationalism which with many Scotsmen almost forbade assent to the Act of Union.

The General Assembly of the Church of Scotland practically possessed (as has been already pointed out) under the Constitution of 1690 a real veto on the passing of any Act of Union brought before the Scottish Parliament if such Act affected in any way the position of Presbyterianism as the established

religion of the State. Hence the Whig statesmen,
who on the whole guided the Parliament of 1703–
1707, tacitly recognised the necessity for obtaining
at least the assent, if not the active support, of the
General Assembly to any Treaty of Union which
could be ratified by the Parliament of Scotland.
Many Presbyterians no doubt, even though as favourable to the Union as was Carstares, must have felt
keen anxiety lest the formation of one Parliament
for the whole of Great Britain, and a Parliament
therefore in which the Episcopalians would possess
a large majority and have a prominent influence,
might expose Scotland to the peril either of the
disestablishment of the Presbyterian creed, or even of
an attempt to force upon her an Episcopalian Church
as the national Church of Scotland.[1] The Tory
legislation indeed of 1712, which revived patronage
in the Church of Scotland, proved that this fear was
no mere panic. But every Whig who in Scotland
wished to maintain the Revolution Settlement, and
certainly every Presbyterian who was not absolutely
blinded by fanaticism, must have perceived in 1707
that an Act of Union afforded the only effective
protection against a second restoration which, like
the restoration of 1660, would be perilous to the
Protestantism of England, and fatal to the Presbyterianism of Scotland. The belief, moreover, which
has now come to prevail that religious or theological
differences of opinion need not give rise to vehement
discord, and still less to civil war, within the limits

---

[1] There was the more risk of this calamity because at the beginning
of the eighteenth century almost all Scotsmen agreed that there ought
to exist in Scotland some one Church recognised by the State as the
representative of the nation.

of a really progressive State, though all but unknown to the mass of Englishmen and Scotsmen towards the end of the seventeenth century, had already been accepted by the wisest men of the eighteenth century. The leaders of the Church of Scotland therefore between 1703 and 1707 were, though with natural anxiety, compelled by their belief in Protestantism to accept an Act of Union necessary for the safety of the national Church of Scotland.

It should be remembered, for it is of the greatest importance to bring dates before our minds when considering such a transaction as the passing of the Act of Union, that at the accession of Anne, Louis XIV. was at the height of his power, and that the ally of the Stewart claimant was the great ruler of the day who threatened the independence of every free State in Europe, and, by the revocation of the Edict of Nantes, had reopened in its bitterest form the persecutions which gave a death-blow to the power of Protestantism in France and threatened the Protestantism of other European States. The Protestantism of Scotland was thus a force always telling in favour of the Union.

(3) *The Pressing Need of Scotland for Material Prosperity and therefore for Free Trade.*—During the century which elapsed between 1603 and 1703 a change of feeling or of opinion had taken place among Scotsmen, as indeed among the inhabitants of most of the progressive European countries, which it is hard to define, difficult even with accuracy to describe, and best on the whole, where possible, to explain by illustration. This gradual revolution may be expressed rather than defined

by terming the seventeenth century an age of theological or religious interests, and the eighteenth
century an age of secular interests. Neither term
can lay claim to much accuracy. Men do not
forego their care for physical comfort, for mercantile
prosperity, or for wealth because they are also
vehemently and sincerely interested in religious
conflicts. Englishmen who fought and destroyed the
Spanish Armada fought zealously for Protestantism,
but they also appreciated to the full the advantage,
public or private, of seizing Spanish gold ships.
Englishmen, moreover, who were zealous Catholics,
and often suffered much for their religion, shared
fully in resistance to the Armada and in triumph over
its defeat. The wise and patriotic statesmanship of
Carstares does not give the remotest reason for
supposing that he was less influenced by the religious
dogmas in which he believed than was Knox or
Andrew Melville. What is really true, and may be
avowed, without any injustice to patriots of the
seventeenth or of the eighteenth century, is that
towards the end of the sixteenth, and far into the
middle of the seventeenth century, the public maintenance of what men held to be religious truth was
esteemed by the leading men of their time to be closely
connected with national welfare and even with national
prosperity. Cromwell, as regards Protestants at least,
adopted ideas of toleration shocking to many Scotsmen of sincere but also of very severe piety. He
had certainly before his death advanced very far
in the acceptance of a sort of toleration which had
begun to mark the best statesmen of his time. Yet
Cromwell saw in the issue of a battle an immediate

sign of God's favour, and held his success in war to
be in more ways than one the moral justification of
his policy.   Nor can we the least doubt that the
defeat at Dunbar must to many Presbyterians have
raised sincere doubts as to the wisdom of a policy
which might, if successful, end in the enforcement
of Presbyterianism upon English Episcopalians and
English Independents.   All one can with fairness
say is that during the hundred years or so (1603–
1707) with which this essay mainly deals, the wiser
people in England and in Scotland were coming
to form a new estimate of the relation between the
national maintenance of what each man considered
orthodox or true religious belief, and the national
attainment of civil order, prosperity, and indeed welfare.   One Englishman of profound insight certainly
got to see before the end of the seventeenth century
that the quarrels between Presbyterians and Prelatists
lay at the root of the hostility which kept apart
two countries which would be greatly benefited by
being united into one State :

> But who considers right, will find indeed,
> 'Tis Holy Island parts us, not the Tweed.
> Nothing but clergy could us two seclude,
> No Scotch was ever like a bishop's feud.
> All Litanies in this have wanted faith,
> There's no *deliver us from a bishop's wrath.*[1]

And William Carstares, and scores of Scotsmen like
him, we may feel assured, re-echoed the conviction of
Andrew Marvell.

The contrast between the theological enthusiasm

[1] *Poems and Satires of Andrew Marvell*, vol. i. (1892), "The Loyal
Scot," p. 129.

prevalent during the sixteenth, and during most of the seventeenth century, and the secular enthusiasm prevalent during the whole of the eighteenth century, is well illustrated by two examples :

During the great Civil War, Scotland was full of passionate zeal for the Solemn League and Covenant. Scotsmen wished both to maintain Presbyterianism at home and to impose it upon England, and even upon Ireland. Yet Cromwell and Laud, hostile to one another as they were, almost equally detested the forcing of this League and Covenant upon England. But, as we must remember, earnest religious men, whether they were Scottish Covenanters, English High Churchmen, or English Independents, for the most part agreed in holding that a nation's national prosperity might, or rather did certainly, depend upon the national adoption of a true theological creed. Herein lay the difficulty of maintaining any form of consistent toleration. By, or indeed before, the beginning of the eighteenth century Scotsmen had convinced themselves that the fortune of Scotland depended far more upon the foundation of a colony on the Isthmus of Panama than on the maintenance of the Solemn League and Covenant. But even in this matter religious enthusiasm still faintly mingled with the vehement desire to found a New Caledonia; a supply of Bibles was sent out for the use of South American Indians, who certainly neither could nor would read them. In truth, New Caledonia and the African Company were merely the visible signs of the longing for wealth and for material prosperity.

The second and the most telling example of the growing predominance of secular over theological

interests is the passionate longing for free trade with
England which, in the course of the seventeenth
century, produced results to which we have already
referred.

Macaulay, with his unrivalled power of pressing
home a plain fact so that the dullest of students
cannot miss seeing its bearing, thus sums up with
unforgettable plainness, but with, possibly, too much
emphasis, the way in which the longed-for restoration
of free trade told with immense force in favour of
union with England.

" It may seem strange that a large portion of
" a people, whose patriotism, exhibited, often in a
" heroic, and sometimes in a comic form, has long
" been proverbial, should have been willing, nay
" impatient, to surrender an independence, which had
" been, through many ages, dearly prized and manfully
" defended.   The truth is that the stubborn spirit
" which the arms of the Plantagenets and Tudors had
" been unable to subdue had begun to yield to a very
" different kind of force.   Custom-houses and tariffs
" were rapidly doing what the carnage of Falkirk and
" Halidon, of Flodden and of Pinkie, had failed to do.
" Scotland had some experience of the effects of a
" union.   She had, near forty years before, been united
" to England on such terms as England, flushed with
" conquest, chose to dictate.   That union was insepar-
" ably associated in the minds of the vanquished people
" with defeat and humiliation.   And yet even that
" union, cruelly as it had wounded the pride of the
" Scots, had promoted their prosperity.   Cromwell,
" with wisdom and liberality rare in his age, had
" established the most complete freedom of trade

" between the dominant and the subject country.
" While he governed, no prohibition, no duty,
" impeded the transit of commodities from any part
" of the island to any other. His navigation laws
" imposed no restraint on the trade of Scotland. A
" Scotch vessel was at liberty to carry a Scotch cargo
" to Barbadoes, and to bring the sugars of Barbadoes
" into the port of London. The rule of the Protector
" therefore had been propitious to the industry and
" to the physical well-being of the Scottish people.
" Hating him and cursing him, they could not help
" thriving under him, and often, during the adminis-
" tration of their legitimate princes, looked back
" with regret to the golden days of the usurper." [1]

*Third Thought.—The circumstances which told
against the Union may be thus summed up.*
  (1) *Failure of the Union of Crowns to bring
        prosperity to Scotland.*
  (2) *The increasing strength of Scottish nation-
        alism.*
  (3) *The Massacre of Glencoe.*
  (4) *Hatred of England excited by the failure of
        the Darien scheme.*

  (1) *Failure of the Union of Crowns.*[2]—The Union
of Crowns, bringing as it did the hope of internal
peace, must among Scotsmen have excited the
expectation of peaceful progress and prosperity.
After the lapse of a century, the all but universal
opinion of Scotsmen was that this hope had been
disappointed. Contemporary writers are unanimous in

[1] Macaulay, *History of England*, iii. 253, 254.
[2] See especially Mackinnon, ch. ii. pp. 15-19

charging the political system, established in 1603, as the main cause of the national depression that culminated in the poverty and misery of the last decade of the seventeenth and the opening years of the eighteenth centuries.[1]   This belief may not have been entirely well founded, but in all matters depending upon public feeling the prevalence of an idea is for many purposes of far more importance than its strict truth.   And the conviction of patriotic Scotsmen that their country had as regarded material prosperity lost much by the union of the Crowns, hardly admits of dispute.   "Partly " through our own fault, and partly through the " removal of our Kings into another country," says Fletcher of Saltoun, " this nation, of all those that " possess good ports and lie conveniently for trade, has " been the only part of Europe which does not apply " itself to commerce ; and possessing a barren country " we are sunk to so low a condition as to be despised of " all our neighbours and made incapable to repel an " injury, if any should be offered." [2]   He states that there were formerly as many ships owned in the ports of Fife as were now possessed by the whole of Scotland, while most of these once prosperous Fife burghs were, he says, in his day little better than so many heaps of ruins.   According to the same authority, before 1603, Scotland carried on considerable commerce with Spain, and drove a great trade in the Baltic with her fish.   Upon the union of the Crowns, all this went to

[1] Mackinnon, p. 15 ; cf. Fletcher, " First Discourse concerning the Affairs of Scotland," *Political Works*, p. 81 ; Lindsay's *Interest of Scotland Considered*, p. 197 ; Seton, *Essays upon the Present State of Scotland* (1700), p. 77 ; Acts of Commission of Parliament on Communication of Trade, A.P.S. x. App. 107-148 (1699–1701).

[2] " First Discourse concerning the Affairs of Scotland," *Political Works*, p. 81.

decay; Scottish money was spent in England, and
not in Scotland, and the furniture, the clothes and the
equipages used by rich Scotsmen were bought in
London, and to sum the matter up in Fletcher's
words, " though particular persons of the Scots nation
" had many great and profitable places at court, to
" the high displeasure of the English, yet there
" was no advantage to our country, which was totally
" neglected, like a farm managed by servants, and
" not under the eye of the Master." [1]

The last years of the seventeenth century had been
marked by a series of bad harvests. Thousands of
persons had been reduced to destitution. Parliament
did what it could to alleviate Scottish misery. An
Act of 1696 offered a premium of 20 shillings per boll
on victual imported.[2] Emigration to Ulster became
common. Many thousands of Scotsmen were turned
into beggars. According to Fletcher these demoral-
ised vagrants rose as high as 200,000. He estimates
the population of the country at 1,500,000.[3] The
records, it has been said by a modern historian, of the
small burghs prove that the national destitution
was not exaggerated. When, in the year 1692, the
Royal Burghs agreed to communicate their exclusive
privileges of trade to those of Barony, on condition of
their undertaking to bear a tenth part of the taxation
leviable on the former, and the Scottish Parliament
accepted the offer, and appointed a commission to

[1] Fletcher's *Political Works*, p. 386 ; Mackinnon, p. 17 ; cf. also the
" Report on the State and Condition of the Burghs of Scotland "
(1692), in the *Miscellany of the Scottish Burgh Record Society.*
[2] A.P.S. x. 64.
[3] Both estimates are certainly a good deal too high. Mackinnon,
pp. 19, 20. See Chap. VIII. Second Thought, *post.*

adjust the terms of the communication, the Commission was overwhelmed with petitions pleading
poverty, and praying for exemption.

Whether Scottish critics at the beginning of the
eighteenth century were right in attributing anything
like the whole of the evils under which their country
suffered, to misgovernment by a King residing in
England, must remain a matter of grave doubt.   All
that need be insisted upon is that for one reason or
another the union of the Crowns had not conferred
material prosperity or settled peace upon Scotland,
and that from this state of things many Scotsmen
naturally inferred that to go farther in the path of
unity and merge the Parliament of Scotland in the
much larger Parliament of England was a desperate
remedy likely to intensify the evils which it was
meant to cure.

(2) *The increasing Strength of Scottish Nationalism.*—This was the main obstacle to the passing of any
Act of Union.   The union of the Crowns had, whatever
its other effects, gone far to prove that, as long as a
Scottish King lived in London, Scotland would to a
great extent be governed, not indeed by Englishmen,
but under English influence and in accordance with
the wishes and the interests of Englishmen.   The
Revolution Settlement showed that the two countries
which made up Great Britain had strong interests in
common, and especially that a Stewart Restoration
might be a deadly blow to Protestantism throughout
the whole island.

But the Revolution itself increased the power of
Scottish nationalism.   The public opinion of Scotland
had obtained since 1689, in her Parliament and in

the General Assembly of the Church, a means of free
and legal expression such as it had never before
possessed.   Free debate in the national Parliament
and in the General Assembly of the Church excited
the sentiment of Scottish nationality, just as, about
eighty years later in Ireland, free parliamentary
debate excited the sentiment of Irish nationality.
Scottish orators (as witness the speeches of Fletcher
of Saltoun, and the patriotic bombast of Lord
Belhaven) began for the first time to address in
Parliament, as Scottish preachers had long done from
the pulpit, the people of Scotland, and even the mob
of Edinburgh.   Parliamentary legislation began, as is
seen in the debates on Union, to interest the whole,
at any rate, of the Lowlands.

It is at first sight surprising to find far more of
parliamentary opposition to the Crown under Anne,
a true Stewart and therefore a Scottish Queen, than
under any one of her predecessors since 1603.   But
there is in reality nothing paradoxical in the matter.
Up to the accession of Anne to the throne, the evils
alleged to result from the union of the Crowns might
be attributed to the character and policy of the
reigning monarch, but Anne's personal merits, from a
Scottish point of view, made it clear that many of
these evils arose from the union of Crowns itself.
It is worth while to consider the justification for this
state of opinion.   As long as James, Charles II., and
James VII. and II. assailed the Presbyterianism of
Scotland it naturally seemed that the evils of government by the Stewarts resulted from the existence
of Kings hostile to parliamentary government both
in England and in Scotland, intensely hostile to

Chapter
III.

Presbyterianism, and, as regards the last two of them, inclined to favour the authority of the Pope. The Revolution, indeed, put an end to all attacks on parliamentary authority or upon Protestantism; it gave new life and power in Scotland to the national Parliament and to the national Church.   It was no accident that the very success of the Revolution should, even in 1689, suggest a union of Parliaments.[1]   The great change which re-established and, in Scotland, increased parliamentary power might be expected to remedy evils attributed to the attempt of despotic Kings to destroy popular liberty in England no less than in Scotland.   William indeed was no despot, but, on the other hand, he was a foreigner unable to conciliate the affection either of his English or of his Scottish subjects.   His whole heart was given to matters of foreign policy.   The ruinous result of the Darien adventure was by Scotsmen attributed to his utter indifference to Scottish interests.   In his case, too, the personal character of the King might be held to explain the failure of the union of the Crowns.   Anne, on the other hand, came to the throne with every advantage.   She represented the Scottish Royal Family.   Whatever her defects, she had no desire to establish despotic power.   She was a Churchwoman in England, but she was no Papist, and, in common with the supporters of the Revolution Settlement, she showed no hostility to Presbyterianism.   These qualities had, at first, their natural effect.   The accession of Anne did something to assuage the hostility to the Revolution Settlement among the Jacobites, who could again call themselves Cavaliers.

[1] See Macaulay, *Hist.* iii. 354, and p. 124, *ante.*

Yet the years which elapsed between Anne's coming to the throne in 1702 and the passing of the Act of Union, 1707, proved that even under a constitutional and a Scottish Queen Scotland would be through the union of Crowns governed rather from London than in Edinburgh. Anne no doubt employed Scottish ministers who attempted with more or less success to gain the support of the Scottish Parliament. But, as every one knew, the vital question whether the Scottish Parliament was, under Scottish law, dissolved by the death of William, or within six months after his decease, was decided in London, and the decision, in fact, depended far more upon the policy and the judgement of Anne's English ministers than upon the opinion of her Scottish advisers. The further inquiry whether at the end of 1702 the Scottish Convention Parliament should be at last dissolved, was, according to popular belief, decided as much by the English Godolphin as by such well-known Scotsmen as the Duke of Queensberry and the Duke of Hamilton. Such incidents deepened the conviction of Scotsmen, Whigs as well as Jacobites, that the union of the Crowns made Scotland, in a sense, dependent on England, without giving to her the material benefits which might be expected from the complete union of Great Britain. We have to-day come to consider Great Britain as one United Kingdom, and are so accustomed to see Scotsmen occupy the highest offices as Prime Ministers of British monarchs, as leaders or Speakers of the House of Commons, and even as Archbishops of the Church of England, that we find it difficult to realise the extent to which in the eighteenth century the influence exercised indirectly by England in the government of Scotland irritated and increased the sensitiveness of Scottish nationalism.

(3) *The Massacre of Glencoe.*—The transactions which have for ever associated the name of Glencoe with treachery and massacre are as well known to Englishmen as any event in the history of Scotland which has not been impressed on the memory of the civilised world by the genius of Sir Walter Scott. We have all learned from Macaulay [1] how the foolish delay of Mac Ian Macdonald in accepting an amnesty tendered by the King left him and his small clan technically in the position of rebels; how his honest efforts to testify to his loyalty were thwarted by accident, and still more by the fraud of his foes; how the basest treachery planned and carried out under the direction of the Master of Stair (Sir John Dalrymple) led to the murder—for it was nothing better—by the royal troops of Mac Ian and his followers at Glencoe. Of the degree of guilt of the persons who carried out, who ordered or condoned the massacre at Glencoe, it is needless, as it is practically impossible, to form any decided opinion. No one can doubt, as apparently no one disputes, that the villainous slaughter of men who had a moral right to claim protection under a pardon or an amnesty is a crime for which the Master of Stair is more directly responsible than any other man.[2]   What does require notice is

[1] See Macaulay, iv. ch. 18, pp. 188-217 ; Bright, *Hist. of England*, iii. 834 ; Burton, vii. 394-413 ; Sir John Dalrymple, *Dict. Nat. Biog.* xiii. 415-420.

[2] It is possible, though by no means certain, that William hardly knew, and did not anticipate the effect of the document which he signed, and which is supposed to justify the massacre.   He certainly never inflicted any punishment upon the chief criminal.   One may

that after about two years the circumstances of the murders committed at Glencoe became known, and were the subject of a parliamentary inquiry. They thus added throughout the Lowlands to the unpopularity of William and of any policy advocated by the King of England. This unpopularity would naturally fall in with the national condemnation, during the ensuing years, of the King's conduct in impeding the attempt of Scotsmen to found a new colony on the Isthmus of Darien. But whatever may have been the amount of indignation felt throughout the Lowlands at the treachery with which the massacre of Highlanders at Glencoe was marked, it seems historically certain that this massacre was industriously used by Jacobites and other opponents of the Revolution Settlement, and of the policy of Unionism in which it resulted, as a means for propagating and increasing the unpopularity of William.

(4) *Hatred towards England due to the Failure of the Darien Scheme.* — The failure of Scotland's attempt to found on the Isthmus of Darien the colony of New Caledonia, the wild hopes it aroused, the tragedy of the failure, and the bitter animosity thereby excited between Scotland and England, have been admirably told in the works of modern historians ;[1] there the oft-told story ought

---

assume that in general Englishmen and Scottish Lowlanders were towards the end of the seventeenth century very indifferent to the methods employed in suppressing disorder in the Highlands, and that indignation over the massacre at Glencoe was closely connected with hatred of the Master of Stair.

[1] See especially Burton, *Hist.* viii. chaps. lxxxiv., lxxxv., pp. 1-78 ; Hume Brown, *Hist.* iii. ch. i. pp. 24-37 ; Lang, *Scotland*, iv. pp. 58-76.

to be studied in detail.[1] Our purpose is simply to
state the facts which explain how it happened that
the ill success of the effort to found a Scottish colony
on the Isthmus of Darien excited in Scotland a de-
testation of England which might well have wrecked
for years every chance of achieving the political unity
of Great Britain.

At the end of the seventeenth, and during the
opening years of the eighteenth century, say from
1690 to 1730, the belief that the commerce and
trade of a state might be infinitely extended by
the formation of huge companies endowed by law
with large trading privileges, prevailed throughout
the progressive States of Europe. The foundation
in England of the East India Company, the creation
of the Bank of England, the gambling over the South
Sea Bubble in 1720, the grand scheme about the same
date framed by John Law of Lauriston for raising up
a Bank of France which was meant to confer unrivalled wealth and power upon that country, but
ended by bringing ruin upon Frenchmen, all belong
to financial schemes of one and the same class. To
these attempts, occasionally successful, but more often
ruinous, to enrich a country by means of companies
supported by a country's resources, belongs the
scheme for the colonisation by Scotland of the Darien
Isthmus.[2]

On 26th May 1695, at the instigation of John
Paterson, a Scottish adventurer of genius, the Parliament of Scotland passed an " Act for a Company

[1] See especially Mackinnon, *The Union of England and Scotland*,
ch. ii. pp. 15-59.
[2] Known now as the Isthmus of Panama.

" trading to Africa and the Indies." [1]   The Act was
touched with the sceptre, and had passed without
opposition.   The intention of its promoters was
that the company should trade with Asia, Africa,
and America.   It was to be supported by a capital
of £600,000, half of which should be purchased
by English and half by Scottish subscribers.   The
company received from Parliament the widest powers
and privileges.   The shares sold rapidly in Scotland
and in England.   On 22nd November 1695 the
subscription lists were closed.   On that very day the
English Parliament met, and on 17th December the
Lords and Commons presented to the Crown an
address pointing out the mischiefs which would result to English traders from the Scottish Act.   The
English subscriptions were withdrawn.   A nominal
capital of £400,000, of which about £220,000 was
actually paid, was in consequence raised by Scottish
subscriptions.   The plan of trading with Africa, Asia,
and America was modified and turned into a plan
for colonising the Isthmus of Darien, and there
founding the colony of New Caledonia, which it was
hoped and believed by Paterson and by Scotsmen
generally would become the centre of the world's
trade and bring wealth and prosperity to Scotland.
For about two years this grand plan was carefully
prepared.   On the 17th July 1698, " ships had been
" procured, stores laid in, and articles of trade (4000
" periwigs among them), such as might tempt the
" cupidity of the natives." [2]   The whole of the Scottish
people, nobles and commoners, the Parliament and
the Church, Jacobites and Whigs alike, believed in

[1] A.P.S. ix. 377-381.   [2] Hume Brown, *Hist.* iii. 32.

the success of the great undertaking, and the first fleet which sailed for Panama left Scotland "amidst the " tears, the prayers, and the praises " of Edinburgh. One patent fact, however, was forgotten, or rather ignored, by every projector and every politician in Scotland. Spain, which in 1698 was a far more formidable power than Scotland, claimed sovereignty over the Isthmus of Darien, and Scotland in effect from the moment that the colonists landed on the Isthmus challenged the might of Spain. Thrice were fleets sent from Scotland, and on each occasion the effort of Scotland to obtain or retain possession ended in ruin. The storms of the sea, plagues on land, the overpowering force of the Spanish navy, all told against the colonists. Once indeed—and it is the only bright point in this tale of misfortune—a small body of Scotsmen, on 11th February 1700, defeated under good leadership and by desperate courage the forces of Spain. This one triumph was in vain ; the Spaniards beset the colony by land and by sea, the situation of the settlers became hopeless, but their courage held out. On the 30th March 1700 the Spaniards offered honourable terms. The colonists were allowed to sail in their own ships, with colours flying and drums beating, and to take with them their arms and ammunition, and all their goods.[1] Ill-luck dogged the adventurers to the last. Two hundred and fifty deaths took place in the departing ships before they reached Jamaica. A hundred more men were drowned in a storm which wrecked the ship after she had reached Jamaica. It may be said almost without exaggeration that the ships and men

---

[1] Hume Brown, iii. 36.

exposed to the risks of the Darien expedition perished, and that the futile enterprise cost Scotland well-nigh 2000 of her sons and over £200,000, which she was ill able to spare.[1]

Why, however, should the ill-luck of Scotland have aroused animosity not only against King William but also against England?

The answer to this question may be summed up in one sentence: In the eyes of Scotsmen, a hopeful attempt to plant a Scottish colony ended in disaster owing, not to the power of Spain, but to the opposition of William as King of England, influenced by the jealousy of the English Parliament, which had no right to control his action as King of Scotland. This feeling is explained, though not wholly justified, by the following facts. From 1695 to 1700 the acts and the inaction of England seemed to Scotsmen to argue contempt for Scottish nationality and indifference to Scottish interests. The Act which in 1695 created the African Company was a Scottish law sanctioned by the King of Scotland, with which the English Parliament had no concern whatever. The remonstrance of the English Parliament against this Act was an insult to Scotland. The admission of William III. as King of England that he had been ill served in Scotland, and the dismissal of the ministers who had let the Act pass into law, was a gross neglect of his duty as King of Scotland. It meant that Scotland was to be governed in accordance with the wishes

Chapter III.

---

[1] Scotsmen overlooked the enmity of Spain, which they should have anticipated, but they did not know what we now know for certain, that until very recent extensions of modern science no European colonists who settled on the Isthmus of Darien had a chance of escaping death from fever.

of the English Parliament.   But this forgetfulness by William of his duty to Scotland was not only an insult but a most distinct injury.   It was immediately followed by the withdrawal of all the English subscriptions.   It led to something far worse.   A circular addressed to the Governors of all the English plantations or colonies, enjoining them to prohibit all His Majesty's subjects from rendering any assistance whatever to the Scottish Company, was forthwith prepared.   This letter was not indeed issued till 1699.   This fact may have seemed to Scotsmen to increase its malignity; it was an additional blow given by England when they were making their last desperate struggle against the power of Spain.   Then, too, the Company had a very fair chance of obtaining at its start help from the wealth of Hamburg.   Yet this help was withdrawn or denied in consequence of a memorial sent in William's name to the Hamburg Senate.   These intimations that the King of England bore no good-will to Scotland's attempt to found a colony worked much actual harm and emboldened the Spaniards to attack Scotsmen who, after all, were not aliens but natural-born subjects of the King, both of Scotland and of England.   The truth, as a Scotsman would have put it, in 1700, was that William as King of England thwarted at the wish of England the very policy which, as King of Scotland, he had sanctioned by an Act of the Parliament of Scotland.   Could an English sovereign have done more to injure Scotland if Scotland had still been governed by a separate King?   Whether the anger thus excited was entirely reasonable is not worth discussion ; that it was natural and that it was strongly felt cannot admit of dispute.   It was

rendered the more vehement because the disappoint- Chapter
ment caused by the Darien calamity was more keen III.
than we now realise. In Edinburgh the news of the one
victory obtained by Scottish prowess was known before
the tidings of final defeat were received, and when at
last hope of success had vanished, the wrath of Scotland seemed unappeasable. Many observers must,
with a correspondent of Carstares, have said to themselves, in June 1700, " God help us, we are ripening
" for destruction. It looks very like Forty-one." It
seemed as if the whole nation was likely to rise in arms
against William III. as it had risen against Charles I.

But this ill-starred expedition had another and,
though a less noticeable, a more important effect. It
proved to the most sensible of Scotsmen, whether
Whigs or Jacobites, that the union of Crowns could
not be allowed on the death of Anne to continue.
Hence it resulted that Scotland was absolutely driven
to choose between the following alternatives : She
must either become, together with England, a part of
the one Kingdom of Great Britain or else return
to the position of things which existed before 1603,
and be a kingdom as independent of, and as foreign
to, England as she had been before the accession of
James to the throne of Elizabeth. In 1705 it became
visible to every one, from the result of the war
between the Parliaments,[1] that if Scotsmen were not
prepared to become again aliens in England, it
logically followed that they must accept the Act
of Union, or some statute which turned Great Britain
into one undivided State, and this conviction was indirectly a result of the Darien scheme and its failure.

[1] Chap. IV. p. 160, *post.*

CHAPTER IV

THE WAR BETWEEN THE PARLIAMENTS [1]

THE SPECIAL CHARACTERISTICS OF THE PARLIAMENT OF 1703

Chapter
IV.

*First Thought. — This Parliament more com-
pletely represented the public opinion of Scotsmen
really interested in politics than any Parliament
which had sat since 1603, and therefore was more
capable of carrying an Act of Union than any
preceding Parliament.*

ON the 6th May 1703 the last of the Scottish
Parliaments met at Edinburgh; it continued in
existence till the 25th of March 1707.

The imagination of historians has been impressed
both by the finality and by the untold importance
of this Parliament's achievements. It abolished the
Parliament of Scotland; it aided in creating the new
Parliament and State of Great Britain. Scotsmen
have naturally dwelt with minuteness on the ceremonies known as the "ryding" which opened the

---

[1] See Mathieson, *Scotland and the Union*, chap. ii. espec. pp. 81-
110; Burton, *Hist.* viii. chap. lxxxvi.; Mackinnon, *Union of England
and Scotland*, chaps. iv., v., vi., pp. 132-198.

first meeting of the last Parliament of Scotland.
They have depicted lovingly the picturesqueness of
the procession, which, in accordance with traditional
custom, passed through the Canongate and the
High Street to the Parliament House. Thus "the
" procession," writes Burton, "according to old
" feudal usage, began diminutively, and swelled in
" importance as it went. The representatives of
" the burghs went first; then, after a pause, came
" the lesser barons, or county members; and then
" the nobles—the highest in rank going last. A
" herald called each name from a window of the
" palace, and another at the gate saw that the
" member took his place in the train. All rode two
" abreast. The Commoners wore the heavy doublet
" of the day unadorned. The nobility followed in
" their gorgeous robes. Each burghal commissioner
" had a lackey, and each baron two, the number
" increasing with the rank, until a duke had eight.
" The Nobles were each followed by a train-bearer,
" and the Commissioner was attended by a swarm
" of decorative officers, so that the servile elements
" in the procession must have dragged it out to a
" considerable length. . . ." [1] These pictures of a bygone age are interesting, but they are misleading.
For the details of a venerable pageant divert the
attention of readers first from some really important
and peculiar characteristics of the last Scottish
Parliament, and next from the instructive paradox
that a bitter conflict between the Parliament of
Scotland and the Parliament of England, which all
but gave rise to civil war, in reality did finally

[1] Burton, *Hist.* viii. chap. lxxxv.

promote the close and lasting union of Scotland and England. The special characteristics of this Parliament and the war of the Parliaments, with its effects, form the subject of the chapter.

The Scottish Parliament under the Constitution of 1690 possessed a legal and constitutional authority (especially when acting in harmony with the General Assembly of the Church) which had never fallen to any earlier Parliament.[1] But to this fact a student should add the consideration that a curious combination of circumstances gave to the Parliament of 1703 a good deal more of a representative character and of moral authority than at the moment when Anne ascended the throne (1702) belonged to the Convention Parliament which had sat without any dissolution from 1689 to 1702.[2] This will be clearly seen if we compare the position of the Convention Parliament and the position of this last of Scottish Parliaments, which may well be called the Union Parliament.

The Convention Parliament did a great work. It carried Scotland, without the use of unnecessary violence, through a constitutional revolution. It re-established the national Church of Scotland. It revived the existence of the General Assembly of the Church.

[1] See Chap. II. pp. 90-99, *ante.*
[2] Contrast the time during which the Convention Parliament of England sat with the time for which the Convention Parliament of Scotland sat. The Convention Parliament of England sat for the short period of not quite twelve months; the Convention Parliament of Scotland sat for fourteen years without dissolution, 1689-1702. During that period three new English Parliaments were successively summoned. Add to this that the Convention Parliament of Scotland after the death of William continued sitting and acting for some months in circumstances which left it very doubtful whether its sitting was not in the strictest sense unconstitutional.

It for the first time established a state of things under which the Parliament and the General Assembly found it possible to act together with substantial harmony, and each, in accordance with the convictions of Scottish Presbyterians, to keep within its proper sphere of action. This Parliament, in short, with great wisdom established and put in force the Revolution Settlement. It also proved that it could pass good laws for Scotland. It further showed, as in the violent agitation aroused by the failure of the Darien scheme, that it could ardently sympathise with the wishes and the prejudices of the Scots people. Yet the Convention Parliament, from the beginning, and still more throughout the later years of its existence, suffered under certain defects which gradually undermined the moral weight of its action. The Parliament, when it was brought together as a Convention, did, from the necessity of the case, represent little more than the Whigs of Scotland. On this point one may rely with perfect confidence on the words of a writer never accused of judging too severely the conduct of a party which commanded his sympathy.

"William," writes Macaulay, "saw that he must "not think of paying to the laws of Scotland that "scrupulous respect which he had wisely and "righteously paid to the laws of England. It was "absolutely necessary that he should determine by "his own authority how that Convention which was "to meet at Edinburgh should be chosen, and that he "should assume the power of annulling some judg-"ments and some statutes. He accordingly sum-"moned to the parliament house several Lords who

Chapter IV.

" had been deprived of their honours by sentences
" which the general voice loudly condemned as un-
" just; and he took on himself to dispense with the
" Act which deprived Presbyterians of the elective
" franchise.

"The consequence was that the choice of almost
" all the shires and burghs fell on Whig candidates.
" The defeated party complained loudly of foul play,
" of the rudeness of the populace, and of the partiality
" of the presiding magistrates; and these complaints
" were in many cases well founded. It is not under
" such rulers as Lauderdale and Dundee that nations
" learn justice and moderation." [1]

The Convention Parliament further appointed a
committee for examining the validity of elections.
The members thereof were for the most part Whigs;
they held, in effect, that few persons were duly elected
who were not sound Whigs.[2] The mere lapse of time,
again, had, by the end of William's reign, diminished
the representative character of the Convention
Parliament, which had already lasted, under the
name first of a Convention, and then of a Parliament, for over twelve years. During the short
time for which the Convention Parliament was
continued under Anne, grave doubts existed as to its
constitutional authority. The death of William would
of itself have been a dissolution of the Parliament,
but for an Act [3] which, subject to certain conditions,
enabled his successor to keep the Parliament alive.
These conditions, however, were not in reality complied
with by Anne or by her Ministers. A large body of

---

[1] Macaulay, *Hist.* iii. 248.   [2] See Macaulay, iii. 374.
[3] 1696, c. 17, A.P.S. x. 59, 60.

Jacobites, or at any rate of the Opposition under Chapter
IV. the Duke of Hamilton, seceded from the Parliament on the ground that its continued existence was illegal and unconstitutional.[1] Add to all this that a Parliament prolonged for fourteen years was completely opposed to such parliamentary tradition as existed in Scotland. As already pointed out,[2] general elections of Parliament were hardly known till about the middle of the seventeenth century. In earlier times, a Parliament generally existed for a session only, and the members of Parliament for shires were elected for a year only, and were members of the Parliament (if any) convened within that year for which a member was elected.[3] Contrast now with the position of the Convention Parliament the far stronger position of the Parliament which met at Edinburgh in 1703. This Parliament, which might well be called the Union Parliament, was the immediate result of a general election. And this election[4] was admittedly one in which the Government under the leadership of the Duke of Queensberry interfered very little with the freedom of the electors. Hence the Scottish Parliament of 1703 represented all the parties into which Scotland was then politically divided.[5] Whether they were or were not represented in their true numerical proportions is a point on which it

---

[1] See Mathieson, *Scotland and the Union*, pp. 74-76.
[2] See Introduction, pp. 11-13.
[3] See Introduction, pp. 12, 13, *ante*. The Convention called together in England by William III. in 1688 converted itself into a Parliament by its own authority in 1689, and this precedent, if so it can be called, was followed by the Scottish Convention of 1689. But the English Convention Parliament (if we may so call it) was dissolved within a year.
[4] Carried on 1702–3.   [5] See p. 159, *post*.

is now impossible to form an opinion. It is also a point which was little considered by the men of 1703, and in itself is of no great importance. What is certain, and is worth insisting upon, is the fact, proved by the debates on the Union, that the leading parties of the day could each make their voice heard within the walls of the Parliament House. Except by persons willing and ready when occasion offered to rebel against the Revolution Settlement and effect a restoration of the Pretender, the constitutional authority of the Parliament of 1703 was beyond question. We may go further than this. The Parliament of 1703 had derived from England much of the doctrine, and even more of the practice, of parliamentary sovereignty. Anne was not in a position to retain long in office any Scottish ministry which could not command the support of the Scottish Parliament. Scotsmen, too, had learned from England the methods by which a Parliament might appropriate to itself royal authority ; they had learned to refuse the grant of taxes, and had practically adopted from Westminster the dogma that the remedy of grievances must precede the granting of revenue. No doubt the General Assembly of the Church of Scotland did, under the Constitution of 1690, still limit the political omnipotence of the Parliament ; but the Parliament of 1703 had received from the Convention Parliament a policy under which the Assembly and the Parliament worked together, and could, by keeping each to its own sphere, immensely increase their collective authority. The growth, lastly, of parliamentary life had by 1703, as it has in all countries where it has flourished, developed the growth of the party system.[1] It is here well to note the parties into which the Scottish Parliament of 1703 was, in effect, divided. These were, first, the Court party, or, as we should say, the Ministerialists; secondly, the Country party, or, in modern phraseology, the Opposition, that is to say, a body of men who, without supporting the Government, were in no sense rebels, but looked, as they themselves avowed and probably believed, wholly to the interest of the country, and in fact were mainly influenced by zeal for Scottish nationalism; and, thirdly, the so-called New party, known generally as the Squadrone Volante, whose members professed to stand outside other party divisions, and held, as they believed, a casting vote, which could determine the success either of the Ministerialists or of the Opposition. This Squadrone Volante was apparently a small body of members broken off from the Country party. The fourth and last party consisted of the whole body of Jacobites, who, speaking generally, included all the Episcopalians. This body, influential though it was, can hardly be treated as in strictness a political party, for it was made up of men who hardly pretended loyalty to the principles of the Revolution Settlement. They were in spirit not a constitutional Opposition but rebels. They were prepared, if fortune favoured them, to bring about by force of arms the restoration of the Pretender in Scotland. Of course, this division into political parties cuts across, and is logically confused by, the religious division of Scotsmen into Presbyterians, Episcopalians, and

[1] The "Club" of 1689, which seems to have been a mere faction of leaders allied together to promote their personal interests or power, had, happily for Scotland, broken down. (See Macaulay, iii. 298, 348, 349, 378, 687.)

Roman Catholics.   But one may roughly count the
last two classes for the most part among Jacobites,
and, as became revealed by the debates on the Union,
one may consider that the large mass of Presbyterians
supported, though often with considerable hesitation,
the Unionist policy of the Government, though, of
course, the most ardent Presbyterians found it almost
impossible, as Covenanters, to support an uncove-
nanted King, and detested a Presbyterian Church
grounded on the non-recognition of the National
Covenant or the Solemn League and Covenant.   From
whichever point of view, then, the matter be considered, the Parliament which passed the Act of
Union was characteristically representative of Scottish
opinion.

The War between the Parliament of Scotland and the Parliament of England

*Second Thought.—A bitter conflict between the
Parliament of Scotland and the Parliament of
England led to the lasting union of Great Britain.*

The circumstances of the day gave to the Parliament of 1703 the means of attacking the Parliament
of England and of forcing upon its attention the
wishes of Scotsmen.   These circumstances deserve
special attention.   The wisest statesmen in each part
of Great Britain were Unionists ; they felt that
political unity obtained by pacific and legal means
could alone promote the prosperity and maintain the
independence of the whole island.   But this ideal of
a completely united British State commanded little
popular support in England and was distinctly un-

popular in Scotland. Every Englishman, however,
who supported the Revolution Settlement, and
many who did not support it, desired the continuance of the Union of Crowns, and also demanded the continued grant of supplies by the
Scottish Parliament for the support of a Scottish
army. All England, in short, speaking broadly,
desired that the whole island should be ruled by one
monarch, that peace on the Border should be
maintained, and that France should be unable to
count upon the alliance of Scotland in a war with
England. But, at the beginning of 1703, it was
certain that, on the death of Anne, the Union of
Crowns would come to an end. The last of her
children was dead ; that she should give birth to
any more children was highly improbable. The Act
of Settlement of 1701, 12 & 13 Will. III. c. 2,
vested the succession to the Crown of England in
the Princess Sophia of Hanover or the heirs of her
body, being Protestants. But this Act of the English
Parliament in no way affected the succession to the
Crown of Scotland. The Scottish Crown would not,
therefore, in the absence of further Scottish legislation,
descend to the House of Hanover. Hence it was
absolutely necessary, in the eyes of Englishmen,
that the Scottish Parliament should provide for the
succession of the House of Hanover to the Scottish
Crown, and also should vote supplies for the maintenance of an army in Scotland.

Meanwhile, as already pointed out,[1] Scotland
ardently desired free trade with England and full
participation in the advantages accruing to England

[1] See pp. 113, 132, *ante.*

from her growing colonial Empire. If, however, the existing Union of Crowns, without a Union of Parliaments, was to be maintained by a Scottish law, the vast majority of Scotsmen were determined that severe checks should be placed on the prerogative of the Scottish King. For such checks seemed to them to be the only means by which to prevent a Scottish King from becoming the instrument through which Scotland would be governed in accordance with the advice of an English ministry supported by an English Parliament. It was certain too that in the Parliament of 1703 the Country party would, on the necessity for such checks, act in combination with the Jacobites, and thus command a majority for declining to consider the regulation of the succession to the Crown, and also for curtailing after the death of Anne the prerogatives of the Scottish King. These circumstances, and especially the knowledge that, at any moment, the death of Anne would, of itself, put an end to the Union of Crowns, placed in the hands of the Scottish Parliament the means for constitutionally compelling the Parliament of England to give ear, at any rate, to the wishes of Scotland, *e.g.* in respect of perfect free trade between the two countries. This power might be exercised in at least four different ways. First, the Scottish Parliament might deny to Anne supplies necessary for carrying on the government and maintaining the military defence of Scotland; secondly, it might refuse, or merely omit, to pass any law regulating the succession to the Crown of Scotland on the death of Anne; thirdly, it might pass an Act which should so restrict the prerogative of the

Scottish King that, even in the event of a retention of the Union of Crowns, English ministers should have hardly any opportunity for interfering in the administration of Scottish affairs ; and fourthly, it might pass an Act which should make it certain that, on the death of Anne, the Union of Crowns should come completely to an end.

When the Scottish Parliament met, on May 6, 1703,[1] the Duke of Queensberry, as High Commissioner, was the real head of the Government, or, if we may venture on a convenient anachronism, was Prime Minister. He was the most successful parliamentary leader in Scotland. He committed some grave errors, but the carrying of the Act of Union was due to his judgement, his boldness, and his skill in the management of Parliament. He was a Unionist. He apparently intended to bring the question of union at once before the Parliament.[2] The Parliament, however, assembled in no humour to negotiate a union. It used every weapon which fortune had placed in its hands. It at once declined to deal with the question of the succession. At any moment, therefore, the death of Anne might bring the Union of Crowns to an end, and thereby cause a civil war between the northern and the southern parts of Great Britain. The chance of this calamity was increased by several considerations. Louis XIV. had already acknowledged the title of the Pretender to the Crowns both of England and of Scotland, and Louis, before his defeats by Marlborough, was in

[1] See p. 152, *ante.*
[2] See pp. 125-126, *ante,* as to the failure of negotiations for union between Nov. 1702 and Feb. 1703.

164   *THE UNION OF ENGLAND AND SCOTLAND*

Chapter
IV.

command of the greatest military force existing in any part of Europe.   A French invader would, it was certain, after the death of Anne, be supported by English no less than by Scottish Jacobites.   The Scottish Parliament also refused to grant supplies.

Further, the Parliament, against the will of the Government, introduced two Acts [1] or, rather, Bills. The first of these, which ultimately became the Act for the Security of the Kingdom, was intended as a threat to dissolve the Union of Crowns on the death of Queen Anne.   It occupied the greater part of the first session of the new Parliament, and, at the close of the session, on September 16, 1703, it was submitted for ratification by being touched with the sceptre and so receiving the royal assent.   It was, however, omitted from the Bills which the Commissioner touched with the sceptre, and he intimated that " it is fit Her Majesty should have " time to consider upon some things that are laid " before her." [2]   The scope of the measure, and its effect when it was ratified in the following year, will be explained later in this chapter ; [3] meanwhile, it is sufficient to say that the employment of the royal veto caused fierce and widespread indignation.   The second of the two measures which indicated the determination of the Parliament to defy the wishes of the Government received the royal assent on September 16, 1703, and became the Act Anent

---

[1] In Scotland the word " Act " was used before a measure passed into law by receiving the royal assent, and indeed from the date of its first introduction into Parliament.   As one of these measures did not, for some time, receive the royal assent, it is convenient to employ the term " Bill."

[2] A.P.S. xi. p. 112.   [3] See p. 167, *post.*

Peace and War. The aim of this enactment was Chapter
clear. It was intended to ensure that, even should IV.
the Union of Crowns continue after Anne's death:
(1) no King or Queen of Scotland should have power
to make war on any State without consent of the
Scottish Parliament; (2) no declaration of war made
without such consent should be binding on the subjects
of the Kingdom of Scotland (though the Crown would
be justified in using its powers to suppress internal
insurrection or to repel foreign invasion); (3) treaties
of peace, commerce, and alliance must be negotiated
by the sovereign with the consent of the Estates of
Parliament.[1] The assent of the Crown to the Act
Anent Peace and War was given against the wishes
of the Queen's English ministers, but was held by
the Duke of Queensberry to be a necessary concession
to the demands of the Scottish Parliament. It considerably diminished the prerogative of the Scottish
Crown, and was intended to prevent future interference by an English Government in the foreign
policy of Scotland. It did not, however, have any
immediate effect, because it was to come into operation only in the event of the Queen's death without
issue. The concession did not induce the Parliament
to grant supplies, and the Commissioner, in adjourning
the Parliament, expressed his regret that the House
had not " given the supplies necessary for the main-
" taining of Her Majesties forces and preserving the
" peace and safety of the Kingdom." [2]

[1] 1703, c. 6, A.P.S. xi. 107. This Act Anent Peace and War was
accompanied by another Act which admitted French wines, duty free,
into Scotland, and this at a time when the Queen of England was
waging war with the King of France.
[2] A.P.S. xi. 112.

To understand the progress of the war between the Parliaments one must note shortly several important events which took place between September 16, 1703, when the Act Anent Peace and War received the royal assent, and August 5, 1704, when the Act of Security received the royal assent. These events greatly increased the animosity between Scotland and England.

The mysterious intrigue known in England as the Scots' Plot,[1] and in Scotland popularly called the Queensberry Plot, had, between these dates, become known throughout each country. The details thereof do not at this time of day greatly concern a constitutionalist employed in examining transactions connected with the passing of the Act of Union. It was common knowledge in the opening years of the eighteenth century that Scotsmen high in public life were plotting for the restoration of the Pretender. The High Commissioner, Queensberry, in 1703 accused the Duke of Atholl, his leading opponent, of joining in a treasonable plot, but the Duke of Atholl was able to show reason for believing that Queensberry himself had at that very moment countenanced rebellion against Anne. It is more than probable that each of these noblemen was the victim of frauds carried out by two of the most unscrupulous and traitorous conspirators[2] in an age when treachery and treason were common. It is equally possible that the two noblemen each tried to secure both the safety and

---

[1] See Mathieson, *Scotland and the Union*, pp. 90, 91, and Mackinnon, chap. v.

[2] Namely, Simon Fraser, who in 1746 as Lord Lovat was, after a life of intrigue and violence, beheaded for treason; and Robert Ferguson, known as the Plotter.

the pecuniary advantages of avowed loyalty to Anne, and also the goodwill of the Pretender, who might by a restoration become the acknowledged King of every part of Great Britain. Everything about the Plot is mysterious; it produced, however, several un- doubted results. Queensberry, though a politician of rare ability, was proved, on the most favourable view of his conduct, to have been the dupe of a scoundrel, whom no man of sense ought to have trusted. The Duke therefore necessarily ceased to hold the position of High Commissioner. The Scots' Plot, whatever the interpretation put upon it, proved to Englishmen that a large number of Scotsmen might any day provoke a civil war and rouse the Jacobites of England to arms. The English Parlia- ment was filled with indignation. The House of Lords, at the instigation of Anne's English ministers, opened a more or less judicial inquiry into the Plot, and thereby in the eyes of Scottish patriots trenched upon the independence of Scotland. The inquiry was resultless.

On July 6, 1704, the Scottish Parliament met for its second session, with the Marquis of Tweeddale instead of Queensberry as High Commissioner. The Parliament thereupon struck another blow in the conflict with the English Parliament, and refused supplies to the Crown unless the Crown gave its assent to the Bill for the Security of the Kingdom. On August 5, 1704, the Bill was touched with the sceptre, and became the law of the land. The character of the famous Act has been thus sum- marised :

" Its main provisions, as it was passed, were these,—

" That on the death of the Queen without issue, the
" Estates were to name a successor from the Protest-
" ant descendants of the royal line of Scotland, but
" the admitted successor to the crown of England was
" excluded from their choice, unless ' there be such con-
" ' ditions of government settled and enacted as may
" ' secure the honour and sovereignty of this crown
" ' and kingdom—the freedom, frequency, and power
" ' of Parliaments—the religion, freedom, and trade of
" ' the nation, from English or any foreign influence.'
" It was made an act of treason to administer the
" coronation oath without instruction from the
" Estates. By a further clause, to come in force
" immediately, the nation was placed in a state of
" defence, and the able-bodied population were
" ordained to muster under their respective county
" heritors, or burgh magistrates."[1]

The aim of the Act was clear. The Scottish
Parliament was utterly dissatisfied, as were also the
people of Scotland, with the working of the mere
Union of Crowns. The Act was to ensure that
some arrangement as to the relation between Scotland
and England satisfactory to Scotland should be
arrived at, or else that Scotland should on the death
of Anne become a separate and independent country,
subject to a king, who should in no case be the same
person as the King of England. Many of those who

---

[1] Burton, *History of Scotland*, viii. pp. 92, 93 ; see also Mathieson,
Scotland and the Union, pp. 83, 84. The Act of Security, as ratified,
was precisely the same as the measure to which the royal assent had
been denied in 1703. Its first reading was carried on July 25, 1704,
and the second reading on August 5. On the same day, the process
of legislation was completed by a vote approving the Bill, and it
was also touched by the sceptre. No amendments to it were moved
in 1704.

THE WAR BETWEEN THE PARLIAMENTS   169

voted for the Act of Security probably wished that Chapter IV.
Scotland should have both complete independence and
complete separation from England.   Leaders such as
Fletcher of Saltoun may have thought that independence might be secured to Scotland while maintaining a Union of Crowns, combined with very great
restrictions on the power in Scotland of the Scottish
King.   Whatever were the exact schemes entertained
by those who demanded the passing of the Act of
Security, it certainly embodied a policy which no
English Unionist, and indeed no Scottish Unionist,
was willing to accept.

The English Parliament was at last completely
aroused to the dangers with which the Scottish Act
Anent Peace and War and the Act for the Security of
the Scottish Kingdom menaced England.   The English
Parliament at once therefore passed the so-called
"Alien Act," which finally received the royal assent
on the 14th of March 1705.   This statute is called by
three different names; each of these gives a different
aspect of the same enactment.   In the Statutes at
Large it is entitled "An Act for the effectual
"securing the Kingdom of England from the apparent
"dangers which may arise from several Acts lately
"passed by the Parliament of Scotland."   This title
tells us the motive with which the Act was
passed.   In the chronological table of the Statutes
the Act is brought under the head of "An Act for
"the Union of England and Scotland."   This name
tells us the actual result to which the Act ultimately
led.   The Act is popularly known by the name of the
Alien Act; this nickname designates the means by
which the English Parliament succeeded in inducing

the Scottish Parliament to consider the advisability of at any rate negotiating for a treaty of Union.

It is always hard to express in clear and untechnical language the meaning of a peculiar and complicated statute. But the general results of the so-called Alien Act may, it is submitted, be thus summed up :

First—The Act offered to the Scottish Parliament the opportunity of negotiating with the English Parliament for a treaty of Union between England and Scotland.[1]

This end was attained by empowering the Queen to nominate commissioners (conveniently termed English commissioners) to negotiate for such treaty whenever the Scottish Parliament should have passed an Act for the appointment of commissioners (conveniently termed Scottish commissioners) to negotiate with such English commissioners for such treaty of Union. It was, however, provided that the Queen should not exercise such power until an Act should be passed by the Kingdom of Scotland authorising the appointment of such Scottish commissioners.

Secondly—The Alien Act enacted that from and after the 25th day of December 1705 (Christmas Day) and until the Scottish Parliament should have passed an Act settling the Crown of Scotland upon the person who, in the event of the death of the Queen without issue, would be entitled to succeed to the Crown of England under the Act of Settlement, 1701, 12 & 13 Will. III. c. 2 [namely, the Electress Sophia of Hanover, or the heir of her body being a Protestant], every native of Scotland, subject to very limited exceptions, should be taken as an alien born out of

[1] See 3 & 4 Anne, c. 7, ss. 1-3, 12.

the allegiance of the Queen of England;[1] and further, Chapter
that from and after the said December 25, 1705, till IV.
the passing by the Scottish Parliament of such Act
regulating the succession to the Crown of Scotland as
aforesaid, the trade between Scotland and England
should be in many most important matters [2] prohibited
under legal penalties.[3]

The name by which the Alien Act is popularly
known, and its provisions, make it appear to modern
Englishmen and Scotsmen a strange and severe
statute, but if properly understood it will appear to
be a prudent and statesmanlike measure. It is carefully drawn so as not to trench upon the independence
of Scotland or the sovereignty of the Scottish Parliament. It does not contain a word which exceeds the
admitted right of England to legislate so as to avert
damage which might result to the country from
Scottish laws. What is of more consequence, the
Act does not even attempt to impose upon Scotland
the passing of an Act of Union. It really places
before the Parliament of Scotland an option between
two different policies, either of which Scotsmen might
accept without loss of dignity or sacrifice of national
independence. The one is willingness to negotiate
with England, as the Parliament of Scotland already
had done in 1702, for a treaty of Union. In such
negotiation the Parliament of Scotland, like the
Parliament of England, would have every opportunity

---

[1] 3 & 4 Anne, c. 7, s. 4.

[2] Namely, the importation of horses, etc., into Scotland from
England, the importation of Scottish cattle from Scotland to England,
the importation of coal from Scotland into England, and of Scottish
linen from Scotland into England.

[3] 3 & 4 Anne, c. 7, ss. 2-9.

of criticising the terms of any proposed treaty, and, if necessary, of refusing to embody the treaty in an Act of the Scottish Parliament. The other policy, to which no Scottish Whig could reasonably object, was to join in settling the Crown of Scotland, as had been done under the Revolution Settlement, upon the person entitled to succeed to the Crown of England. All that England tried to insist upon was that there should either be a closer union between the two countries, or that the Union of Crowns, which had been treated as permanent since the accession of James to the Crown of England, should be continued. Scotland, in fact, was left full freedom either to continue the Union of Crowns by settling the question of succession, or to create such a union of the two countries as Scotsmen and Englishmen might, on the whole, find conducive to the benefit of the whole of Great Britain.   All, in fact, that the English Parliament tried to enforce was that Scotland should not break up the Union of Crowns as it had existed for more than a century, and at the same time decline even to consider the advantages to be gained by the closer political union of England and Scotland.   Let it be particularly observed that if Scotsmen had preferred, as some of them no doubt did, to settle immediately the succession to the Crown without trying to treat for a closer union of the kingdoms, there is nothing whatever in the Alien Act which would have injuriously affected the position of any Scotsman, or have diminished the independence of Scotland and her Parliament.   What English states-men really insisted upon, and in this every Whig throughout the two countries agreed, was that the

Union of Crowns ought to be maintained, even though Scotland was not inclined to create a union of the two kingdoms. The Alien Act was passed with the very object of making plain to Scotsmen that either the settlement of the succession or the consideration of an Act of Union was to England, as to Scotland, a political necessity. The Act received the royal assent on March 14, 1705.[1]

This date is worth attention, for it reminds us of transactions which illustrate the bitter resentment excited in Scotland by the failure of the attempt to colonise the Isthmus of Darien. The African Company, though the colony of Darien was ruined, still attempted to keep up their trade. One of their vessels, the *Annandale*, which they were to charter for the East India trade, happened to be in England, where the ship was seized at the instance of the English East India Company. This excited indignation in Scotland. Shortly afterwards an English ship, the *Worcester*, under Captain Green, put into the Firth of Forth, and the secretary of the African Company, in revenge for the treatment of the *Annandale*, carried out with a body of followers a plot to seize the ship. A report arose that the crew of the *Worcester* had committed piracy on a vessel called the *Speedy Return*, which belonged to the African Company, and had murdered Captain Drummond and the crew. The rumour spread like wildfire throughout Edinburgh. Green and his crew were put on trial at Edinburgh in March 1705 for murder. Captain

---

[1] The Alien Act, 3 & 4 Anne, c. 7, unfortunately appears in the Statutes at Large and in the chronological table of the Statutes as an Act of 1704.

Green and his companions were easily convicted by a
Scottish jury. There was no evidence that any of
the defendants had murdered Drummond and his
crew. It was never proved that Drummond had been
killed ; there is a good deal of evidence, though not
perhaps conclusive, that Drummond had been seen
alive long after the date when the supposed murder
by Captain Green and his crew was alleged to have
been committed. The Queen sent orders that Green
and the other men convicted should be respited.
The populace of Edinburgh were determined that the
execution should take place.   The Scottish Privy
Council sympathised with the feeling and certainly
feared the violence of the mob.   On April 11 Green
and two of his crew were hanged.   They were,
to speak plainly, the victims of a judicial murder.
Forbes of Culloden, one of the justest of Scotsmen,
attended the victims to their death, and even carried
the head of Captain Green to the grave.   A more
fearful example of mob law never occurred in a
civilised country.   Its importance lies in the evidence
which it supplies of popular sentiment in Scotland.
A judicious writer adds that "it is a remarkable
" instance of the slight communication and sympathy
" between the two countries, and also of English
" unconsciousness of the formidable condition of
" Scotland, that the fate of Captain Green and his
" crew had little more interest to the wide English
" public than if it had been an affair with Algerian
" pirates." [1]

[1] Burton, viii. 109.   But see Captain Alexander Hamilton's *New
Account of the East Indies* (1727) for some evidence that Green was
guilty of piracy in 1703.   Cf. Roughead's *Riddle of the Ruthvens, and
other Studies*, pp. 363-390.

However this may be, Scottish statesmen had Chapter IV.
learned the lesson which the English Parliament
meant to convey to them by the Alien Act; the time
had come when Scotland, if she would neither legislate
so as to maintain the Union of Crowns nor negotiate
for a union of kingdoms, must try to stand alone as
a separate State and thus sacrifice every advantage
which she had gained or had hoped to gain from the
accession of James to the throne of England. The
Scottish Parliament reassembled on June 28, 1705.[1]
The High Commissioner had again been changed and
was now the Duke of Argyll. To use modern
expressions, the Duke was Prime Minister, but
Queensberry soon became a member and a predominant
member of the Government. The Queen, in her
letter of June 18,[2] most earnestly urged upon the
Parliament the settling of the succession to the Crown
and the promotion of a union between England
and Scotland. On August 25 the Act for a treaty
with the kingdom of England was read.[3] On September 1 the House proceeded to the subject of the
nomination of Commissioners to treat for a union.[4]
The real question at issue was whether the Scottish
Commissioners should be nominated by the Parliament
or by the Queen. It was thoroughly understood
that the Duke of Hamilton, as leader of the Opposition, would advocate their nomination by the
Parliament, and could probably carry a motion to
this effect. The decision one way or other was of
vital importance. A Commission nominated by the

[1] See A.P.S. xi. 205.
[2] Read in Parliament, July 3. See *ibid*. 213, 214.
[3] See *ibid*. 224.
[4] See *ibid*. 237 and App. p. 86.

Chapter
IV.

Parliament would certainly contain a certain number of Jacobites, and probably also of men who, though not Jacobites, were opposed to any very close union between England and Scotland. If, on the other hand, the nomination were left to the Queen, the names of the Scottish Commissioners would be in fact mainly determined by the Queen's English ministers, and the Scottish Commissioners might probably consist almost wholly of Whigs, or at any rate of men not opposed to union with England. Late in the evening of September 1, when most of the Jacobites, in other words of the Duke of Hamilton's followers, had left the House, the Duke suddenly proposed and carried a resolution that the nomination of the Commissioners should be left to the Queen.   On September 21, 1705, the Act giving such nomination to the Queen was touched with the sceptre, and the Parliament was prorogued.[1]   To students who know the historical course of subsequent events it may seem that the resolution of September 1, 1705, decided the carrying of the Act of Union.   To

[1] A.P.S. xi. 292, 295, c. 50. With the question, What were the motives of the Duke of Hamilton in recommending nomination by the Queen? we need not greatly concern ourselves. Those who think that his treachery or tergiversation is undoubted may be right, but they should weigh one or two facts : (1) All the members of the commission to treat for a union in 1702 had been nominated by the Queen. (2) The Alien Act, 3 & 4 Anne, c. 7, ss. 1 and 2, left the nomination of the English Commissioners to the Queen, and might be construed as suggesting, if not requiring, the nomination of the Scottish Commissioners by the Queen, and as it was intended to accept the proposal for treating for a union contained in the Alien Act, it might be expedient to put the acceptance in a form not open to any objection. (3) If the Duke was acting treacherously to his supporters, and in opposition to the wish of the Parliament, why should no resistance have been made to the passing of the Act, c. 50, which three weeks later gave legal effect to the resolution proposed by the Duke ?

contemporaries it appeared for months later that the policy of unionism was little better than a dream or chimera pursued by the English ministers. The one thing which is certain is that the action of the Scottish Parliament was met generously by the Whigs of England. The English Parliament met on October 25, 1705; on November 27, at the suggestion of Lord Somers, the sections of the Alien Act offensive to Scotsmen were immediately repealed. The war between the Parliaments was thus brought to a close. The road was open for the appointment of Commissioners for the drafting by them of the Treaty and the passing by the Parliament first of Scotland, and next of England, of the Act of Union.

Third Thought.—The war between the Parliaments produced or confirmed the conviction on the part both of Scotsmen and of Englishmen that the Union of the Crowns (as it had existed since 1603) was no longer maintainable.

The War of the Parliaments produced one most important result. In 1702, and even in 1703, many supporters of the Revolution Settlement, both in England and in Scotland, thought that the most prudent course for both countries was to leave unchanged the Union of Crowns, if the Scots would settle the Crown of Scotland upon the House of Hanover. The War of the Parliaments convinced such men that the maintenance of the Union of Crowns was an impossibility. This change of opinion was natural, and not unreasonable. Many English Whigs in 1702 thought that the Union of Crowns

gave to England most of the advantages, in relation
to Scotland, which were requisite for the prosperity of
England.   It had at any rate secured peace on the
Borders, and practically it had prevented any
alliance between Scotland and France.   Many English
traders were not by any means anxious to allow free
trade between Scotland and England, or to share with
Scotland the gains which accrued to England from
her foreign colonies and foreign possessions.   Many
Englishmen would therefore at the beginning of
Anne's reign be naturally inclined to practise the
easy policy of what is called " letting well alone."
But such English advocates of *laissez-faire* may
well have changed their views by 1705.   The Darien
expedition proved that the colonial policy of Scotland might well come into conflict with the colonial
policy of England.   The Scottish Act Anent Peace
and War and the Act of Security had proved that
in case of such a conflict Scotland might well be
inclined to re-establish Scottish national independence,
and possessed, as long as the succession to the Scottish
Crown was unsettled, the legal means of attaining
this end.   But Scottish independence might at any
moment mean actual war between Scotland and
England, and a war in which Scotland would be
supported by the power of France and by an alliance
with the English Jacobites.   Scotsmen, on the other
hand, had long doubted the benefit to their country
of the Union of Crowns.   On this point many Scottish
Whigs agreed with many Jacobites, perceiving that
this particular kind of unity did not really prevent
Scotland from being governed, in many respects, by
English ministers, while it denied to Scotsmen Free

Trade and other advantages which, might arise from their becoming, to the full extent, citizens of Great Britain. Hence the English Alien Act exactly hit its mark. It showed every Scotsman really interested in public life that England was prepared to take vigorous measures in defending her own interests; that at the very lowest the Union of Crowns must be made permanent, and that a closer union was the only method of securing Scotland from war, or the threat of war with England. Hence arose a general conviction that the mere Union of Crowns, as it had existed since 1603, did not meet the wants of either country. This conviction did not ensure success in the attempt to create absolute political union between the two countries, but it did take from the opponents of union half the strength which generally and legitimately belongs to a party which on really conservative grounds opposes a revolution; for the power of such a party lies in the right to assert that the existing state of things is on the whole satisfactory.

CHAPTER V

THE COMMISSIONERS AND THE TREATY OF UNION

First Thought.—The Commission was appointed for the purpose not of collecting information about a Treaty of Union, but of preparing such a contract or treaty of Union as might obtain the assent both of the Parliament of Scotland and of the Parliament of England

IN modern times, parliamentary Commissions are constantly appointed for two different ends. One of these ends is to collect information with regard to some subject which it may ultimately be desirable to regulate by Act of Parliament: such, for example, was the object of the Commission appointed to ascertain what is precisely the existing law of England with regard to divorce, and what are the opinions prevailing as to the changes (if any) by which such law might be amended. A Commission appointed with this object may conveniently be called a Commission of inquiry. The other end or object for which a Commission may be formed is the preparing or the drafting of a Bill, to be laid before Parliament, as to the principles whereof there is thought to exist a certain amount of general agreement. Such was the

object of the Commission for the Amendment of the
Poor Law, on whose Report the Poor Law Amendment Act, 1834, 4 & 5 Will. IV., c. 76, was substantially grounded. A Commission appointed with
this object may be conveniently termed a Commission
for legislation.[1] It is worth while to insist upon this
difference between a Commission of inquiry and a
Commission for legislation ; and this for two reasons.

The one reason is that the character of the persons
who ought to form part of a Commission differs
according to the object of the Commission: in the
case of a Commission of inquiry the Commissioners
may with advantage consist of persons holding
entirely different and even opposed views in respect
of the topic which the Commission is called upon to
consider; for this difference of opinion will facilitate
the obtaining of information about the facts which
require to be ascertained. In the case, on the other
hand, of a Commission for legislation it is pre-
eminently desirable that the Commissioners should
agree on the principles and the aim of the law which
they are called upon to prepare or draft.

The other reason for insisting upon the distinction
between the two kinds of Commission is that the
Commission nominated for the preparing or drafting
the Treaty of Union was not a Commission of inquiry,
but emphatically a Commission for legislation. The
Commissioners were nominated by the Queen acting,
as every one knew she would, under the advice of
her English and her Scottish ministers, who were all

[1] Of course a Commission may be both a Commission of inquiry
and a Commission for legislation, but this combination of different,
though not absolutely inconsistent objects often leads to unsatisfactory
results.

Unionists.   The Queen's ministers were determined
that the Treaty of Union should ensure permanent
political unity to the whole of Great Britain.   They
wisely, therefore, made up their minds that the Commission whose business it was to draft the Treaty
should not contain any appreciable number of members who wished not to produce, but if possible to
prevent, the political unity of the whole island.   The
adoption of this principle of appointment[1] was in
accordance with the dictates of ordinary good sense.

This statement must not be taken to mean that
serious differences of opinion did not arise between
the English and the Scottish Commissioners, or that
these differences did not receive full and fair consideration.   Its true meaning is that these differences of
opinion were confined to disagreements which might
arise between Unionists, or more strictly between the
Whigs of Scotland and the Whigs of England.

*Second Thought.—The Treaty of Union, as also
the Act of Union which embodies it, is a real treaty
or contract between England and Scotland, and
has the leading characteristic of a contract between
individual persons.*

This Thought is one of essential importance.   It
has no reference whatever to any fictitious contract
which thinkers of different schools, such as Hobbes,
Locke, or Rousseau, have imagined or feigned as

---

[1] There were several English Commissioners who were appointed
not because of their political opinions, but because their appointment
gave dignity to the Commission, and because it gave a guarantee to
some Englishmen that the Treaty of Union should not contain terms
offensive to some powerful class.   Such distinguished Commissioners
were the Archbishop of Canterbury and the Archbishop of York.

the basis of a State's existence, or as the vindica-
tion of the relation between a sovereign and his
subjects; it has also little to do with the equally
unreal contract which, for the exposure of revolutionary fallacies, has been called up by the rhetoric
and the fancy of Burke when he tells us that " society
"is indeed a contract. . . . It is a partnership in
" all science; a partnership in all art; a partner-
" ship in every virtue and in all perfection." [1] Our
Thought is the assertion of the very plain fact, which,
however, is often forgotten, that the Treaty or the
Act of Union was a real contract, and therefore
possessed a peculiar virtue rarely to be found in any
law, or in those well-known arrangements between
independent States, to which the name of treaties
has become, by usage, appropriate. This special virtue
of a true contract (when made without the use of
fraud or force) between individuals, A and X, is
that, in general, it meets the wishes of each party
to the agreement, and gives to each that which he
deems to be, and which usually is, a real advantage. [2]
The Treaty and the Act of Union being a true contract between the Parliament of England and the
Parliament of Scotland, or between the countries
which they severally represented, was meant to
confer, and did confer a benefit, or benefits, upon
each of the parties thereto. Note, too, while we are
dealing with the matter, that this peculiar virtue

[1] Burke, " Reflections on the Revolution in France," *Works*, vol. v.
pp. 183-184.
[2] This principle certainly applies to all bilateral contracts, which
are the sort of bargains which we have in mind; it probably also
applies to a unilateral contract, though the point is not here worth
working out.

of conferring a benefit upon each party to a true contract does not belong either, generally speaking, to a law, or to those so called but often unreal contracts which are termed treaties. The special characteristic of a law is that it imposes a command under some kind of penalty upon some person or persons, and enforces obedience thereto by the power of the sovereign or State imposing the law. But even a good law does not necessarily benefit, in the ordinary sense of the word, the person upon whom it imposes an obligation. "Thou shalt not steal" is a good law and is enforced by penalties in every civilised State, but it would be a strange confusion of thought and a misuse of language to say that this law confers a benefit upon the thief whom it sends to prison or the gallows. A treaty, again, between two nations who have been fighting one another has the appearance of a contract, and in some few cases it may be a real agreement and confer a benefit upon each of the parties who sign it. But in the vast majority of cases the victor in a severe war who compels his opponent to accept a treaty attempts to get a gain for himself, but hardly professes to be the benefactor of the vanquished State. It would be absurd to say that by the treaty which took Alsace from France Germany conferred a benefit upon France. This assertion would be true only in the sense in which a robber who demands your money or your life confers a benefit upon you when he takes your purse and rides away without shooting you through the head. This comment upon our Thought may appear to be lengthy; it will not be wasted if it impresses upon our readers the fact that the Treaty of Union, and the Act of Union which embodied and amended the Treaty, aimed at conferring, and as we shall see, did in truth confer real benefits both upon Scotland and upon England.

Third Thought. — The Articles of the Treaty agreed upon by the Commissioners formed the basis of, and are almost wholly embodied in, the Act of Union.

The result of this fact is that the general effect of the Treaty and of the Act of Union is best and most conveniently considered in Part III., which treats of the Act of Union and its leading provisions,[1] and also of the general results, bad or good, of the Act of Union.

Fourth Thought.—There are certain characteristics of the Commissioners and of the Treaty which are most easily dealt with in this chapter, namely—

(1) *The Character of the Commissioners.*
(2) *The Commissioners as representatives both of England and of Scotland.*
(3) *Special difficulties encountered by the Commissioners.*
    (a) *The Appellate Jurisdiction of the House of Lords.*
    (b) *The Safeguards for the Churches.*
(4) *The Work of the Commissioners.*

[1] See Chap. VII., *post.*

(1) The Character of the Commissioners

The Commission was composed of thirty-one Englishmen and an equal number of Scotsmen representing the Ministry, the Judiciary, and the Parliaments of each country. Each body [1] contained many names of the highest distinction. The English representatives included Godolphin, Somers, Halifax, Harley, Sunderland, and Sir Simon Harcourt; the Dukes of Newcastle, Devonshire, Somerset, and Bolton; the Speaker of the House of Commons, the Lord Keeper, and the two Chief Justices. Among the Scottish members were the Lord Chancellor (Seafield), the Duke of Queensberry, the Earls of Mar, Loudoun, Stair, and Rosebery, Lord Archibald Campbell (Earl of Islay and afterwards third Duke of Argyll), the President and three of the Judges of the Court of Session, and the Lord Provost of Edinburgh. The Commissioners were for the most part Whigs [2] or men who were at that date co-operating with the Whigs, and, as has already been pointed out, it was natural, and indeed necessary, that the Commission which prepared the Treaty of Union should be chosen from the party who desired the political unity of Great Britain. One professed Scottish Jacobite was indeed included in the list, to his own surprise and that of other people. This was George Lockhart of Carnwath, who, probably, as he himself believed, was selected for what he

[1] For names of Commissioners see Appendix C.
[2] Bishop Burnet regarded the English Commissioners as well chosen, but remarked that "those who came from Scotland were not "looked on as men so well affected to the design" (*History of His Own Time*, ii. 446, original edition).

regarded as at least a dubious honour, in the hope that he might be induced to change his political allegiance. His Jacobitism was in opposition to the traditions of his family, and he was the nephew of one of the English Commissioners, Thomas, fifth Lord Wharton (afterwards Marquis of Wharton). Lockhart accepted the nomination, but continued to act in the Jacobite interest by conveying to his friends information useful for political purposes. In the end, he did not appear at the meeting held for the signature of the report of the Commissioners.

With the exception of Lockhart, the members of the Commission set to work with good will, vigour, and intelligence, and, indeed, they represented the best ability which Great Britain could supply. They were, too, as is well known, supported by men of high talent outside the Commission. The Duke of Argyll, whose omission from the list of Commissioners caused some comment, had in fact refused to accept nomination unless the Duke of Hamilton, to whom he was bound by some promise, should also be nominated, but Argyll's services in promoting the appointment of a Commission were recognised in 1705 by his creation as Baron Chatham and Earl of Greenwich in the English peerage, and he gave the negotiations his enthusiastic support. The Duke of Marlborough, whose pre-eminence in the field of statesmanship some students of history regard as not less remarkable than his genius in the conduct of war, notoriously desired the policy of Union. He had been one of the Commissioners appointed in 1702, and his son-in-law, Sunderland, though not always in agreement with Marlborough's political views, represented them in this connexion, and could bring the authority of the great Duke to bear upon his fellow-Commissioners. The Scottish members were strengthened by the knowledge that the policy of Union was ardently supported by the most statesmanlike of the ministers of the Scottish Church, Carstares, who did as much for the Union as Queensberry himself by preventing opposition in the General Assembly.

It is particularly noticeable that the Commissioners met in the spirit of men seriously engaged on a grave and weighty achievement. A circumstance, small in itself, is, when we consider the habits of the times, sufficient to show the businesslike spirit in which the framing of the Treaty was carried on. Lockhart was reported on his return to Edinburgh to have remarked that " none of the English Commissioners during the " Treaty had one of the Scots so much as to dine " or drink a glass of wine with them." [1]

The Commissioners sat in London from April 16 to July 22, 1706, and their work was completed in three months. It was thoroughly well done. The Treaty was so drafted that it was completely the basis of the Act of Union, and, though amended by the Scottish Parliament in some points, all, or almost all, of which were for the advantage of Scotland, did give 'to England and to Scotland alike the special advantages which each of the contracting parties particularly wished to secure.

---

[1] *Mar and Kellie Papers.*   Hist. MSS. Comm. p. 371.

(2) Commissioners as Representatives both of England and of Scotland

It might be thought that the Commissioners, being almost every one of them Whigs, would have looked to the interests of their party and have little concerned themselves with the special interest either of England or of Scotland. But that idea is groundless. The Scottish Commissioners and the English Commissioners were no doubt Whigs, but a Scotsman, though a Whig, was above all things a Scotsman, whilst an English Whig was above all things, at any rate as regards Scotland, an Englishman. Indeed, though all Whigs, speaking broadly, were Unionists, a Scottish Whig in many of his opinions differed essentially from an English Whig.

Chapter V.

The status of the members of the Commission as the representatives of two independent kingdoms engaged in making a Treaty was emphasised by the procedure they adopted. Sir John Clerk, of Penicuik, one of the Scottish Commissioners, thus described their methods of deliberation :

"The Commissioners of both nations met in " different apartments in the Royal Palace of West- " minster, which commonly goes under the name of " the Cockpit. There was one great room where they " all met when they were called upon to attend the " Queen, or were to exchange papers, but they never " met to hold conference together, except once, when " the number of the Scottish representatives for the " two Houses of the British Parliament came to be

" debated, all their transactions were reduced in
" writings concerted in separate apartments." [1]

It might again be imagined that, because of this
sense of different nationality, a Scottish Commissioner
would look only to the interest of Scotland, whilst an
English Commissioner would have his mind wholly
fixed upon the interest or wish of England. But this
danger was averted because the Commissioners as
a whole, whether Scotsmen or Englishmen, were
Unionists and wished the Treaty of Union to pass
into law. All of them equally knew that no Treaty
would ever be passed as an Act of Parliament by
the Parliament of each country which did not pay
careful respect to the interests, the feeling, or even
the prejudices both of Scotsmen and of Englishmen.

The more the Act of Union is studied, the
more apparent the fact will become, that the Commissioners tried hard to represent, and succeeded
in representing, the wishes of the Unionists of each
country. They did indeed more than this: They
took infinite care not to offend, in the Parliament of
Scotland or in the Parliament of England, any large
minority of Unionists which by uniting with the
Jacobites might prevent the Treaty from becoming,
as was necessary, an Act passed both by the English
and by the Scottish Parliament.

It is sometimes suggested, and with formal truth,
that neither the Parliament of England nor the
Parliament of Scotland did, from a modern and a
democratic point of view, adequately represent the
population of either of these countries. So be it.
Every fair-minded historian will admit that these

1 Clerk of Penicuik's *Memoirs* (Scot. Hist. Soc.), pp. 58-59.

Parliaments did represent the wishes of Englishmen and of Scotsmen in so far as they took a part in the political life of the country. The actual terms of the Treaty obtained for England and for Scotland the advantages which each country particularly desired.

(3) Special Difficulties encountered by the Commissioners

(a) *The Appellate Jurisdiction of the House of Lords.* — On no subject was Scottish nationalism more sensitive than on the slightest claim of English Courts to exercise jurisdiction in Scotland. The Scottish Commissioners of 1670 had objected to the creation of an appeal to a Parliament sitting in London.[1] It looked like the revival of the claim of an English King to exercise sovereignty in Scotland. Every word of the new Treaty implied that, speaking broadly, the law and the judicial system, both of England and of Scotland, should remain unchanged except in so far as they might either of them be altered by Act of the British Parliament created by the Act of Union. Special care was taken by Article XIX. of the Treaty "that no Causes in " Scotland be cognoscible by the Courts of Chancery, " Queen's Bench, Common Pleas, or any other Court " in Westminster Hall; and that the said Courts, or " any other of the like nature, after the Union, shall " have no power to cognosce, review, or alter the " Acts or sentences of the Judicatures within

[1] Mackenzie's *History of Scotland*, p. 204.

Chapter
V.

"Scotland, or stop the execution of the same."[1]
These words look full enough to exclude every possible
intervention by any English Court in any cause tried in
Scotland. Is it possible, however, that the Commissioners deliberately left open an appeal from the
highest Court in Scotland—the Court of Session—to
the House of Lords? The legal reader who examines
with care the words cited will see that this question,
strange though it seems, could certainly be raised.
The words just cited do not mention the House
of Lords. They exclude verbatim the jurisdiction of
" the Courts of Chancery, Queen's Bench, Common
" Pleas, or any other Court in Westminster Hall";
but a moment's thought, or a very little knowledge
of law, shows that the House of Lords neither was
nor indeed is, a Court in Westminster Hall. It is a
Court which exists wherever Parliament happens to
be sitting, and the men living in 1706, or 1707,
could, many of them, remember the meeting of an
English Parliament, and a very notable English
Parliament, during the reign of Charles II., held not at
Westminster but at Oxford. This must have been
known to many leading Scottish lawyers and statesmen no less than to Lord Somers. The Commission
further, as stated by Defoe,[2] considered how far the
House of Lords ought to be a Court of Appeal from
any Scottish Court, and could not come to any clear
decision on the matter.

Did the Commissioners, one asks, intentionally
leave a difficult question open and undecided? The

[1] See Act of Union, Article XIX. s. 1, embodying this provision.
[2] Defoe, *History of the Union*, pp. 158-160. Cp. Defoe as to Sacramental Tests, pp. 340, 347.

most obvious, and possibly the truest reply is that Chapter
V. such was their intention, and that prudence sug‑ gested the wisdom of leaving to the decision of future events [1] the answer to a dangerous inquiry which after all might not arise for years. There must have seemed much good sense in leaving a curious point of constitutional law practically unsettled until by the lapse of twenty years or more every one should have become accustomed to the work‑ ing of the Act of Union. For on the one hand it would probably be a benefit to Great Britain that it should possess one Court of Appeal to which important cases might be brought from every part of the British Kingdom for decision, whilst on the other hand it must have seemed highly imprudent, while the carrying of the Act of Union was in doubt, to raise a most irritating, though somewhat speculative, ques‑ tion about appeals to the House of Lords. For it must be remembered, what Cameronians at any rate never forgot, that Bishops formed a part of the House of Lords, and that in the judgements of that Court Bishops even during the eighteenth century sometimes took part. The scrupulosity of Davie Deans, and Cameronians like him, could hardly tolerate a Parliament in which Bishops had seats. It must, therefore, have seemed wise not to institute, in so many words, a Court of Appeal which would excite the enthusiastic opposition of Scottish patriots, because in fact, though not in theory, it sat at West‑ minster, and would arouse the still more fanatical

---

[1] In strictly international treaties of the ordinary kind such leaving of difficult questions to be answered by the future is a common and sometimes a wise course of action, or rather of inaction.

opposition of religious zealots, because it included Bishops among its members. The teaching of history in the shape of events occurring within four or five years after the passing of the Act of Union appears to deride the prudent ambiguities of cautious statesmen. Four or five cases indeed in which questions of private rights alone were concerned were brought up from the Court of Session on appeal to the House of Lords within a very short time after the passing of the Act of Union, and apparently excited little attention and no popular discontent.[1] But in 1709 James Greenshields raised the question as to the right of appeal to the House of Lords from the Court of Session in the most dangerous form conceivable, that is to say, in the shape which made it necessary to decide not only how far the Episcopalian form of worship could, under the Union, be lawfully exercised in Scotland, but also, if the matter be put briefly, how far the national and Presbyterian Church of Scotland could check the growth of Episcopalianism within Scotland. Greenshields was a Scotsman who had been ordained by the deprived Bishop of Ross, but who for fourteen years had been a curate in the north of Ireland, and, as such, had, with questionable sincerity, taken the Oath abjuring the Pretender. He came to Edinburgh and set up an Episcopalian meeting-house with a view to determining whether or not his political qualifications would protect him in using the Book of Common Prayer. At that time there were thirteen Episcopal chapels in and around

---

[1] See Mathieson, *Scotland and the Union*, p. 198, note i. Lockhart, i. 346-348 ; Reports of Scottish Appeals in the House of Lords, i. 12-15.

Edinburgh. In some of these, the English Liturgy was read. Greenshields would probably have gone unpunished had he not, with a view apparently to raise the question of right, set up his chapel exactly opposite the Church of St. Giles, Edinburgh, and if he had not obtruded his presence on the four congregations which assembled there by making his Episcopalian services begin and end at the same time as theirs. A complaint was signed by some 200 persons and presented to the Commission of the General Assembly of the Church of Scotland. A late Act of the Assembly enjoined the prosecution of all who had introduced the use of set forms, and Greenshields having been cited before the Presbytery, and having denied its jurisdiction, was suspended on September 7, for officiating as a minister without warrant and for violating the uniformity of worship established by law. On refusal to comply with the sentence after endorsement by the magistrates, he was imprisoned. The Court of Session when applied to for his release, upheld the judgement of the magistrates. On December 29, 1709, Greenshields appealed to the House of Lords. In 1711, judgement was given by the House of Lords in favour of Greenshields. The judgement appears on the whole to have excited less outcry in Scotland than might have been expected. The judgement did in fact acquire or preserve toleration for Episcopalian worship in Scotland.[1]

It is now, however, quite clear that the Commissioners, when by an ambiguity of language they gave under the Treaty of Union an opening for an appeal

[1] See Mathieson, pp. 194-197.

from the judgement of the Court of Session to the House of Lords, were consciously raising two difficult questions : First, what was the existing law of Scotland as to appeals from the Court of Session to the Scottish Parliament ? and, Secondly, whether it was expedient to allow appeals from the Court of Session to the House of Lords ?

As to the question of Scottish Law. It is uncertain whether under Scottish law there did or did not exist, before the Union, an appeal from the Court of Session to the Parliament of Scotland. The College of Justice was the direct lineal descendant of a Committee of the Estates, and its constitution depended upon an Act of Parliament. The Scottish Parliament maintained throughout its history its early traditions as a Court of law. Hence it was for a long time an open question whether its judicial powers still included the right of hearing appeals from the law Courts. An Act of 1457 had prohibited appeals from the Judicial Committees of the Estates, but it was uncertain whether this prohibition extended to the existing Courts which had replaced these Committees. The question was raised in 1674 in circumstances described in Sir George Mackenzie's *History of Scotland*. The Earl of Callander, who had been unsuccessful in a plea against the Earl of Dunfermline, was advised to appeal to the Parliament, which " would be glad to draw to itself the last and supreme " decision of all causes. This appeal displeased most " sober men, who considered that by this method the " nobility, who always governed Parliaments, would " thereby too much influence private causes." [1] The

---

[1] Mackenzie, pp. 268 and 269.

King, on the advice of Lauderdale, who was the Chapter
nephew of the Earl of Dunfermline, insisted on V.
maintaining the supreme authority of the College
of Justice and forbade appeals.[1]

It was still uncertain whether what was known
as a " Protestation for Remeed of Law " was included
in this Prohibition; this process differed from an
appeal in that it did not involve a suspension of the
execution of the sentence. The decision of Charles
II. was regarded as an illustration of the dangerous
increase in the royal prerogative during his reign, and
indeed the royal letter of 1674 based the decision on
the ground that the maintenance of the authority
of the College of Justice, as representing the King's
person and authority, was " indispensably necessary
" for our service." It was therefore inevitable that
the question should be raised after the Revolution, but
the authors of the Claim of Right contented themselves
with stipulating that " it is the right and privilege of
" the subjects to protest for remeed of law to the King
" and Parliament against sentences pronounced by
" the Lords of Session, providing the same do not
" stop execution of these sentences." Proposals to
define by Statute the cases in which such protesta-
tions were competent were made in 1695 and 1700,
but no definition was made and the question was
still, to this extent, unsettled when the Commissioners
met.

The result, therefore, had been that, at the time

---

[1] A.P.S. ix. 353, x. 214. Professor R. K. Hannay kindly refers
us for further discussion of this intricate question to Stair's *Institutions*, iv. Tit. i. ; Campbell's *Acts of Sederunt*, xxix. ff., the Privy
Council Register, Third Series, vol. iv. p. 631, and A.P.S. ix. 177,
App. 159-60.

when the Commission was sitting, there existed a difference of opinion between a group of eminent Scottish lawyers and the Court of Session on the question how far there existed an appeal from the decisions of the Court to the Scottish Parliament; and we may fairly suppose that the Scottish Commissioners told their English colleagues that such an appeal did exist under the law of Scotland. This view would doubtless make the Commissioners as a body believe that they were introducing no great innovation in giving to the House of Lords a jurisdiction already possessed by the Scottish Parliament. The historical truth of this view is well open to question, but it would to many men of politically sound judgement have been an apology for the ingenious device by which the very section of the Act of Union, which seemed to exclude the jurisdiction in Scotland of any English Court, really though silently endowed the House of Lords with jurisdiction already exercisable by the existing Scottish Parliament, of which the peers of Scotland were a part.

As to the question of expediency. Of course it was a perfectly fair inquiry whether it was expedient to give to the House of Lords sitting at Westminster the position of a Court of Appeal for deciding questions of Scottish law. The creation of such jurisdiction, it might be argued, would be equivalent to referring the most difficult points of Scottish law to English lawyers unacquainted with the law of Scotland. But there were strong reasons which might induce Scottish lawyers to think that the existence of an appeal from the Court of Session to the House of

Lords was justifiable on grounds of expediency. As a
matter of fact it has worked admirably. The decision,
for example, in Greenshields' case did much towards
securing the same amount of religious toleration in
Scotland as the Revolution of 1688 had practically
established in England. Experience shows further
that the existence of one Court of Appeal for the whole
of the United Kingdom has done a great deal towards
establishing legal unity throughout every part of
Great Britain, and this without destroying the
different character of English and of Scottish law
in cases such as the law of marriage, where the
national feeling of each country has been opposed
to a unification of law when it runs against the
popular sentiment either of England or of Scotland.
No better historical testimony to the expediency of
making the House of Lords a Court of final appeal
from the judgements of the Court of Session can be
found than is given in a note by Sir Walter Scott to
the *Bride of Lammermoor*. It clearly represents his
own opinion as a Scottish historian.

"The power of appeal," he writes, "from the Court
"of Session, the Supreme Judges of Scotland, to the
"Scottish Parliament, in cases of civil right, was
"fiercely debated before the Union. It was a privi-
"lege highly desirable for the subject, as the examina-
"tion and occasional reversal of their sentences in
"Parliament, might serve as a check upon the Judges,
"which they greatly required at a time when they
"were much more distinguished for legal knowledge
"than for uprightness and integrity.

"The members of the Faculty of Advocates (so
"the Scottish barristers are termed) in the year

" 1674, incurred the violent displeasure of the Court
" of Session, on account of their refusal to renounce
" the right of appeal to Parliament; and, by a very
" arbitrary procedure, the majority of the number
" were banished from Edinburgh, and consequently
" deprived of their professional practice for several
" sessions, or terms.   But, by the Articles of the
" Union, an appeal to the British House of Peers
" has been secured to the Scottish subject, and that
" right has, no doubt, had its influence in forming
" the impartial and independent character which,
" much contrary to the practice of their pre-
" decessors, the Judges of the Court of Session
" have since displayed." [1]

(b) *The Safeguards for the Churches.*—The Commissioners, by the Acts empowering the Queen to
nominate them, were forbidden to treat of any
alteration in the worship, discipline, or government
of either the Church of England or the Church of
Scotland.

The origin of this exclusion is probably to be
traced to the letter (1689) from the Scottish Convention to King William, already quoted,[2] in which
the Convention expressly excepted from consideration
any alteration of the system of Church government
as it should be established at the time of the Union.
No similar stipulation was made in the Act of 1702,
authorising the Royal nomination of Commissioners,
but the Scottish Parliament, on the day (June 25)

---

[1] Waverley Novels, xiv., *The Bride of Lammermoor* (New ed.
1895), p. 250.   The incident to which Scott refers followed the
Royal decision just quoted, and is fully narrated by Sir George
Mackenzie.

[2] See p. 124, *ante.*

on which the Act was passed, addressed a letter to Queen Anne, calling her attention to the reservation made in 1689, and expressing their confidence that "Your Majesty, both in the naming of the Commis-"sioners, and in the whole procedure of the Treaty, "will have a gracious and careful regard to the main-"taining of the Presbyterian Government of the "Church as now established by Act of Parliament "and ratified by your Majesty in this Session of "Parliament."[1] A further safeguard was provided in the last Clause of the Act of 1702, that nothing done by the Commissioners should "be of any strength or "effect whatsoever" until it had been confirmed by an Act of the Scottish Parliament. A similar precaution was taken in the Act for a Treaty with England, passed by the Scottish Parliament in 1705,[2] and, on the English side, in the Alien Act of 1704, which, in suggesting the appointment of a Commission, stipulated that it should not "treat of or "concerning any alteration of the Liturgy, rites, "ceremonies, discipline, or government of the Church, "as by law established within this Realm (England)." As the discussion of the Treaty progressed in 1706, emphasis was laid upon this restriction by English supporters of the project of Union, who feared that the scheme might be wrecked by a High Church movement to avoid the recognition of the Presbyterian establishment in North Britain.[3]

The real effect of this curtailment of the authority

---

[1] A.P.S. xi. pp. 26, 27. On the question of the liability of Scotsmen to the English Sacramental Test, see pp. 202, 248, 255, *post*.

[2] A.P.S. xi. p. 295.

[3] The Earl of Stair to Carstares, April 26, 1706, *Carstares Papers*, p. 750.

of the Commissioners was, as every Whig must have foreseen, to make sure that any ecclesiastical matter dealt with under the Act of Union should, as regards England, be determined in accordance with the wishes, or certainly not in opposition to the wishes, of the English Parliament, and as regards Scotland in accordance with the wishes, or certainly not against the wishes, of the Scottish Parliament, or rather of the Scottish Parliament acting in harmony with the General Assembly of the Church of Scotland. No one can doubt that the Parliament of England desired the maintenance of the Church of England as by law established, or that the General Assembly desired the maintenance of the Church of Scotland as by law established. It is the special glory of the Whig statesmen throughout Great Britain that they recognised at the beginning of the eighteenth century, what every one acknowledges at the beginning of the twentieth century, that it was not necessary either for England or for Scotland that one and the same form of religious creed and worship should be maintained throughout the whole of the United Kingdom of Great Britain.

The maintenance of the Sacramental Test in regard to the Scotsmen holding certain offices in England, and especially the post of M.P. in the British Parliament, did not fall strictly within the provision which excluded the Commissioners from dealing with the discipline or government of the Church of England or the Church of Scotland, and they did discuss the topic of the Sacramental Test without coming to any definite conclusion. One may safely conclude that they thought it best to let the matter be decided

in regard to the Church of England by the English
Parliament, and with regard to the Church of Scotland by the Scottish Parliament, and probably they
foresaw that as regards seats in the British Parliament, the Church of England would take care that
the Sacramental Test should be maintained in the
British Parliament. The matter was in reality
determined by the Scottish Parliament with the
tacit assent of the Scottish Church so as not to
offend English feeling.[1]

(4) The Work of the Commissioners

The business of the Commissioners was to draft
a Treaty which should be laid before, and in its
substantial provisions be passed as a Bill first,
by the Parliament of Scotland, and next by the
Parliament of England. To Unionists, as were
almost all the Commissioners, and to men of
strong common sense and great practical ability,
as were many of them, the nature of the business
in hand, almost of necessity, must, whether they
were conscious of the fact or not, have dictated the
policy which is patent in every line of the Treaty,
and of the Act of Union in which that Treaty was
finally embodied. This policy was, under the proposed
Union, on the one hand to give to England and Scotland respectively the benefits which each country
mainly desired; and on the other hand, to make no
change in the institutions of either country which
was not necessary for the securing of these benefits
to each country and for ensuring and keeping in

[1] See Chap. VI. pp. 219, 232, *post.*

existence the complete political union of the two countries as one united Kingdom of Great Britain.

The coming to an agreement on the terms of the Treaty, and the final drafting thereof, which was entrusted to four Commissioners, was in itself an extraordinary feat.

Some sixty Englishmen and Scotsmen, who fairly represented the enlightenment and the statesmanship of Great Britain, had come together, and by the mere power of reasonable discussion combined with a *bona fide* purpose of uniting two hostile countries into one powerful and peaceable State, had succeeded in producing an agreement which, if it did nothing else, laid before the Parliaments of England and of Scotland a plan of national unity which, since it conceded to each country many things which each country ardently desired, was, on the face of it, a scheme which deserved to be candidly considered by the national legislature of each country. Even if the people of neither country had actually accepted the terms offered to their consideration in the Treaty as drawn by the Commissioners, the mere framing of a scheme of concord between two States which for centuries had been engaged in perpetual conflict would have been a great step towards future unity. But the work of the Commissioners came to much more than this. The terms which it offered were, in the case of England, so essentially reasonable, that even when modified to a certain extent by the Scottish Parliament, they were, as we shall see, in effect accepted and ratified by the Parliament of England without a single change.

But this work of extraordinary skill was also a

work of extraordinary rapidity. The Commission by whom it was carried out met on the 16th April and signed the draft Treaty on the 22nd July 1706. Yet no one can doubt that the debates carried out in private by eminent statesmen left very few points of importance unconsidered, and exhibit a form of legislation much more likely to produce satisfactory results than has often been achieved by democratic Parliaments where debates carried on in the hearing, so to speak, of every elector who can buy a newspaper exhibit much more of noise than of thought, and much more of partisanship than of prudence. The Commission by whom the Treaty of Union was drawn up may be not unfairly compared with the Convention which framed the constitution which, in 1787, was accepted by the citizens of the United States of America.

CHAPTER VI

THE PASSING OF THE ACT OF UNION BY THE TWO PARLIAMENTS

First Thought.—Students of to-day fail to realise the immense difficulty at the beginning of the eighteenth century of passing the Act of Union.

A MODERN student who wishes to understand the difficulties which beset the passage of the Act must bear constantly in mind two considerations :—

1st. The Act was in itself a piece of legislation quite unlike any statute which had been passed before 1707 by any Parliament either of England or of Scotland, for it combined two distinct characteristics not to be found in any law hitherto passed by the Parliament of either country. It was of necessity both a *bona fide* treaty or agreement between the two countries, and it had also to be an Act or statute regularly and peaceably passed by each of the separate Parliaments of England and of Scotland. The Act of Union was, in short, intended not only in name but in truth, to be at once the ratification of a Treaty and the passing of an Act by the two Parliaments. A critic may object that the Instrument of Government[1] whereby

[1] See Gardiner, *Constitutional Documents of the Puritan Revolution*, p. 314.

Scotland was incorporated in the Commonwealth of England, Scotland, and Ireland anticipated this twofold character of the Act of Union of 1707. The objection is plausible, but at the bottom unsound. The incorporation of Scotland in the Commonwealth of England was an act of conquest and of power; it represented the wise policy of conquerors prepared to deal with Scotland in what, from their own point of view at least, was a liberal and a statesmanlike spirit. But it is absolutely vain to contend that the compulsory union under the Commonwealth, whatever be the form by which it was carried out, was the result of a real agreement between the Parliament of Scotland and the Parliament of England. The objection is not even formally true, since no true Scottish Parliament ever assented to the Cromwellian Union.

2nd. The Act had to be passed by each of two Parliaments which themselves were not friendly to each other, and represented two nations which for centuries had been enemies. This fact can hardly be too strongly insisted upon. Scottish nationalism had been strengthened by war with England, whilst the independence of Scotland had been a constant peril to England.

Second Thought. —The Treaty on which the Act of Union was based was drafted in England by the English and the Scottish Commissioners.

THE DRAFTING OF THE TREATY OF UNION IN ENGLAND

The Treaty, which ultimately formed the basis of

the Act of Union, was drafted in England. This work however was in no sense the work of the English Commissioners alone; it was the work both of the English and of the Scottish Commissioners. It was understood that the Treaty, when drafted, would first be submitted to the Parliament of Scotland, which would assent to it by passing it as an Act with such amendments as that Parliament thought desirable. It was certain that, if the Parliament of Scotland, either formally or in substance, rejected the Treaty, it would not be passed into an Act by the English Parliament, and would thus fall to the ground; and it was also obvious that the Treaty would fall to the ground if it was not incorporated in the Act of the English Parliament.

The English Commissioners, however, stood in a relation to the English Parliament somewhat different from and stronger than the relation of the Scottish Commissioners to the Scottish Parliament. This is a matter of some consequence which has not been sufficiently noted. The Act, if passed at all, must be passed, as the whole Commission knew, by the Whigs of England and by the Whigs of Scotland. The English Commissioners did perfectly represent the Whigs and moderate Tories, who were Unionists and formed the majority of the English Parliament. Such Commissioners were as well fitted to speak in the name of the English Parliament, as would be, in modern times, a British Cabinet fully supported by a majority of the House of Commons. Indeed, they occupied a stronger position than many later ministries have held; for, besides the support of the House of Commons, they had, in respect, at any rate, of

Unionism, the goodwill of the Queen and the support of the House of Lords, and, at the beginning of the eighteenth century, the constitutional authority of the House of Lords was far greater than it has been at any time since the Reform Act of 1832. Hence the English Commissioners could say, and did say authoritatively to their Scottish colleagues, what were the terms of union which must certainly be contained in any Act of Union which would have a chance of obtaining the assent of the English Parliament, and also the terms which, if insisted upon by Scotsmen, would make it impossible to carry an Act through the English Parliament. Thus the English Commissioners at once informed the Scottish Commissioners that any proposed union must be an incorporation of the two kingdoms into a unitary and not a federal state, even though Scotsmen expressed a preference for some kind of federative union.[1] A federal union, besides the other objections to it,

[1] " The first grand point debated by the Commissioners for Scotland " among themselves was whether they should propose to the English a " Federal union between the two nations, or an Incorporating union. " The first was most favoured by the people of Scotland, but all the " Scots Commissioners, to a man, considered it ridiculous and impractic- " able, for that in all the Federal unions there behoves to be a supreme " power lodged somewhere, and wherever this was lodged, it henceforth " became the States General, or, in our way of speaking, the Parliament " of Great Britain, under the same power and authority as the two " nations are at present. And in things of the greatest consequence to " the two Nations . . . it was impossible that the Representatives or " their suffrages in both nations could be equal, but must be regulated " in proportion to the power and riches of the several public burdens " or taxations that could affect them ; in a word, the Scots Com- " missioners saw that no Union could subsist between the two nations " but an incorporating perpetual one. But after all the trouble we gave " ourselves to please the people of Scotland, we knew at the time that it " was but losing our labour, for the English Commissioners were posi- " tively resolved to treat on no kind of union with us but what was to " be incorporating and perpetual " (Clerk of Penicuik's *Memoirs*, p. 60).

would not have met the political necessity which
was in the minds of Queen Anne's English advisers.
One of their main objects was to commit Scotland,
irrevocably, to the Hanoverian Succession, and to
leave no legislative body in Scotland which might
put forward a moral, even if not a legal, claim to
reopen the question after the death of the Queen.
Further, after some discussion, the English Commissioners insisted that the English Parliament would
not consent to give to Scotland a greater representation in the House of Commons than forty-five
members, a number increased, to satisfy the Scots,
from the original English suggestion of thirty-eight.

The Scottish Commissioners, however, could not
be nearly as assured of the terms which the Scottish
Parliament would accept or reject, as were the
English Commissioners in respect to the feeling
or the conduct of the English Parliament:[1] and
this for several reasons. The Jacobites were in the
Scottish Parliament a much more powerful body
than in the Parliament at Westminster: the Scottish
Parliament was divided into more than two parties,
and it was always possible that at any moment,
till the Act was actually passed by the House of
Parliament, the Jacobites by a temporary alliance
with some other party, such for instance as a body of
zealous Presbyterians who deprecated any sort of
union with a country which maintained an Episcopalian
Church, might reject the Treaty of Union. As a
matter of fact, indeed, the " Squadrone Volante," the

[1] Here Parliament means the King and the two Houses which
technically make up the Parliament of the United Kingdom of
Great Britain. See p. 1, *ante*, and compare Dicey, *Law of the
Constitution* (8th ed.), p. xviii.

principles and policy whereof were doubtful and obscure, might on several occasions have caused the rejection by the Scottish Parliament of the Act of Union. The Scottish Commissioners, therefore, could not do much more than assent to proposals which they thought it probable the Scottish Parliament might accept. Everything depended upon the issue of the debates of the Parliament of Scotland, and much also upon the extent to which the General Assembly might accept, or refrain from opposing, provisions made with regard to the Presbyterian Church of Scotland. But there were two points which the Scottish Commissioners knew to be essential to the acceptance of the Treaty, and with regard to these they were not prepared to accept any compromise. The first was freedom of trade; the second, the retention of Scots law and of the Scottish Law Courts. When the English representatives insisted upon an incorporative, or, as it was then termed, an incorporating, union, the Scots replied that they could accept the proposal only with the provision " that all the " subjects of the United Kingdom of Great Britain " shall have full freedom and intercourse of trade " and navigation." [1] At a later stage they made a similarly emphatic statement with regard to the law, and the English accepted both demands. The Scottish Commissioners knew that, without the first of these provisions, the mercantile interest would wreck the Treaty, and that, without the second, the opposition of the lawyers, powerful in any Parliament, would prove fatal to the scheme. The English Commissioners, on their part, were able to reply that if the

[1] Defoe's *History of the Union*, pp. 118 *et seq.*

Scots agreed to an incorporating union and the settlement of the Crown of the United Kingdom upon the House of Hanover, and so met the wishes of Englishmen, the Parliament of England would be willing to meet the wishes of Scotland with regard to the establishment of Free Trade throughout the United Kingdom and between the United Kingdom and all the colonies and dependencies of the Crown of England.

The fact that the English Commissioners were agents authorised by a Parliament, which they represented, to make a treaty on behalf of that Parliament, while the Scottish Commissioners could only hope that a Parliament, which they very imperfectly represented, would accept their recommendations, explains the extent to which the Treaty drafted by the Commissioners was a definite tender of a contract of union by the English Parliament to the Scottish Parliament. It also explains the circumstance, very singular in itself, that the English Parliament, on receiving the Act of Union which, after elaborate discussion and amendment, had been passed by the Scottish Parliament, debated the measure in both Houses, but did not alter one word of its provisions.

Third Thought.—The Treaty of Union, as settled by the Commissioners, was discussed and amended by the Scottish Parliament, and having been so amended, was passed by such Parliament and assented to by Anne as Queen of Scotland, and thus became the Scottish Act of Union.

The Debate, Amendment, and Passing of the
Act of Union by the Parliament of Scotland

Under this head it is convenient to include, in the
first place, the course of procedure properly so called,
that is, the steps taken at different dates in voting
upon and passing the Act, and next, a short account
of certain critical occasions in the voting and the
passing of the Act.

(a) *The Course and Dates of Procedure.*—On
the very day when the Act which gave to the
Queen the nomination of the Commissioners to treat
for the Union was passed, September 21, 1705, the
Scottish Parliament was adjourned till October 3,
1706. This adjournment of itself calmed the excitement which created, and was increased by, the war
between the Parliaments. It gave an opportunity for
the English Parliament to repeal the offensive clauses
of the so-called Alien Act. It was an advantage that
the Scottish Parliament should not be sitting at
the time when the Commissioners were nominated, or
indeed until they had finally drafted the Treaty of
Union. This document was duly signed by the Commissioners[1] on July 22, 1706. Many persons, one
supposes, must have known its general drift, but the
Treaty was not in any way published till one of the
three copies thereof, each of which was signed by
the Commissioners, was delivered to the Parliament
of Scotland on the said October 3, 1706. It was
thereupon printed by order of the Parliament. With
this day begins the dealing of the Scottish Parliament

[1] With the exception of Lockhart (cf. *supra*, p. 187).

with the Act, or, as we should say, the Bill, which embodied and also amended the Treaty.[1]

The following dates may with advantage be borne in mind. They show that the Parliament proceeded with deliberation. On the 3rd October 1706 the Articles were for the first time read out in Parliament.[2] Then there was a pause. They were read again on the 12th of October,[3] and from the 15th[4] to the 30th of October[5] they seem to have been the subject of general discussion in Parliament. On November 1, 1706,[6] the voting on the Articles, or in other words the voting of the clauses of the Bill, began. But the vote of each member was conditional upon the whole of the Articles being ultimately voted. From the 1st November 1706[7] till the 14th of January 1707,[8] the voting on the Articles, combined with the discussion of and voting on amendments, went on. On 16th January 1707,[9] the Bill, or Act of Union, *i.e.* the Articles as amended, was read by the House a second time, and being touched with the sceptre became, as far as Scotland was concerned, the Scottish Act of Union and the law of the land. But the Act, though assented to by the Crown, had a curiously conditional character. For it is enacted that " the " approbation and ratification of the foresaid Articles " and Act [*i.e.* the Articles and Act of Union] shall be " nowayes binding on this kingdom [Scotland] until

---

[1] The Treaty drafted by the Commissioners was, as regards the Parliament of Scotland, the Bill which after amendment by the Parliament, and assent thereto by the Queen, became the Act of Union as passed by that Parliament.

[2] A.P.S. xi. 302.   [3] *Ibid.* 307.   [4] *Ibid.* 307.
[5] *Ibid.* 311.   [6] *Ibid.* 311.   [7] *Ibid.* 401.
[8] *Ibid.* 402.   [9] *Ibid.* 414 (b).

" the said Articles and Act be ratified, approven, and
" confirmed by Her Majesty with and by the authority
" of the Parliament of England." [1]

(*b*) *Critical Occasions in the Passing of the Act.*

(1st) *As to the Passing of the First Article,
Nov. 2–4, 1706.*—The first Article of Union in its
material part runs as follows :

" That the two Kingdoms of Scotland and England
" shall upon the first day of May next ensuing the date
" thereof, and forever after be united into one King-
" dom by the name of Great Britain."

This provision lies at the basis of the whole Act
of Union.   It was defended and attacked with great
vigour.   The one speech made in the Scottish Parliament which has obtained permanent fame or notoriety
is the celebrated oration of Lord Belhaven.[2]   Even
now calm-headed Scotsmen differ greatly as to the
terms in which it ought to be described.

" It would," writes Burton, " be impossible to
" stumble on this production, in any shape, without
" acknowledging in it the work of an artist.   In de-
" spite of Scotticisms, Gallicisms, overstretching class-
" icality, and monstrous affectation, it would stand
" beside any efforts of later English oratory; and prob-
" ably, were it examined at an age so distant as not
" to give the later speaker the benefit of a distinctly
" perceptible adaptation to acknowledged convention-
" alisms, it would be found to have few competitors
" among them in the essentials of heroic oratory—
" rapid and potent diction, impassioned appeal, bold
" and apt illustration." [3]

[1] A.P.S. xi. 414.
[2] *Parl. Hist.* vi., 1702–1714, App. No. I. cxlii-cliv.
[3] Burton, viii. 151.

Chapter
VI. Mathieson, however, describes the same speech, delivered on Saturday, November 2, as "the greatest, " the most popular, if also the most turgid, and over- " strained of all Belhaven's political harangues."[1]

Mackinnon, who gives the fullest account of the great debate commenced on Saturday, November 2, and finished on Monday, November 4, tells us that Belhaven's celebrated oration " was couched in the " pathetic tone of a seer; and both for its pathos " and its periods, was accounted the great speech of the " Session.   To us, it smacks too much of the mock " heroic to be true eloquence.   Our somewhat queru- " lous Cato drew a melancholy picture of the future, " as it appeared to his pessimistic eye.   Church, nobil- " ity, barons, burghs, . . . and Caledonia, the mother of " all, appear clad in sackcloth, to curse the folly that " has lost to them the proud privileges of independence, " and exposed them to the galling woes of national " subordination. . . . Then comes the image of the " hapless Caledonia, like Cæsar, sitting in the midst " of our Senate, ruefully looking round about her, " covering herself with her royal garment, attending " the fatal blow, and breathing out her last with a " ' *Et tu quoque, mi fili.*' "[2]

Even if we bear in mind the maxim which forbids discussions concerning questions of taste, one thing is undeniable, and is of importance.   His lordship between two of the most pathetic parts of his harangue was overwhelmed with emotion, and begged the favour of a little time to " drop a tear as the prelude to so " sad a story."[3]   After a lengthy pause, filled by the

[2] Mackinnon, pp. 292-295.   [3] *Parl. Hist.* vi. p. cli.

discordant voices of other speakers, Belhaven again Chapter
perorated, arguing against the folly of agreeing to the VI.
general motion of an incorporating union without
first discussing the provisions thereof.[1]   This specimen
of high debate mingled with irregular and confused
procedure, shows that the Scottish Parliament had
even in its last days not attained elementary skill in
the conduct of debate.   It could be carried off its
feet by the most ordinary arts of pompous rhetoric.
Belhaven's fervent and pathetic patriotism was
answered by the short reply of the Earl of March-
mont in one sentence : " Behold, he dreamed ; but
" lo ! when he awoke, he found it was a dream ! " [2]
One is not surprised to learn that Belhaven's vehement eloquence is reported not to have affected a
single vote in Parliament.   The Scottish parliamentary system, though as a school for debate it had
existed for not more than sixteen years, had raised
up with extraordinary rapidity that well - known
scheme of party government which, as far as English
experience goes, is the inseparable accompaniment of
the supremacy possessed by a debating, and a more
or less elected, Parliament.   When the first Article of
Union was put to the vote there were one hundred
and sixteen members in its favour and eighty-three
against it.   The "Squadrone Volante" had thrown their

[1] " Is not the Scottish Constitution, on the contrary, ' subject to
" ' regulations or annihilations,' and the Scots, in return, awarded the
" honour of paying English debts, and ' of having some few persons
" ' for witnesses to the validity of the deed, when they are pleased to
" ' contract more ? '   ' Good God, what !   Is this an entire surrender ? '
" Our orator sinks down in overwhelming emotion, and begs the favour
" of a little time to shed a tear in silence, as the prelude to so tragic a
" conclusion " (Mackinnon, *Union of England and Scotland,* p. 295).
   [2] See, for the debate, Mackinnon, pp. 292-297.

weight on to the side of the Union. As far as the
wishes of the Scottish Parliament went, it might now
be assumed that the Treaty would be ratified and
become, as it did, the Act of Union. It is worth
while here to note that the preponderance of the
majority in favour of the Union in this test case, as
in subsequent divisions, was to be found among the
nobles. The barons, or county members, stood as
regards the First Article as thirty-seven to thirty-
three, and the representatives of the burghs were
thirty-three to twenty-nine. Throughout the voting
for and against the Union the measure supported by
the Government commanded invariably a majority
in each of the three Estates.[1]

(2nd) *As to the Security of the Established
Church of Scotland, November 4–12, 1706.*—Then
came up for decision a matter of extraordinary
difficulty. The Commissioners who drafted the
Treaty, as we have seen, were forbidden to deal with
" the worship and discipline and government of the
" Church of Scotland as now by law established."
Any arrangement contained in the Act of Union as
to the Church of Scotland must, it was realised, be
thoroughly acceptable to the people of Scotland, and
certainly could be brought about only by leaving such
arrangement to be determined by the Parliament of
Scotland acting in harmony with the Established
Church of Scotland.[2]

---

[1] See Burton, viii. 153.

[2] And similarly, of course, no arrangement with regard to the
Church of England could be acceptable to the English people which
was not accepted by the English Parliament, which, in this unlike the
Scottish Parliament, contained the authorised representatives of the
Established Church.

The General Assembly of the Church of Scotland was not sitting in November 1706, but the Commission with power to act on behalf of that Assembly was sitting, and at the request of the Commission, an Act, or Bill, as we should say, was introduced into Parliament for providing for the security of the Church. That Bill granted such security as the leading members of the Commission thought at first sufficient. They were acting under the influence of Carstares, the most sagacious of ecclesiastical statesmen. This Act for the security of the Established Church may be thus briefly recapitulated : " It " guaranteed to the Scottish people the Presby- " terian creed, worship, discipline, and government, " ' without any alteration in all succeeding gener- " ' ations.' It required all office - bearers of the " four universities, which were likewise guaranteed " to Scotland for all time, to acknowledge the civil " government and conform to the Presbyterian " creed and worship. It absolved all Scotsmen " from taking any oath or test within the " Kingdom of Scotland, inconsistent with their " religious principles, and bound the Queen's suc- " cessors ' in all time coming ' to take an oath to " inviolably maintain and preserve the government, " worship, discipline, rights, and privileges of the " Church." [1]

It contained further a most unprecedented provision, which ratified beforehand whatever provision might be inserted by the English Parliament in the Act of Union for the protection of the Church of

[1] Mackinnon, *The Union of England and Scotland,* pp. 303, 304.

England.[1]   The Whigs of both countries had at last learned the full wisdom of the dictum that

'Tis Holy Island parts us, not the Tweed.

They were fully determined that neither Bishop nor Presbyter should have power to raise a religious war which might break up the political union of the two countries.

(3rd) *The Passing of the Twenty-second Article.*— In spite of debating, and other causes of delay, Article after Article of the Treaty was ratified and passed.   From the 7th to the 9th of January 1707, Article XXII. was under discussion.   It refers to the number of Peers, namely 16, and of the members for burghs and shires, namely 45, who were to be representatives of Scotland in the Parliament of Great Britain.   It was felt that here the Opposition must fight 'its last battle.   The plan of proceeding was carefully arranged.   The Opposition were to rally

[1] See Mathieson, *Scotland and the Union*, p. 186.   The Act declares that " the Parliament of England may provide for the security of the " Church of England, as they think expedient to take place within " the bounds of the said Kingdom of England, and not derogating " from the security above provided [*i.e.* provided in the Act of Union] " for establishing of the Church of Scotland within the bounds of this " Kingdom [*i.e.* Scotland]" (A.P.S. xi. 414).   If the whole provision be put into plain words, the Act of Union, as passed by the Parliament of Scotland provides that an Act passed by the Parliament of Scotland for the security of the Established Church of Scotland shall form an essential part of the Act of Union, and that, further, the Parliament of England shall be at liberty to insert in the Act of Union any Act which the English Parliament deems needed for the security of the Church of England in England, so long as such last-mentioned Act does not trench upon the security provided for the Church of Scotland, and that the Act to be thus passed by the Parliament of England, being ratified beforehand by the Act of Union, shall not need any further ratification by the Parliament of Scotland.

with their whole force. If they were defeated, the Duke of Hamilton was to enter his protest and, at the head of his followers, withdraw from Parliament. When the day of final action arrived, he pleaded a severe toothache as an excuse for not coming to the Parliament House. Pressure was put upon him to appear in Parliament. He came to the House. The Government carried the Article by a decided majority. The Duke then refused to enter his protest. The whole demonstration broke down and the parliamentary opposition to the Treaty was practically at an end.

The number of the representatives to be given to Scotland, in the British Parliament, whether as Peers in the House of Lords, or as members of the House of Commons, was a matter deliberately determined by the Treaty of Union, and obviously concerned the interest of England no less than of Scotland. It was also completely understood that the number of these representatives, being once settled by the Commissioners, was an essential part of the Treaty and could not be changed by an Act either of the Scottish or of the English Parliament. But care was at the same time taken that the Scottish Parliament should, whilst it remained in existence, and after the passing of the Act of Union, but before the Act came actually into force, have the power of determining by Act of the Scottish Parliament several important questions with regard to such representatives. Thus, while the Scottish Act of Union was passed by the Scottish Parliament on January 16, 1707, the Act for settling the manner of electing such Peers and members to represent

Chapter
VI.

Scotland in the British Parliament was passed on February 5, 1707,[1] and, as it may be convenient here to add, the 16 Peers and the 45 M.P.'s to represent Scotland in the first British Parliament were in fact elected by and from among the members of the then existing Scottish Parliament.[2] This transaction is a typical one. It exhibits the desire of the supporters of the Union to make as little unnecessary change as possible in Scottish Institutions. It left to Scotsmen, for example, the distribution of seats among shires and burghs, and went far to ensure that every city or shire which was represented in the Parliament at Edinburgh should have some part at any rate of representation in the Parliament which was to meet at Westminster.

(4th) *Pamphlets, Petitions, Addresses, Riots, which threatened to become Civil War against the Passing of the Act of Union.*—Let no man imagine that the different stages of the passing of the Act of Union by the Scottish Parliament were gone through during a period of calmness, of quiet, or even of peace. From the moment when it was known to the public that the Act involved a corporative union of the two Parliaments in the Parliament of Great Britain, it aroused active and vehement opposition in Scotland. Many Scotsmen had supposed that the unity of Great Britain would be secured by a federative Union which would leave the English Parliament and the

---

[1] A.P.S. xi. 425, c. 8.

[2] This was done nominally on the ground that the Peers and Commoners forming part of the then existing English Parliament were to remain part of the British Parliament, but in reality on the ground that this arrangement made all but sure that the 61 representatives of Scotland who would form part of the first Parliament of Great Britain should be Whigs or Unionists.

Scottish Parliament each in existence.[1]   No one, it is true, knew exactly what a federative Union meant. We must remember that the only forms of federal government much known to Scotsmen, or indeed to Englishmen, were supplied by Holland and Switzerland.   One speaker in the Scottish Parliament referred to Sweden and Denmark as "united by a federal " compact under one monarch," [2] but the constitution of the United Provinces seems to have been in the minds of the Scotsmen who demanded a federal union. Alike in Holland and in Switzerland, separate states were joined together by a sort of more or less federal alliance, but the world had not yet seen anything like federalism as it has existed for more than a century among the United States, or as it now exists in the Dominion of Canada, and in the Commonwealth of Australia.   It is, at any rate, of importance to note that no definite scheme of federal government was ever put forward by the opponents of the Act of Union, nor was there any such plan which on its own merits had been brought to the knowledge, or had received the support of, the Scottish people.   The demands for a Union which should not be an incorporative Union were little more than an expression of dislike, natural enough on the part of Scotland, to the abolition of the Scottish Parliament.   No fair-minded person can dispute that, with a large number of Scottish electors, the Act of Union was unpopular. Petitions against it poured in from burghs, parishes, and shires.   The pamphlets which attacked the Act

[1] See Burton, viii. chap. lxxxvii. pp. 1361-64; Mathieson, *Scotland and the Union*, pp. 116–124, and cf. the quotation from Sir John Clerk, p. 209, *ante*.

[2] *Parl. Hist.* vi. App. cxli.

of Union were numerous. Those in its favour were comparatively few. One of the latter gives incidentally a picture which probably represents one aspect of the state of feeling among opponents of the Union accurately enough:

"In a corner of the street one may see a
"*Presbyterian Minister*, a *Popish Priest*, and an
"*Episcopal Prelate*, all agreeing together in their
"discourse against the Union, but upon quite
"different views and contradictory reasons. The
"*Minister*, because he fears the Presbyterian Church
"Government will be ruined, and so great encour-
"agement will be given to Popery and Prelacy.
"The *Priest*, because his darling hopes will be
"disappointed, by the settling the succession in the
"Protestant line. And the *Prelate*, because he
"knows the Parliament will make such a security
"for the Presbyterian Church Government, as that
"it cannot be altered in *Scotland* without sapping
"the Foundation of the Union, and shaking the
"whole fabric of the *British* Constitution."[1]

The existence of pamphlets and petitions on either side establishes the fact, which is of consequence, that readers in Scotland—at all events in the Lowlands, where alone public opinion can be said to have existed—must have been, in proportion to the population, a larger body than the reading public in England, and that it was worth while to appeal to the feeling and the understanding of a more or less educated electorate. Still, when the matter is analysed, though the mob in Edinburgh was certainly opposed to a measure which threatened to diminish

[1] Quoted in Clerk of Penicuik's *Memoirs*, p. 244.

the importance and wealth of Scotland's capital, and
though the majority of the electors may have looked
with more fear than liking on the policy of Unionism,
no one can now answer with anything like certainty
the question how far the majority of Scotsmen
in 1707 can be counted among the opponents of
Unionism.   At Edinburgh, at Glasgow, and in some
other parts, violent riots, which threatened the rise
of civil war, expressed the indignation of Scottish
nationalism against its apparent destruction by the
Act of Union.   At one moment the supporters of
the Act felt their lives in danger; it is even said
that preparations were made for sending English
troops into Scotland for the support of order.   Yet
all the efforts of Scottish nationalists ended in
failure.

(5th) *The actual Passing of the Act of Union
by the Scottish Parliament on January 16, 1707.*—
On January 16, 1707, the Scottish Act of Union, as
amended by the Scottish Parliament, was passed by
the Estates of Scotland, and on being touched with
the sceptre, became the Scottish Act of Union.   But,
as we have already noted, the Act itself provides
that the Articles of the Treaty, and the Act in which
they are embodied, shall have no authority in Scotland until they, as so amended by the Scottish Parliament, should have been passed by the Parliament
of England.[1]   This conditional form in which the
Scottish Act was passed certainly warrants the
conclusion that any material change made by the
English Parliament involved a necessity for the
return of the Act to the Scottish Parliament in

[1] See A.P.S. xi. 414.

order to obtain its assent to such change. Many Englishmen and Scotsmen imagined that the Parliament of England would in some respect amend or alter the Act as passed by the Parliament of Scotland, and that, in this case, the Act would have to be sent again to Scotland and be liable to further debate and amendment, and even rejection, by the Scottish Parliament. This expectation, not in itself unreasonable, may have facilitated the passing of the Act in Scotland. It certainly accounts in part for the rapidity with which, and the mode in which, the Act was dealt with by the English Parliament.[1]

It has been said that, as far as Scotland was concerned, " the Union was in fact carried by the Parlia-" ment with the assistance of the Church [2] against the " country."

Fourth Thought.—How far was the Union carried by the Scottish Parliament against the wish of the Scottish people ?

This question in reality raises at least three different inquiries which ought to be distinguished from each other.

First Inquiry.—Is it true that the Act of Union was carried in Scotland by bribery ?

This question was long ago raised by Jacobites, who gave to it an affirmative answer. It has been countenanced also by the language of a writer generally so moderate and judicious as Hallam. He describes Scottish Unionists as making a " great sacrifice of

[1] See p. 230, *post.*
[2] On the claim of the General Assembly to represent Scottish opinion, see pp. 80-89, *ante.*

"natural patriotism," and that his meaning may not
be misunderstood adds the following statement : " The
" Union closes the story of the Scots Constitution.
" From its own nature not more than from the gross
" prostitution with which a majority had sold them-
" selves to the surrender of their own legislative exist-
" ence, it has long been odious to both parties in
" Scotland." [1]   We may add, what may without hesitation be admitted, that in 1707 the parliamentary
statesmen neither of England nor of Scotland can as a
class claim credit for pecuniary disinterestedness or for
condemnation of conduct which, at any rate at the
end of the nineteenth century, would have been stig-
matised as corrupt.   But we have to go a great deal
further than this in order to maintain the truth of
the charge that the majority of the Scottish Parliament sold their own legislative existence.   The subject
has in late years been carefully investigated,[2] and
while it is undeniable that political venality at the
time when the Act of Union was carried existed both
in England and in Scotland, it is also true that
Jacobites were certain to bring the charge of corruption against the men who had passed the Act of Union,
and thus, in effect, had defeated every plan for restoring the exiled Stewarts.   To assert that " bribery
" carried the Union would be a contention absurd on
" the face of it.   If one thing is apparent from the
" correspondence of the Scottish statesmen who were
" mainly responsible for its accomplishment, it is that
" they were profoundly convinced of its necessity in

---

[1] Hallam, iii. (ed. 1872) 340.
[2] See especially Burton, *Hist.* viii. 178-184 ; Hume Brown, iii.
126, 127 ; and Hume Brown, *Scotland and the Union*, pp. 126-128.

" the interest of both kingdoms." [1]   It has also been
made plain that a large amount of the payments made
to Scottish officials during or after the passing of the
Act of Union was in reality the payment of salaries
or other debts due to them from the Crown, and to
accept payment of a debt is a very different thing
from the taking of a bribe.

Second Inquiry.—Why was it that the majority
of the Scottish Parliament could never succeed in
defeating any material provision of the Act of Union ?

The obvious cause of this failure lies on the surface.
It is that the Opposition consisted of two parties
who agreed in objecting to the Union, but disagreed
on almost every other question of policy. The Jacobites
hated the Union, but they longed for the restoration
of the Stewarts, and detested the Revolution Settlement.   A very large number of Presbyterians disliked
the Union in that it destroyed the Scottish Parliament, but were determined at any cost to maintain
the Revolution Settlement. A few fanatics for Presbyterianism, known as the Cameronians, were bitterly
opposed to the Act of Union, because it was treachery
in their eyes to the Solemn League and Covenant,
but no Presbyterian could forget the " killing time "
or desire a Restoration any more than Davie Deans
could have imagined an alliance with Viscount Dundee.
The moment that a Jacobite, who might well be an
Episcopalian or a Papist, urged a Presbyterian to
uphold against the Government the securities and
the privileges of the true Presbyterian Church, persuasion which savoured of hypocrisy was sure to raise
alarm.   Jacobites and Presbyterians could not vote

[1] Hume Brown, iii. p. 127.

together in Parliament; they could still less take up
arms together against a Government which secured
the Church and thereby gave irresistible strength to
the Revolution Settlement. When the day was nearly
approaching for the Union Bill being touched with
the sceptre, and thus becoming the law of the land,
the Government feared that the enthusiasm of the
Cameronians for the League and Covenant might
enable them to enter into an unholy alliance with
Jacobites longing for a restoration of the Stewarts and
for the triumph of Episcopacy. But this fear was
groundless, and the supposed co-operation of fanatics
who hated one another more than they each hated the
Whigs turned out to be an impossibility.

Third Inquiry.—What was it in the state of
opinion which made men who disliked the Treaty of
Union hesitate to offer vigorous opposition to the
passing of the Act of Union?

The answer to this question does not admit of
being given with absolute certainty, yet to any
modern critic who thinks the matter over with care
it ought not to be very difficult to conjecture the
existence of feelings which might make an honest
opponent of the Union hesitate to give effect by deed
or vote to the fulfilment of his own desire. The
wretched poverty and the discontent of Scotland were
patent. The union of Crowns had in popular estima-
tion been of no benefit to Scotland. But freedom of
trade under Cromwell had opened to Scotland the
chance of material prosperity. A true lover of his
country, and there were hundreds of such among
Scottish Jacobites, might wish to reject the Union
and yet not be able to support the moral responsibility

Chapter VL of causing the rejection of a policy which at any rate offered wealth and prosperity to Scotsmen.   The Duke of Hamilton's hesitations, or, as many would say, treachery, need explanation, and an unbiassed critic might suggest that the parliamentary leader of the Jacobites himself could not bear the responsibility of thwarting a policy which might after all further, as it did further, the prosperity, the happiness, and the welfare of the Scottish people.   Hesitation no doubt means weakness.   But feebleness of resolution is a vice not unknown to politicians.   It is conceivable at least that ambition may sometimes and without great guilt be thwarted by the dictates of conscience.

THE DEBATE ON AND PASSING OF THE ACT BY THE PARLIAMENT OF ENGLAND

Fifth Thought.—The Act so passed and assented to by the Queen of Scotland was after debate but without any amendment (with one exception authorised by the Scottish Act of Union) passed by the English Parliament, and finally assented to by Anne as Queen of England,[1] and thus became the Act of Union for the whole of Great Britain.

The Treaty and Act of Union as passed by the

---

[1] The apparent paradox that the Scottish Act which embodied the Treaty of Union as amended by the Scottish Parliament was discussed but not in reality altered by the English Parliament is explained at pp. 208-212, *ante.*   The Treaty was drafted in England, and as ratified and enacted by the Scottish Parliament contained all the provisions for the benefit of England held to be essential by the English Commissioners, and these Commissioners represented the wishes of the Whigs who had a majority in the English Parliament.   A single amendment would have risked sending the Bill back to the Scottish Parliament for reconsideration.

Parliament of Scotland was ratified or accepted by the Chapter
VI. English Parliament without the repeal of a word.[1]

The Whigs in a body voted for the Act in both Houses, and it was supported even by some of the Tory members for the northern counties.[2] The opposition of the High Church party to an Act which ratified the existence of an Established Presbyterian Church in Scotland proved to be very ineffective.

" When the Act for securing the true Protestant " religion and Presbyterian Church Government " was debated in the Committee in the House of " Lords, several Lords, and four Bishops, spoke very " warmly against ratifying, approving and confirming " it, though they were not against giving the Scots a " security that it should be maintained among them. " But the Archbishop of Canterbury [Tenison] said, " he had no scruple against ratifying, approving and " confirming it within the bounds of Scotland. That " he thought the narrow notions of all Churches had " been their ruin; and that he believed the Church " of Scotland to be as true a Protestant Church as " the Church of England, though he could not say it " was so perfect. Several of the Bishops spoke very " much in the same strain, and all of them divided " for ratifying, approving and confirming the Church " Act, except the four that spoke against it, and the " Bishop of Durham [Lord Crewe] who went away " before the vote. The other High Church Bishops " were not at the House that day." [3]

The parallel Act or Bill ratifying the privileges

---

[1] The provisions for the security of the Church of England were ratified and approved of by anticipation in the Scottish Act of Union. See pp. 219-220, *ante.*

[2] *Carstares Papers*, pp. 759-760.   [3] *Ibid.*

of the Church of England was introduced in the
House of Lords on February 3, 1707, by Archbishop
Tenison. It differed from the Scots Act in imposing
a sacramental test upon Scotsmen in England. This
possibility had been foreseen in Scotland, but the
Scottish Parliament had deliberately refrained from
taking any action in the matter. Defoe explains the
self-restraint shown by the Scots in not imposing a
test in Scotland by the objection of the Scottish
clergy to "imposing any oath or acknowledgment
" of the Church, as a test of civil employment," and
in relating the decision not to take any precautions
against the imposition of a test in England, he tells
us that many members of the Scottish Parliament
believed the imposition of such a test to be inconsistent both with the Treaty of Union itself and
with the Act for Securing the Church of Scotland,
which ordained that no oath, contrary to their principles, should be imposed upon members of the
Church of Scotland. In the end "it was thought
" that to meddle with this matter might do much
" more harm than good." [1] In the absence of any
stipulation to the contrary, the sacramental test was,
by the Act of Security for the Church of England,
imposed upon Scottish members of Parliament.

The astounding circumstance of the adoption of
the Treaty of Union by the English Parliament without any change, except what was implied in the Act
of Security for the Church of England, is thus stated by
one of those few historical writers who can summarise
the results of extended knowledge in a few sentences.

"Scarcely would the union have threaded the

[1] Defoe, *History of the Union*, p. 469.

" opposition of the High Churchmen and Tories in
" the English Parliament if they had been allowed
" to debate the articles in detail. The Bill might
" have been in committee till the day of doom.
" But that danger was eluded by the ingenuity of
" Harcourt, afterwards Chancellor, who framed a Bill
" with the Treaty recited in the preamble, and a single
" enacting clause. To make all fast, in addition to the
" Acts imposing the abjuration oath, an Act was passed
" declaring it treason to impugn the settlement of the
" Crown under the Act of Union or the right of
" Parliament to limit the succession. This was aimed
" against the Jacobite enemies of the union and the
" succession in Scotland. It stamped the monarchy
" as parliamentary." [1]

But draftsmanship, however skilful, cannot, we all
know, be an effective substitute for statesmanship,
and the words of Goldwin Smith themselves raise
a curious inquiry : How did it happen that the
Parliament of England could pass in a week or two
unchanged, though not absolutely undiscussed, an Act
which in the Scottish Parliament had for about four
months been the subject of violent debate and inces-
sant discussion ? The substantive answer to this question can be obtained only by a careful consideration
of the Treaty of Union agreed to both by the English
and by the Scottish Commissioners. That Treaty
secures to England all the advantages which Englishmen demanded as the necessary price of assent to
the Union. These were the unity of Crowns—the
unity of Parliaments—the limited number of Scottish
representatives in the new British Parliament—the

[1] Goldwin Smith, *The United Kingdom*, ii. p. 139.

equality of taxation for the inhabitants of the whole of the United Kingdom, and, to put the matter shortly, the absolute political unity of Great Britain, combined with the parliamentary supremacy of England in the Parliament of the United Kingdom. Each of these advantages was secured to Englishmen by the Act of Union as passed by the Scottish Parliament. That Act also obtained for Scotland the exact advantages, *e.g.* freedom of trade and the security of the established Presbyterian Church, which were the payment demanded by Scotsmen for the sacrifice of the old Scottish Parliament. It was clear that to touch any provision of the Bill would in fact be a rejection of a contract arrived at on each side with the greatest trouble. It would have in common fairness involved the sending back of the Act of Union to Scotland for reconsideration. No Unionist could foresee with confidence the result of a reopening of an elaborately arranged international contract. English Whigs at any rate, though not enthusiastic for the Union, did ardently desire the fruits of Union with Scotland. The Whigs had a majority in each House of Parliament; the Union was desired by the Queen; the policy of the Union was supported by the statesmanship and by the victories of Marlborough. Blenheim and Ramillies shattered the forces of Louis XIV., and also drove through Parliament unquestioned that Act of Union which on the 6th March 1707 created the new and United Kingdom of Great Britain.

PART III

THE ACT OF UNION AND ITS RESULTS

CHARACTER OF PART III

This Part treats of the following topics :

Character of Part III

    I. The Act of Union itself as illustrated by its general character and provisions.[1]

    II. The objections to the Act of Union.[2]

    III. The acceptance of the Act of Union.[3]

    IV. The success of the Act of Union.[4]

[1] See Chap. VII. *post.*   [2] See Chap. VIII. *post.*
[3] See Chap. IX. *post.*   [4] See Chap. X. *post.*

CHAPTER VII

THE ACT OF UNION—ITS GENERAL CHARACTERISTICS AND LEADING PROVISIONS

Chapter
VII.
Thought.—The Act of Union is at once a most revolutionary and a most conservative statute.[1]

In every line of the Act[2] is visible the determination of its authors to stick at no change, however revolutionary, which was necessary for creating the absolute political unity of Great Britain, but to introduce no change, however salutary in itself, in the institutions either of England or of Scotland which was not necessary for the creation of such unity.

THE REVOLUTIONARY CHARACTER OF THE ACT OF UNION

The Act carried through four revolutionary or fundamental changes in the constitution of England and of Scotland.

---

[1] See particularly Chap. V. p. 182, *ante*, as to the extent to which the Act was the embodiment of a distinct and real contract between the Parliament of England and the Parliament of Scotland respectively. Cf. 5 Anne, c. 8.

[2] Lecky, ii. pp. 22-90, contains an excellent general appreciation of the Act of Union, 1707.

(A) The complete political union of the two Kingdoms.

(1) They became the one United Kingdom of Great Britain. (Art. I.)

(2) The Crown was settled after the death of Queen Anne, in default of her issue, on the Electress Sophia of Hanover, and the heirs of her body being Protestants; and Papists were entirely excluded from the succession. (Art. II.)

(3) The United Kingdom became wholly and solely represented by one and the same Parliament, viz. the Parliament of Great Britain (Art. III.), in which Scotland was represented by 16 Peers in the House of Lords, and 45 members in the House of Commons returned by Scottish constituencies (Art. XXII.).

(4) The legislative and ultimate executive power in Scotland was transferred from the Parliament of Scotland, which had never been either in theory or in fact a supreme or sovereign body, to the Parliament of Great Britain, which inherited both the tradition and, in legislation, the practice of supreme or sovereign authority.

These leading provisions brought under head (A) created the State of Great Britain, and further gave to England by the Act of Union the advantages which English statesmen had mainly desired. The Act secured, as far as any law could do so, constant peace throughout the United Kingdom, placed the government of Great Britain wholly in the hands of one King and Parliament, and, whilst giving to Scotland a real representation in the two Houses of the British Parliament, made certain that the British

Parliament should remain in character a substantially English body. This last result of the Union certainly lasted till 1800, and was not materially disturbed till 1832. Up to that date it was hardly possible that members not elected by English constituencies should keep in office a Cabinet acceptable only to a minority of English parliamentary representatives.

(B) Complete freedom of trade was established for all subjects of the United Kingdom throughout the United Kingdom, and all the Dominions and Plantations belonging thereto.[1] (Arts. IV., V., VI.)

At the time when the Act of Union was passed no Dominion or Plantation of England had, it may be assumed, authority to tax goods imported in English ships from England. Curiously enough the establishment of free trade from 1845 onwards, combined with the wide legislative powers given to the Parliaments of the Dominions, has to a certain extent curtailed the advantages supposed to be secured to Scotsmen and Englishmen under the Act of Union. Taxes may be, and are now, imposed by the Parliament of a Dominion on goods imported from the United Kingdom.

The Act of Union, further, was intended to establish equality of taxation by the British Parliament in Scotland and in England, and efforts were certainly made to allow for the comparative

[1] " That all the subjects of the United Kingdom of Great Britain " shall, from and after the Union, have full freedom and intercourse " of trade and navigation, to and from any port or place within the " said United Kingdom, and the Dominions and Plantations thereunto " belonging ; and that there be a communication of all other rights, " privileges, and advantages, which do, or may belong to the subjects " of either Kingdom, except where it is otherwise expressly agreed in " these Articles." (Art. IV.)

poverty of Scotland by lightening the taxes imposed
upon her.[1]

(C) Complete security for the Church of Scotland
combined with equal security for the Church of
England.

From one point of view this may be called the
most revolutionary innovation to be found in the
Act of Union. The way in which that Act provides
security at once for the national and Presbyterian
Church of Scotland and also for the national and
Episcopalian Church of England is a piece of most
original statesmanship. Each Church derives the
strength of its position from the Act of Union. We
may also say that each Church is made to guarantee
the maintenance of the other. Such legislation gets
rid once and for all of the delusion, which had made
the political unity of Great Britain all but impossible,
that no country could be politically united without
the establishment, within the whole of its territory,
of one and the same form of Christian doctrine and
worship.[2]

The provisions brought under (B) and (C) embrace
in reality the main direct advantages obtained by
Scotland. They were distinctly the price offered and
paid by English Unionists in return for the corporate
union of the two countries. This complete unity
was not popular in Scotland, because it permanently

[1] " Great as was the inequality of the value of land in the two
" countries, when the English commissioners agreed that the land tax
" in Scotland should be less than a fortieth of that contributed by
" England, they were certainly straining a point in favour of the
" poorer country " (Hume Brown, iii. 107).

[2] As to enactments which, from different points of view, may be
regarded as having at once a revolutionary and a conservative character, see pp. 246, 254, *post.*

placed the government of Great Britain in the hands of a Parliament in fact sitting in London, and of an Executive, or as we now term it, a Cabinet, appointed, if not in strictness by, yet mainly in accordance with the wish of, the British Parliament. This seemed to be, though in truth it was not,[1] the sacrifice of Scottish nationality; it was really the sacrifice of a different thing, namely, Scottish political independence.

The advantages gained by Scotland, though they turned out in the main a great benefit to the whole of Great Britain, were very considerable, and in fact in the course of less than fifty years created a kind of material and intellectual prosperity hitherto unknown in Scotland. Before the lapse of a century, *i.e.* before 1800, they had given to the whole of Great Britain a strength and wealth absolutely unknown before the Union, and also had laid the foundations of the present British Empire. The so-called expansion of England is in reality the expansion of Great Britain. As the war with Napoleon proved, the British Empire had in 1815 become the most powerful State in the world, and could resist the whole force of the Napoleonic Empire, which meant at one time little less than the armed power of the whole of Continental Europe except the Spanish Peninsula.

(D) The transference of the government of Scotland from a non-sovereign to a sovereign Parliament.

The extension to Scotland of the supreme authority of Parliament is not recorded by a single word in the Act of Union. It may well be doubted whether,

[1] See Chap. X. p. 322, *post*.

either in England or in Scotland, it was clearly
realised or perceived. English statesmen no doubt
assumed that the British Parliament would possess
after the Union the same theoretical and practical
authority which the English Parliament already
possessed, and which it was coming more and more
constantly to exercise throughout England. Scottish
Parliamentarians were probably not unwilling to
exalt the parliamentary power in which they were to
share. It is quite conceivable, moreover, that they
themselves did not fully appreciate the difference
between the authority of the Scottish and the
authority of the English Parliament. We have
already dealt generally with this subject,[1] and it is
unnecessary here to do more than remind readers that
the Scottish Parliament had never in reality exercised
anything like the authority which for generations had
been asserted and enforced by the Parliament of
England. The transference in Scotland of authority
from a non-sovereign to a sovereign Parliament is
one of those changes which, just because it was not
expressed in any legal enactment, deserves the more
attention. English statesmen and English lawyers
have occasionally found serious difficulties in dealing
with problems raised by the relation of Church and
State in Scotland, but the perplexities have arisen,
not from any desire to interfere with Scottish law,
or with Scottish religious convictions, but from the
unwillingness of Englishmen, statesmen and judges
alike, to admit that a Church, or any society existing
for the maintenance, *inter alia*, of certain religious
beliefs, can possess, in regard to such beliefs, any

---

[1] See Introd. pp. 19-23, *ante*.

authority which can transcend an Act of Parliament or which may enable the Church to enforce any contract held invalid by the House of Lords sitting as a Court of Appeal from Scotland. Englishmen, in short, have, like many English jurists, an intellectual difficulty, derived really from their being accustomed to the sovereignty of Parliament, in admitting the possibility of any division of sovereignty between Church and State.

A modern Englishman or Scotsman finds it hard to realise how thorough-going and in the strictest sense "revolutionary"—if we exclude from that term the idea of a political change carried through by physical violence—the Act of Union seemed to the inhabitants of Great Britain in 1707.[1] For no inhabitant of Great Britain can, without a considerable effort of imagination, picture to himself the state of things under which England and Scotland had been politically independent countries, and under which each country was still, in spite of the union of the Crowns, animated by a good deal of mutual hostility produced by almost constant warfare which had lasted for between three hundred and four hundred years.

The Conservatism of the Act of Union

The Act of Union carried through by legal means an immense revolution; it created a new State, namely the United Kingdom of Great Britain. But it was the most conservative of revolutionary

---

[1] For the relation between England and Scotland between 1603 and 1707 the reader should consult the statement as to the character of Part I., which precedes Chap. I. pp. 27-29, *ante*.

measures. To put the matter shortly, it repealed every law or custom of England or of Scotland inconsistent with the political unity of the new State, but it did not make or attempt any change or reform which was not necessary for the creation of the new United Kingdom.

The conservatism of a law must, in the main, consist in what the law does not enact. Hence it is not easy to exhibit to a student the way in which the authors of the Act of Union deliberately left alone many matters, some of which they might conceivably have reformed or changed. The wisdom of this omission to deal with any matter outside the real scope of the Act will be apparent to historically minded persons. But, whether this avoidance of unnecessary reforms be praised or blamed, its working and existence can be shown only by illustrations. These examples of a negative policy may be most easily understood if they be drawn first from the way in which the conservatism of the Act affected England, and next from the way in which it affected Scotland.

As to England.—With the one exception [1] of the introduction of representatives of Scotland into what had been the English and now became the British Parliament, no English political institution whatever was changed. Not a single small or rotten borough was deprived of a member; not a single unrepresented English town gained under the Act of Union representation in Parliament.[2] The Act of Union in no

[1] See Articles of Union XXII., XXIII., and Act, s. 22.

[2] This fact is the more noteworthy if we observe that during the Interregnum under the Constitution of 1653, a very complete, and in some respects a very skilful measure of parliamentary reform was

way whatever touched the dignity, the doctrine, or the property of the Church of England.

As to Scotland. — Examples of even excessive conservatism abound : Except as to the number of Scottish representatives, the parliamentary system of Scotland was kept in existence,[1] and the arrangements as to the election of the representatives of Scotland were, as we have seen, purposely left for determination by the Parliament of Scotland. The heritable jurisdictions then existing in Scotland,[2] and the rights and the privileges of the Royal burghs were kept alive;[3] and ample security was given against alteration in the worship, discipline, and government of the Church of Scotland.

Any student will perceive that the provisions of the Act of Union providing for the security of the Church of Scotland and of the Church of England respectively, have been already used as illustrations of the revolutionary or thorough-going character of the Act, and that here they are treated as illustrations of the conservatism of the same Act. The apparent contradiction is intentional, for it brings into view that the very same enactment may in the Act of Union be at once revolutionary or thorough-going and yet be even more distinctively marked by conservatism.

---

brought into existence by Cromwell and the leading Puritan statesmen. See *The Instrument of Government*, 1653 ; Gardiner, *Constitutional Documents of the Puritan Revolution.*

[1] See Articles XXII., XXIII., and the Act of Union, s. 22.

[2] Articles XIX., XX.

[3] Article XXI. "That the rights and privileges of the Royal " Burghs in Scotland, as they now are, do remain entire after the " Union, and notwithstanding thereof." This looks as if it ensured the burghs against diminution in electoral power, but clearly must be read as subject to Article XXI.

This combination of different though not really opposed characteristics is most easily seen by any thinker who contemplates as a whole the ecclesiastical legislation of the Act of Union.

The ecclesiastical provisions of the Act were in the strictest sense revolutionary, for they introduced a totally new relation between the Church of Scotland and the Church of England. But these provisions were even more truly conservative, for their aim and effect was to secure for the people of Scotland the maintenance of the Church which in respect of doctrine and government they preferred, and at the same time to secure for the English people the Church which in respect of doctrine and of government the English people preferred. The statute, moreover, made these provisions a fundamental and essential part of the Treaty of Union. One can hardly doubt that they were meant to be immutable parts of that Treaty. Under the Act the people of Scotland guaranteed to the people of England the maintenance of the Episcopal Church of England, whilst the people of England guaranteed to the people of Scotland the maintenance of the Presbyterian Church of Scotland.

If proof is wanted that to some Whig statesmen, at any rate, it seemed that ecclesiastical peace between the two countries making up Great Britain could be best secured by making the Act of Union the security to each country for the maintenance of the national Church which it preferred, particular attention should be paid to the way in which the celebrated Test Act of 1672, 25 Car. II. c. 2, was deliberately made by the Parliament of Scotland applicable to Scotsmen who in England (e.g. as Scottish M.P.'s in the British

Parliament) came within its terms. The Scottish
Parliament not only suggested that the English
Parliament should provide whatever security for
the Church of England the English Parliament might
deem necessary under the Act of Union, but also
during the debates on the Act of Union at least twice
rejected proposals that Scotsmen in England should
not be subject to any additional religious test.[1] And
this view that the Sacramental Test imposed upon
Scotsmen in England indirectly was a security for
the maintenance of the national and Presbyterian
Church in Scotland, finds curious expression many
years later than the Union in a eulogy of the Test
Act, not by a religious fanatic, but by Dr. Alexander
Carlyle, who represented and probably exaggerated
what one may call the theological Liberalism of
Scottish Moderates.[2]

"Nay, Moderator, . . . I think I could show that
" the Test Act, instead of an evil, is a blessing. The
" Test Act has confirmed the Union. The Test Act
" has cured Englishmen of their jealousy of Scotsmen,
" not very ill-founded. The Test Act has quieted the
" fears of the Church of England. The Test Act has
" enlarged and confirmed the principles of toleration;
" so far is it from being a remnant of bigotry and
" fanaticism as the memorial would represent. The
" Test Act, Sir, has paved the road to office and
" preferment. The Test Act, Sir, for there is no end
" of its praises, is the key that opens all the treasures
" of the south to every honest Scotsman."[3]

[1] See 1707, A.P.S. xi. 377; cf. also 320.
[2] See *Autobiography of A. Carlyle*, p. 580.
[3] Carlyle, speech in the General Assembly, 1791: *Autobiography*,
p. 580. This passage should be compared with Dr. Somerville's *Life*

The character, and especially the conservatism, of the Act of Union is noteworthy, and gives rise to the following observations :—

First Observation.—The statesmen of 1707 had learned a good deal of wisdom from the failure of the Commonwealth to found a permanent union between Scotland and England.

The Union under Cromwell was founded upon the conquest of Scotland by England, and not upon a contract between Scotland and England, but the statesmen of the Commonwealth, as we have seen, were not only Unionists but Reformers. Hence they attempted to abolish by law all the effects of vassalage in Scotland, and especially the heritable jurisdiction possessed by owners of land, and Cromwell probably raised the character of the Scottish Courts by giving seats thereon to English lawyers. He maintained, further, better order in the Highlands than had been maintained by any Scottish King, and probably than was maintained by any British King up to 1745, and he gave to Scotsmen free trade throughout the whole of Great Britain. This benefit

---

and Times (pp. 225 *et seq.*). On Somerville's motion, the General Assembly, in 1790, protested against the Test Act, and, in May 1791, Sir Gilbert Elliott presented to the House of Commons a petition from the General Assembly, and moved for a Committee to consider how far the provisions of the Test Act extended, or ought to extend, to persons born in Scotland. The motion was rejected by 120 votes to 62 (*Parl. Hist.* xxix. 488), but Somerville remarks that "there has " not, perhaps, occurred a single instance of the enforcement of the " statute since the debate." The General Assembly of 1790 based its petition partly on the ground that " the extension of the Test Act of " Charles the Second to members of the Church of Scotland was a " violation of the privileges stipulated to them by the Treaty of " Union," and partly on the general plea that the practice was " injurious to the interests of religion and morality."

was more or less appreciated by Scotsmen, but Cromwell and the statesmen of the Commonwealth apparently thought that real reforms, *e.g.* the abolition of hereditary jurisdictions, were likely to ensure popularity in a country where they were introduced by the power of England. This is a delusion by which Englishmen have again and again been misled in their dealings with lands conquered or annexed. The statesmen of 1707 were, as regards Scotland at any rate, not guilty of this mistake. They knew that the best chance of creating real moral and political unity throughout Great Britain by the Act of Union depended upon leaving the ordinary habits and prejudices of its inhabitants as little affected by the Act of Union as possible. Hence, except in the settlement of more Scotsmen in England than an Englishman liked to see there, the Act of Union hardly affected at all any change either in the law of England or in the ordinary course of an Englishman's life. So again in Scotland as regards the daily life of most Scotsmen, Scottish law was hardly at all affected by the Act of Union, and any Scotsman, who neither lived in Edinburgh nor took an active part in political life, might well, as far as his habits, feelings, or prejudices were concerned, forget the fact that Scotland and England had been transformed into the one United Kingdom of Great Britain. No doubt the inhabitants of Edinburgh felt the loss of the Scottish Parliament. This was inevitable, but, after all, they had, most of them, never cared much about the Parliament, and many of them felt the retention of the regular and annual meetings at Edinburgh of the General Assembly of the Scottish Church to be a more important matter than the transference of the Scottish members to the Parliament at Westminster. Here, in short, we come again across the all-important fact that the Parliament of Scotland had never become the centre of Scottish public life.

To the disappearance of the Scottish Parliament must be added the abolition of the Scottish Privy Council and the revival of the Commission of the Peace. Article XIX. of the Treaty of Union provided " that, after the Union, the Queen's Majesty, and her " Royal successors may continue a Privy Council in " Scotland, for preserving of public peace and order, " until the Parliament of Great Britain shall think fit " to alter it, or establish any other effectual method " for that end." In the first session of the United Parliament a Bill was introduced "for rendering " the Union of the two Kingdoms more entire and " complete." It provided for the abolition of the Privy Council of Scotland after May 1, 1708, and for the conferment upon Justices of the Peace of certain powers which had belonged to the Council. The Privy Council as the instrument of an absolute monarchy had been greatly detested in Scotland, and even after 1690 it was regarded as, and to a large extent was, the means by which the policy of the Sovereign's English advisers was made effective in Scotland. Bishop Burnet says that memories of government by Council after the Restoration "had " been no small motive to induce the best men of " that nation to promote the union, that they might " be delivered from the tyranny of the Council," and the Duke of Roxburgh told Lord Dartmouth that " this was the main inducement that he and most of

" the nobility had to come into the Union, finding it
" impossible to have any redress against the High
" Commissioner and Council, let their proceedings
" be never so unreasonable or tyrannical." [1] The
abolition of the Privy Council, therefore, caused little
or no irritation in Scotland. The main objection to
the Bill was that the powers given to the Justices
of the Peace encroached upon the heritable jurisdictions, but the encroachment was no greater than
had been customary under the rule of the Council.[2]
A Commission of the Peace had been issued by King
James in 1617, and had been confirmed in 1661, but
the system had never been in effective operation in
Scotland, except for a few years after 1655, when
Cromwell appointed Justices with the same powers as
in England. The English system was introduced in
1708 but does not appear to have met with any
serious opposition.

Second Observation. — The statesmen of 1707,
though giving full sovereign power to the Parliament
of Great Britain, clearly believed in the possibility
of creating an absolutely sovereign legislature which
should yet be bound by unalterable laws. From one
point of view, which is clearly realised by most
modern jurists, the attempt to limit absolutely
sovereign power involves something like a contradiction of ideas. For a true Sovereign, whether called
Emperor, King, or Parliament, who can change every
law, can also change the very law which limits his
authority, *e.g.* the Articles of Union which make the
maintenance of the government, etc. of the Church

---

[1] Burnet's *History of His Own Time*, ed. of 1823, v. pp. 351-52.
[2] Burnet, v. 350-51.

of Scotland an absolute condition of the validity of the Union.[1] But though, logically, there is a contradiction between the creation of a really sovereign legislature which nevertheless cannot repeal the whole or certain parts of a statute which creates this sovereign power, the enactment of laws which are described as unchangeable, immutable, or the like, is not necessarily futile. The declaration contained in the Act for Securing the Protestant religion and Presbyterian Church government within the Kingdom of Scotland, which is embodied in the Act of Union, that "this Act, with the establishment thereof shall " be held and observed in all time coming as a " fundamental and essential condition of any Treaty " or Union to be concluded betwixt the two Kingdoms " [of Scotland and England] without any alteration " thereto," is not unmeaning. It represents the conviction of the Parliament which passed the Act of Union that the Act for the security of the Church of Scotland ought to be morally or constitutionally unchangeable, even by the British Parliament. This declaration would morally strengthen the force of the opposition by a large part, and, *a fortiori*, by a majority, of the Scottish people to any change of the Act for securing the Protestant religion and the Presbyterian Church government within the Kingdom of Scotland. A sovereign Parliament, in short, though it cannot be logically bound to abstain from changing any given law, may, by the fact that an Act when it was passed had been declared to be

Chapter VII.

[1] See, for example, the Act of Union, ss. 2-6, reciting the Scottish Act for the Security of the Church of Scotland, and ss. 7-9, reciting the English Act for the Security of the Church of England, and ss. 10, 11, etc.

unchangeable, receive a warning that it cannot be changed without grave danger to the Constitution of the country.[1]

Third Observation.—The conservatism of the Act of Union may have seemed to some Scotsmen to have been to a certain extent illusory. The provision of the Act of Union which gives to the House of Lords an appellate jurisdiction from the judgements of the Court of Session [2] is drawn in a form which must have made it appear, to readers who were not lawyers, to be an enactment specially intended to secure Scottish Courts against appeals to any Court in England, whereas in fact it created, and was probably intended to create, an appeal from the highest of such Courts to the House of Lords wherever it might happen to be sitting. So again the Act for securing the Protestant religion and Presbyterian Church government within the Kingdom of Scotland appears at first sight to protect any Scotsman against being made liable to any oath, test, or subscription inconsistent with such true Protestant religion and Presbyterian Church government, worship, or discipline.[3] But this protection extended only to any oath, test, or subscription within the Kingdom of Scotland, and left a Scotsman (*e.g.* when a Scottish member of the British House of Commons) liable to the Test Act, and thus to be called upon to receive the Sacrament in accordance with the provisions of that Act.

Scotsmen often objected to this result of the

---

[1] Compare remarks as to nature of sovereignty, Chap. II., Ninth Thought, p. 99, *ante,* and Introd. pp. 19-22, *ante.*

[2] See Chap. V. p. 191, *ante,* and the Act of Union, s. 1, Art. XIX.

[3] 1707, c. 6, A.P.S. xi. 402.

Act of Union, but it is fair to observe that these consequences of the Act are not so much in reality exceptions from as, when well considered, illustrations of the peculiar conservatism of this great enactment. This remark holds specially true with regard to the way in which religious tests are therein treated. The authors of the Act were specially anxious not to interfere with the habits, customs, or laws to which the people of England and of Scotland respectively were in general accustomed. This wish made it necessary to save Scotsmen in Scotland from tests inconsistent with the tenets of Presbyterianism. It made it equally necessary to save Englishmen not only from being subject to tests to which they were not used, but also to the introduction into England of religious tests of a form which might offend members of the Church of England. The Act for the security of the Church of England made the maintenance of the Test Act part of the security demanded by that Church, and it is more than likely that the English clergy would have been offended, and would have felt the security of the Church of England diminished, if a Scottish M.P. when required to comply with the Test Act, had been allowed to do so by receiving the Sacrament in the manner prescribed by the Church of Scotland. It is even possible that a religious Scotsman may, even if he approved of a Sacramental Test, have rather preferred that the Sacramental forms imposed upon a man who receives the Sacrament for the sake of holding political office, should be the forms prescribed by the Church of England, and not the forms prescribed by the Church of Scotland. Why not, it may be

Chapter
VII.

said, abolish the Sacramental Test altogether? The answer is plain though morally it is unsatisfactory. Such a step might well have been fatal to the passing of the Act of Union.

CHAPTER VIII

OBJECTIONS TO THE WORKING OF THE ACT OF UNION

First Thought.—At the time when the Act of Union came into force it did not command popularity either in England or in Scotland.

THE unpopularity of the Act of Union with many of the inhabitants of Great Britain need excite no surprise. It was in the circumstances of 1707 perfectly natural.

Every argument which told against the passing of the Act also deprived it of popularity. The Jacobites in the south no less than in the north of Great Britain hoped for, and in many cases expected, a Stewart restoration. They all execrated an Act which, if it succeeded, was fatal to their hopes. Many Whigs must have doubted whether, on the death of Anne, it would be possible for an unknown German Prince to be placed on the throne, or even if he was placed there, to hold his own against a claimant who was obviously the legitimate King both of England and of Scotland. Englishmen no doubt, at the actual moment when the Act received the Royal Assent, felt that the Union was a triumph for England, and a triumph which on the face of it immensely increased the power of Great Britain. Yet even Englishmen who were not Jacobites may have looked upon the Union as a very dubious political experiment. These doubts were in part excited by a belief of which we now do not appreciate the force, namely that the unity of two countries could not be secured unless throughout the State to be formed by their union there was maintained one national Church, be it Protestant or Catholic, of which the whole people of such State should be members. This opinion that the unity of a State and the concord of its citizens could only be preserved by unity of religious, or rather of theological, belief, was entertained by statesmen, no less than by theologians, at the end of the seventeenth century. But the Act of Union was based upon the maintenance of a national and Episcopal Church in England, and of a national and Presbyterian Church in Scotland. How therefore, sensible men asked themselves, could real concord or unity exist throughout the State of Great Britain?[1] This weakness in the Act of Union is thus described by Swift :

---

[1] This difficulty was in 1707 increased by the existence of many Scotsmen who remembered how Charles II. had enforced Episcopalianism upon Scotland, and of many Englishmen who had heard from their fathers how Scotland had tried to force Presbyterianism, as interpreted by Covenanters, upon England. The conviction, be it noted, that it is hard to form one State out of two countries, the inhabitants whereof entertain essentially different theological beliefs, contains an element of truth. The attempt to combine Belgium and Holland as one State was recommended by considerations of obvious political expediency. But it failed, and this want of success was in part at least due to the historical prevalence of Protestantism among the Dutch and of Roman Catholicism among the Belgians. On the other hand, differences of faith have not destroyed the unity of Switzerland.

The Queen has lately lost a part
Of her *Entirely English* [1] heart
For want of which by way of botch,
She piec'd it up again with Scotch.
Blest revolution ; which creates
Divided hearts, united States ;
See how the double nation lies
Like a rich coat with skirts of frieze :
As if a man, in making posies,
Should bundle thistles up with roses.
Who ever yet a union saw
Of kingdoms without faith or law ?

Henceforward let no statesman dare
A kingdom to a ship compare ;
Lest he should call our commonweal
A vessel with a double keel :
Which, just like ours, new rigg'd and mann'd,
And got about a league from land,
By change of wind to leeward side,
The pilot knew not how to guide,
So tossing faction will o'erwhelm
Our crazy double bottom'd realm.

Swift has written many more powerful pieces of satire, but, as usual, he hits a real weakness in a policy which he opposes. Further, English traders were no friends to free trade with Scotland. They dreaded the energy and, in their judgement, the unscrupulosity of their Scottish rivals ; the merchants of London, within a few weeks of the passing of the Act of Union, were confirmed in their fear of Scottish competition by the craft with which Scotsmen found in the Act of Union itself the means of underselling,

[1] Quoted from Queen Anne's Coronation Medal.

even in London, the wealthy merchants of England.[1]

To Scotsmen, even though Whigs, the Union, just
because it was an English triumph, seemed to be a
Scottish defeat; and this sentiment was reinforced
by the widespread suspicion [2] (which we know now
to be substantially unfounded) that the Whig leaders
had been induced to vote for the Act of Union by
bribery. Here, indeed, we reach the root of Scottish
aversion to a Treaty and an Act which conferred
immense benefit upon the whole of Great Britain.
Scotsmen of all classes dreaded subjection to England.
This fear was natural. The Union did destroy the
national independence of Scotland.[3] But during the
greater part, if not the whole, of the eighteenth
century, no distinction was drawn between political
independence and what we now call nationalism.[4]
Hence at the time of the Union it was all but
impossible for any Scotsman not to feel that the
Treaty which offered solid material advantages to
Scotland, destroyed Scottish nationality and undid
the work of Wallace and Bruce. This feeling is best
described in the words of Scott:

"At the period of the Union [1707] every reader
"must remember the strong agitation which per-
"vaded the minds of the Scottish nation, who could

[1] See p. 269, *post.*
[2] This suspicion was increased by the slow payment of the in-
demnity due to Scotland. On the question of bribery, see p. 226,
ante, and Hume Brown, *The Union of England and Scotland,*
pp. 126, 127; App. iv. p. 200; Hume Brown, *History of Scotland,*
iii. 126-128.
[3] As also of England.
[4] The very word "Nationalism," as applied at any rate to politics,
had not in 1707 come into existence. As to Nationalism, see Ch. X.
p. 321, *post.*

" not, for many years, be persuaded to consider this
" incorporating treaty in any other view than as a
" wanton surrender of their national independence.
" So deep was this sentiment, that a popular preacher
" in the south of Scotland, who died about the middle
" of the last [18th] century, confessed to his friends
" that he was never able to deliver a sermon, upon
" whatever subject, without introducing a hit at the
" Union." [1]

Second Thought.—*The evils attributed by Englishmen to the Act of Union were different from and
far less serious than the evils attributed to it by
Scotsmen.*

(A) *Evils attributed by Englishmen to the Act
of Union.*—The advantages conferred upon England
by the Union were undeniable and immediate, for
it manifestly ensured the power and the peace of
Great Britain, whilst leaving English institutions
all but unchanged.[2] The political objections to
the Union entertained by honourable Englishmen
who were not Jacobites, might be reduced to the
one single, though serious, charge, namely, that the
presence of Scottish representatives in the British
Parliament worked great damage to England. This
complaint against the working of the Act of Union
takes two different forms.

The action, in the first place, both of the Scottish
Peers [3] and the Scottish M.P.'s increased, it was

---

[1] Sir W. Scott's Essay on the Regalia of Scotland, " Provincial
Antiquities," *Prose Works*, vii. 338, 339.

[2] See pp. 245-246, *ante.*

[3] The Scottish elected Peers came practically to be nominated by
the Government of the day. We have therefore almost entirely

alleged, the corruption and lowered the character of Parliament. In this matter we may rely with confidence on the language of a Scotsman :

" What I am most grieved about, and cannot see
" where it will land in the issue, is the present state
" of our Parliament members, and the elections to
" them. All is carried on by money ; and a man
" cannot be chosen unless he bestow five or six
" hundred guineas ; and that must be repaid of [*sic*]
" somehow or other. Stanmore told my author he
" had spent five hundred guineas ; and Colonel
" Douglas said to him, he had expended a thousand.
" All must have either a post or three or four
" hundred guineas, called travelling charges, up
" and down. This must in time make Parlia-
" ments mercenary and expose everything to the
" highest bidder, and we may be brought to any-
" thing, or rather sold to anybody who has money
" enough." [1]

The Scottish M.P.'s,[2] in the second place, formed a Scottish clique of men who acted upon one intelligible principle, namely, that they would support the Government of the day,[3] whereby they gained no small advantage for themselves, and, it must in fairness be added, for Scotland. This policy became by degrees so well understood that, when it reached its height, a

---

confined attention for the sake of simplification to the action of the Scottish M.P.'s.

[1] Porritt, ii. p. 10, citing Wodrow, *Analecta*, iii. 228, 229. Lord Dartmouth in his notes to Burnet's *History* remarks that the Scottish representatives in 1708 " were very importunate to have their deserts " rewarded " (Burnet, v. 349).

[2] This means " members representing Scottish constituents " ; they were almost invariably Scotsmen.

[3] Porritt, ii. 8.

Scottish M.P. complained that the Lord Advocate, who generally in practice was the Minister concerned in the management of Scottish affairs and votes, was not a sufficiently tall man for his followers to see which way he voted. " We Scotch members," said this critic, " always vote with the Lord Advocate, " and we therefore require to see him in a division. " Now I can see Mr. Pitt, and I can see Mr. Addington, " but I cannot see the Lord Advocate." [1] The general results of this adherence by Scotland's 45 M.P.'s to the party in power, or in some instances, to the persons likely to come into office, may thus be roughly summed up: From 1707 to 1760 they habitually gave additional strength to the Whigs, and for this plain reason, that for these fifty years or more the Whig party, or some section thereof, held office almost continuously. From about 1760 to 1810, the 45 members generally added to the personal authority of George III., since for this period the King, or the Premiers whom he supported, generally governed the country. From 1811 to 1832, the Scottish vote kept up the strength of the Tories, even though from 1815 to 1832 the supremacy of that party had been undergoing a gradual decline. No

---

[1] Porritt, ii. p. 8. Ramsay of Ochtertyre (1736–1814) frequently refers to the existence of Government control over Scottish elections. In writing, for example, of Lord Milton, Justice-Clerk from 1735 to 1748, he says: " The management of elections, and the counteracting " of plots against the State, fall more properly under the department " of a Secretary of State or his deputies; but as there was no such " minister in Scotland, these parts of his duty were exercised by the " Justice-Clerk, in conjunction with the Lord Advocate. . . . When " he resigned the office of Justice-Clerk in 1748, he retained the " charge of superintending elections, which he considered as his " masterpiece " (*Scotland and Scotsmen in the Eighteenth Century*, i. 89).

doubt it is easy to find instances in which the faithful 45 deserted Ministers still in power, but these exceptions are of the kind which is said to prove the rule. The members from Scotland deserted Walpole in 1736–7 ; they aided in his final overthrow in 1741. But their action, independently of personal intrigues, is explainable. Walpole was deemed, whether justly or not, to be responsible for a measure which threatened Edinburgh with the severest penalties as a punishment for the execution of Porteous by a mob of that city, organised and led by the most respectable of its inhabitants. This act of " Lynch Law" was held by the Government of the day to be nothing better than the murder of a zealous official on the ground of his having discharged his obvious duty, whilst it was held by Scotsmen to be a justifiable act of popular justice needed to prevent a criminal, condemned to death by a Scottish Court, from escaping through a Royal pardon the proper punishment of his crime. In this case—and the fact should be noticed—the Scottish members represented the feeling both of Edinburgh and of Scotland. It should also be noted that Scottish shrewdness had probably perceived that Walpole's tenure of power was, in 1736–7, drawing to its close. The dislike felt by any English party, when in opposition, to the Scottish policy of increasing the parliamentary strength of any existing or of any anticipated Government was natural, and this dislike was increased by the clannishness and the political unscrupulousness by which the influence of the Scottish group was supported and its unity secured. For this group early adopted the habit of using its quasi-judicial authority in determining the validity of an election for the purpose of punishing M.P.'s whose conduct met with Scottish disapproval. Thus in 1708 Sir Henry Dutton Colt, for making some sneering reference to Scotsmen, was punished by the loss of his seat through a combination of the Scots with the Tories. Nearly half a century later, Sir Philip Anstruther, member for the Crail burghs, was the one Scottish member who voted in support of Walpole at the time when Edinburgh was threatened with punishment for the Porteous Riot. He obtained a regiment as the price of his treachery; he was punished by the loss of his seat, and never sat in Parliament again.[1] There is no difficulty in understanding why English parties, as, each in turn, they were in opposition, honestly condemned and detested the support given by Scottish M.P.'s, and no less, on the whole, by Scottish Peers sitting as such in the House of Lords, to the Government of the day. It became very easy therefore for many Englishmen to hold that this policy of strengthening each party when in power was a grave damage to England, or rather to the United Kingdom. The effect thereof upon the history of England has thus been stated by a writer who clearly means to mention instances in which the influence of the Scottish members before the Reform Act has been injurious to the country.

"The effect upon the history of England, during "the eighteenth century and the first quarter "of the nineteenth, of the readiness of the 45

---

[1] Porritt, ii. **13**. See also Lecky, *England in the Eighteenth Century*, ii. 83.

Chapter VIII.

Chapter
VIII.

" members from Scotland to give their unquestioning
" and undivided support to the Minister for the
" time being, always under the discipline of a
" Parliamentary manager, cannot be traced here.
" Parliamentary support so obtained had momentous
" effects on the policy of England towards the
" American colonies, and again on the war with
" France, which followed the French Revolution ; and
" this support from Scotland unquestionably helped
" to give George III. a larger measure of control
" over the House of Commons than had been directly
" exercised by any of his predecessors on the throne." [1]

This language, however, exaggerates the effect on
the history of England produced by the vote of the
Scottish members of Parliament. They admittedly
supported, as a rule, the Government of the day.
They thus gave, *e.g.* to George III. personally, a
good deal more power than had been usually exercised
by his two immediate predecessors. But there is no
reason to suppose that the policy of George III. was
often opposed to the wishes of the English people.
His opinion in general, whether wise or unwise,
represented the principles or prejudices of average
Englishmen. The King insisted upon the necessity
for subduing the thirteen American colonies. The
King detested and defeated the great Coalition between Fox and North in 1784. The King determined,
at great cost to the country, to resist every attempt
to confer upon Roman Catholics the same political
rights as their fellow-citizens. But what candid
historian can deny that the inhabitants of Great
Britain, in each of these instances, approved of and

[1] Porritt, ii. 13.

supported the policy of George III. ? The electors of Bristol, as Burke found to his cost, were determined to enforce the sovereignty of Parliament throughout the American colonies, and pedlars displayed the insolence of Kings. The country, in common with the King, abhorred the Coalition, and in this case the triumph of the King was also the victory of the people. The King supported the war against France whether governed by Jacobins or by Napoleon. In this matter he was supported not only by the electorate, but by the wisest and by the most patriotic of Englishmen. He was supported not only by Tories but by the most sensible of the Whigs, such as Lord John Russell and Sydney Smith. George's bigotry or his narrow-mindedness denied political equality to Roman Catholics. This terrible error was fatal to the chance that the Union between Great Britain and Ireland might be as successful as the Union between England and Scotland. But here, too, the folly of the King was for the most part also the error of his people. Whoever considers the riots headed by Lord George Gordon in 1780, and the fact that, almost up to 1829, statesmen such as Peel and Wellington vehemently opposed concession to Roman Catholics of so-called emancipation, will not only feel certain that the ill-starred folly of George III. was shared by the mass of Englishmen and Scotsmen, but will doubt whether Pitt, without the most active support on the part of George III., could in 1800 have conferred upon Roman Catholics a political equality which in 1829 was conceded to them by the English people only with great reluctance. George, indeed, in 1778 went beyond the liberality

of the average Englishman and made no difficulty
in relieving Roman Catholics from oppressive legislation which was supported by popular sentiment
both in England and in Scotland. The very riots
excited in London by the prejudices of the people were
repressed mainly by the determination of George III.
to show, if necessary, to the country that there was
one magistrate, at least, who knew how to perform
his duty. In truth, the very power of George III. is
a strong proof that in the main he shared the sentiment of Englishmen and Scotsmen. Let this once
be admitted, and the evil done to England by the
consistency with which Scotsmen, from whatever
motives, made it a rule to support the Government
of the day, is greatly diminished. Hear on this
point the words of Bagehot :—

" In the actual working of affairs . . . the elimina-
" tion of [parliamentary] minorities . . . is a process
" highly beneficial. It is decidedly advantageous
" that every active or intelligent minority should
" have adequate spokesmen in the legislature ; but it
" is often not desirable that it should be represented
" there in exact proportion to its national importance.
" A very considerable number of by no means unim-
" portant persons rather disapproved of the war with
" Russia ; but their views were very inadequately
" represented in the votes of Parliament, though
" a few able men adequately expressed their charac-
" teristic sentiments. And this was as it should be.
" The judgement of the Parliament ought always
" to be coincident with the opinion of the nation ; it
" is extremely important that it should not be less
" decided. Very frequently it is of less importance

" which of two courses be selected, than that the one
" which is selected should be constantly adhered to
" and energetically carried through . . . It is there-
" fore no disadvantage, but the contrary, that a
" diffused minority in the country is in general
" rather inadequately represented [in Parliament].
" A strong conviction in the ruling power will give
" it strength of volition. The House of Commons
" should think as the nation thinks ; but it should
" think so rather more strongly, and with somewhat
" less of wavering." [1]

It is a mistake, however, to search too elaborately
for the serious ground of English objections to the
Act of Union. Their strength lay in hostility to
Scotland caused by centuries of conflict, in fear of
free trade, and in dislike to the presence in London
of Scottish adventurers whose poverty, energy, and
clannishness contributed to their success in obtaining
advantages both political and material which were
coveted by their richer English rivals.

(B) *Evils attributed by Scotsmen to the Act
of Union.*—The alleged evils to Scotland may
roughly but conveniently be brought under two
main heads :

I. Immediate and more or less transitory evils.

(i.) *Dispute as to alleged Unfair Trading.*[2]—
The Act of Union was passed on March 8, 1707,
and it came into force on May 1, 1707. The Act

[1] Bagehot, *Parliamentary Reform,* 50, 51. Our recent experience
of war will convince any one that though there may be much to be
said for not going to war, and still more to be said in favour of
prosecuting a war with vigour, the policy of carrying on a war with
feebleness is the worst of conceivable policies.

[2] Cf. Hume Brown, iii. 130-132 ; Mackinnon, ch. x.

undoubtedly[1] established free trade between England and Scotland.   The import duties on goods brought from foreign countries, *e.g.* Holland or France, were, up to the 1st May 1707, lower in Scotland than in England, and such duties were negligently (or in many cases not at all) collected in Scotland between March 6 and May 1, 1707.   Then, too, under regulations of the English Treasury certain foreign goods again exported to a foreign country were exempted from the greater part of the duty payable on importation into England, and Scotland was, up to the 1st of May 1707, in regard to such regulations, a foreign country.   In this state of things, the acuteness of Scottish merchants, aided probably by some English merchants, carried into effect two devices by which, in virtue of the Act of Union, such merchants might, after May 1, 1707, import into England from Scotland goods which had paid no import duties, or very slight import duties, and thus sell them in London cheaper than could English merchants sell the same kind of imported goods on which they had already paid heavy English duties.   The first device was comparatively simple.   The Scottish merchants, between March 6, 1707 and May 1, 1707, and possibly even from an earlier date, began importing into Scotland a large amount of foreign goods upon which was paid little or no duty.   In Scotland the goods remained till June 1707, when they were brought to London and, as Scotsmen maintained, were, under free trade as established by the Act of

[1] Subject to limited exceptions with which for the present purpose we are not concerned.

Union, not liable to any duty whatever, as Scotland had ceased to be a foreign country, and the whole of Great Britain was simply one country. The second device was rather more complicated. Certain goods, for example tobacco, if imported into England, and again exported into a foreign country, were exempted from the greater part of the duty payable under English law. Before the 1st May 1707, 5000 hogsheads of tobacco were imported by certain merchants into England and thence exported into Scotland. These goods were thus exempted from nearly the whole of the import duties then payable under English law. After the 1st May, say during June 1707, this tobacco was reimported into England, and then again the importing merchants claimed freedom from liability to pay any duty whatever. The English Custom House officers in each case claimed the duty, and would not deliver the goods until it was paid. Hence a bitter dispute about the payment of Customs between the Scottish importers on the one side, and English merchants, with whom the House of Commons sympathised, on the other. To a modern critic the state of the case is clear. Scottish astuteness had overreached the dulness of English traders. Scotsmen had violated the spirit of the Act of Union, but they had broken neither any specific provision of the Act nor the law of England. It is quite intelligible that Scotsmen should have maintained that the British Government had no claim to tax goods not imported into England but only carried from one part of Great Britain to another. It is equally intelligible that London traders, suffering from what they would call

a fraud, should ask to be protected against the
dubious exercise of Scottish cunning.   The House
of Commons sympathised with English traders who
had been overreached, if not cheated, but the House
of Lords rejected two Bills, each of which might fairly
be called attempts to vary the provisions of the Act
of Union.[1]   The Government met the difficulty in
another way.   The importers were not compelled
to pay any duty, but the officers of the revenue
were instructed to seize the goods.   Many of them
were condemned as of French (*i.e.* enemy) origin,
and the delay in the sale of the others decreased
their saleable value.   The arrangements, further, for
the collection of the revenue in Scotland itself were
not in working order by May 1, so that the whole
trade of Scotland was stopped for two months for
want of orders to put it into the new course in
which it was to be carried on.[2]   Irritation in Scotland, where an anticipated gain had been turned
into a positive loss, was therefore not less pronounced than in England, and vehement protests
were made by merchants of both nations.   It was
unfortunate enough to make so bad a beginning of
national unity, but it would have been still more
unfortunate if either of the Bills presented by the
Commons had become law.   It was a real gain that
the Legislature as a whole had respected the Act of

[1] Two Bills were rejected by the Lords, both of which proposed
that all foreign goods imported into Scotland after February 1, 1707
should pay duties if imported into England after May 1, 1707
(Burnet, v. 291).   That no provision in the Act forbade the devices
by which the payment of duties was evaded, may have been due to
the determination of the English Parliament to pass the Act of Union
without amendment.

[2] Burnet, v. pp. 324-25.

Union. If one asks for the explanation of this political wisdom it is easy to find. The Whigs were strong in the House of Lords, and in 1707 the Whigs were in office. The Act of Union was their work, and in the eighteenth century the Lords were less affected by popular prejudice than was the House of Commons.

(ii.) *The Transference of Parliament from Edinburgh to London.* — In 1707 Edinburgh was the undoubted capital of Scotland. It was the only town in Scotland which could in reference to the population of that country be called a large city. The population of Scotland numbered at that time possibly 1,000,000, and probably not more than 800,000 inhabitants.[1] The leading towns, which now embrace more than half the people of Scotland, contained but a small part of the population, and were sometimes little better than overgrown villages. Edinburgh numbered about 20,000 persons, whilst Aberdeen, Dundee, and St. Andrews had each a population of about 4000. Perth was slightly larger, and had a certain importance as a garrison against the Highlands. The population of Glasgow was under 13,000. One effect of the smallness of the country was the concentration of social and political influence in the capital. Edinburgh itself suffered immediately from the abolition of the Scottish Parliament. The dignity of the city and the interest of life there was, for the moment at any rate, diminished. There must after the Union have been a fall in the value of houses and land in the old capital of Scotland, for the nobility

[1] Craik, ii. 216, 217.

of the country, in many cases from political and social causes, began to frequent London, and the mercantile prosperity which in later years benefited Edinburgh and other Scottish towns developed but slowly.   Sir Walter Scott, more than a century later, could recall the complaints of old people about the gloom which the year 1707 produced in the capital of Scotland.   Scott himself could speak with great authority, and he was sure that till about 1737 the Union was unpopular in Scotland.   He, however, in 1825 consoled Miss Edgeworth[1] for the apparent desolation of Dublin, owing to the disappearance of the Irish Parliament, by referring to the experience of Edinburgh in like circumstances.   Hence one may certainly infer that the injury caused by the Union to the social life of that celebrated town was not permanent, and Scott's words with regard to the Act of Union itself should never for a moment be forgotten.   "It is a loss," he writes, "however, which " time will make good, if I may judge from what " I have heard old people say of Edinburgh after " 1707, which removed the Crown from our Israel— " an event which, had I lived in that day, I would " have resigned my life to have prevented, but which, " being done before my day, I am sensible was a " wise scheme." [2]

The removal of the Parliament of Scotland from Edinburgh produced, however, deeper evils than merely arresting the prosperity of Edinburgh.   It diminished the influence of Scotsmen on legislation which might affect Scotland.   The intelligence of

[1] Scott, *Familiar Letters*, ii. 311, 312.
[2] *Ibid.* ii. 312.

Scotland was, in 1707, to a great extent centred in her capital city. Many of the leading men of Scotland resided there. The Court of Session sat there. The General Assembly of the Church met there. A leading University had its seat there. Intellectually and morally, Edinburgh represented the feeling of Scotland, or at any rate of the Lowlands, as truly as, and perhaps more truly than, during the eighteenth century London represented the opinion of England. Edinburgh indeed returned but two members to the Scottish Parliament, and after the Union returned but one member to the British Parliament, and both before and after the Union the electorate of Edinburgh was ridiculously small. But, for all that, the opinion of the most important city in Scotland was certain to tell upon the votes of the members of a Parliament, whether Lords, county members, or burgh members, which met in Edinburgh. The opinion of Scotland, in short, was, before the Union, concentrated at Edinburgh, and was guided a good deal by the sentiment of the capital. Even the mob of the capital sometimes gave forcible expression to the national feeling of Scotland, as, for example, when it imperilled the life of the Royal Commissioner because he was supporting the Act of Union,[1] when it insisted upon the judicial murder of Captain Green,[2] or when it actually murdered Porteous.[3] The removal of the Scottish Parliament from Edinburgh must, during the years which immediately followed the Union,

---

[1] See pp. 223-225, *ante.*
[2] See p. 173, *ante.*
[3] See Chap. IX. p. 301, *post.*

have lessened the rapidity with which Scottish
opinion obtained parliamentary expression. But
Dr. Alexander Carlyle declared in 1759 [1] that "the
" member of Parliament for the City of Edinburgh
" was of great consequence, as whoever held that was
" sure of the political government of the country,
" and without it no man would be of any con-
" sequence." The effect of the Union, therefore,
upon the political prestige of the capital was, probably, slighter than many Scottish patriots of 1707
feared that it would be.

In estimating the effect of the removal of the
Scottish Parliament from Edinburgh it must be
remembered that, if distance be measured by time,
Scotsmen might reasonably feel that their Parliament
had been transferred to the capital of a distant
country, whilst Englishmen might with equal reason
consider the appearance of Scotland's representatives
in the British Parliament as the intrusion of foreigners
into an English legislature. Even in 1730 the
methods of travelling in Scotland were primitive.
There were no chariots or stages to be found north
of the Tay. In 1725 the first chaise was seen in
Inverness. Lord Lovat has described his journey
with his two daughters from Inverness to Edinburgh. They met with constant accidents. They took
eleven days to reach their destination. Till 1749
no stage-coach ran between Edinburgh and Glasgow.
It then went twice a week, and took twelve hours
to go forty-six miles. Consider now the state of
travelling between England and Scotland some
eleven years later. In 1760 a stage-coach set out

[1] Carlyle, *Autobiography*, chap. x. ed. of 1910, p. 407.

once a month from Edinburgh to London. It occupied fifteen days upon the road.[1] At the accession of George III. an M.P. coming from the Orkneys to take his seat in Parliament at Westminster spent a much longer time than would now be required by a traveller coming from New York to London. Yet, many years later, Burke argued that the mere question of distance rendered it impossible for an American colony to be represented in the British Parliament.

II. Interference with Scottish institutions and laws.

(i.) *Representation of Scottish Peerage by elected Scottish Peers.*[2]—Under the Act of Union the creation of Scottish Peers came to an end. The 16 Scottish representative Peers were, and still are, elected at the

[1] See Craik, ii. 117.

[2] "Therefore Her Majestie with advice and consent of the Estates "of Parliament Statutes Enacts and Ordains That the said Sixteen "Peers who shall have right to sit in the House of Peers in the "Parliament of Great Britain on the part of Scotland by virtue of this "Treaty shall be named by the said Peers of Scotland whom they "represent their heirs or successors to their dignities and honours out "of their own number and that by open Election and plurality of "voices of the Peers present and of the Proxies for such as shall be "absent the said Proxies being Peers and producing a mandat in "writing duly signed before witnesses and both the Constituent and "Proxie being qualified according to law Declaring also that such "Peers as are absent being qualified as aforesaid may send to all such "meetings Lists of the Peers whom they judge fittest validly signed "by the said absent Peers which shall be reckoned in the same "manner as if the parties had been present and given in the said "List. And in case of the death or legall incapacity of any of the "said sixteen Peers That the foresaid Peers of Scotland shall nominate "another of their own number in place of the said Peer or Peers in "manner before and aftermentioned." (Extract from "Act settling "the manner of Electing the Sixteen Peers and Forty Five commoners "to Represent Scotland in the Parliament of Great Britain," 1707, c. 8, A.P.S. xi. 425.) See also Act of Union, 1707, 5 Anne, c. 8, Arts. XXII., XXIII.

election of each British Parliament to represent the
Scottish Peerage, that is the body of Scottish Peers
being in existence at such election. On the seat of
such elected Scottish Peer becoming vacant, either by
a dissolution of Parliament or otherwise, another
Scottish Peer is to be elected by the existing Scottish
Peerage to fill the vacancy. In consequence of the
strict interpretation by the House of Commons of a
dubious point of Scottish constitutional law, neither
a Scottish Peer nor the eldest son of a Scottish
Peer could, under the Act of Union, sit in the
House of Commons for a Scottish seat.[1]   It was held
by the House of Lords, and therefore was law from
1711 to 1781, that though the Crown could give to
a Scottish Peer the status of what was then [2] called
a British Peer, yet such a Scottish Peer had not, in
virtue of his British Peerage, a right to sit and vote
in the House of Lords. But this decision has been
reversed since 1782.[3]   It was also held down to
1791 that such a Scottish Peer so created a British
Peer had not a right to vote in the election of a
Scottish Peer as one of the 16 representative Scottish
Peers. This right, however, has since 1795 been held
to belong to, and is now exercised by, any Scottish
Peer who has been created a British Peer. The result
appears to be that a Scottish Peer created a British

[1] The disqualification, which was removed in 1832, applied only
to eldest sons and did not extend to a grandson who was the heir-
apparent or to a brother who was the heir-presumptive of a Peer of
Scotland. The eldest son of an English Peer could sit for a Scottish
constituency, and the eldest son of a Peer of Scotland for an English
constituency, at all events after 1800 (cf. Rait, "The Hard Case of
" the Masters," *Glasgow Herald*, January 8, 1916).

[2] Now a Peer of the United Kingdom.

[3] Anson, *Law and Custom of the Constitution*, i. 209-210.

Peer has since 1795 possessed all the rights of a British Peer, or, in later language, of a Peer of the United Kingdom. No part of the Act of Union has, judged by the event, been more open to objection than the provisions with regard to the position of the 16 Scottish Peers. Though in theory and in form elected by the body of Scottish Peers, they were all but invariably between 1707 and 1832 nominated by, or in accordance with the wish of, the Government in power. This was not satisfactory to Scotsmen. Scottish Peers, and in almost every case the eldest son of a Scottish Peer, were excluded from seats in the House of Commons, and the greater number of Scottish Peers would thus have been absolutely excluded from parliamentary life if the exclusion had not been to a great extent evaded after 1781 by their being given British Peerages. But this mitigation or evasion of the effect of the Act of Union was resented by and opposed to English feeling. Yet no part of the Act of Union was more distinctly the Act of the Parliament of Scotland than the provisions relating to the status and representation of the Scottish Peerage. At the beginning of the eighteenth century the Peers, both of Scotland and of England, wished to curtail or abolish the right of the Crown to create new Peerages. They thought they could thus increase their own dignity and power. There was in 1707 no Scottish Walpole to warn Scotland of the danger involved in this mistaken policy.[1]

[1] Oddly enough, the provisions of the Act of Union with regard to the 16 representative Peers of Scotland are almost the only parts of the Scottish parliamentary system which have survived successive Reform Acts from 1832 to 1918 inclusive.

(ii.) *Interference with the Rights of the Church.—* This grievance took in the eyes of Presbyterians various forms.

The restoration of Church Patronage in Scotland in 1712 [1] is the chief and almost the only example of an Act of the British Parliament passed in violation of the Act of Union. For the present purpose it may be enough to say that the theory of Scottish Presbyterianism had always been that the people of each several congregation should elect, or at any rate sanction the appointment of, their minister, though the legislation of the Scottish Parliament had varied greatly as to the persons in whose hands such election or sanction should lie, and as to the degree to which the ancient patrons of Churches should nominate ministers subject to the sanction or the approval of the people. In 1690, however, that is to say, within two years after the Revolution of 1688, the Parliament of Scotland deliberately passed an Act abolishing Church Patronage. [2] With how much deliberation the Act was

[1] See 10 Anne, c. 12 (which in the Revised Statutes is described as 10 Anne, c. 21), with which compare 10 Anne, c. 7 (Rev. Stats. 10 Anne, c. 10), for the protection of Episcopalians in Scotland, and see particularly the Yule Vacance Act, 10 Anne, c. 13 (Rev. Stats. c. 22). It is worth while to note that all these Acts are attributed in the Statute-book to 1711, whereas they were in fact passed in 1712. This is due to the fiction that the Acts of a session date from the first day of the session. See, as to the law of Patronage in Scotland, Mathieson, *The Awakening of Scotland*, ch. iv., especially pp. 145-148; Balfour, *Presbyterianism in Scotland*, pp. 121-133.

[2] See Act concerning Patronage, 1690, c. 53, A.P.S. ix. 196. The statute provided that when any vacancy in any Church occurred —(i.) the Elders and Heritors (landowners) were to choose a person for the approval of the congregation;

(ii.) If the congregation disapproved of the person thus selected, they were to give in their reasons to the Presbytery, by whom the whole matter was to be finally determined;

carried is shown by the strenuous opposition of King William. In 1712 the Act passed by the Scottish Parliament twenty-two years before was repealed and the system of Church Patronage abolished by the Scottish Parliament was restored. It hardly admits of dispute that the Act of 1712, to restore patrons to their ancient rights of presenting ministers to the churches vacant in that part of Great Britain called Scotland, was opposed to the spirit, and probably to the letter, of the Act of Union.

The revival of lay patronage met with consistent opposition from the General Assembly. In 1711 Carstares and two other distinguished Scottish ministers were sent to London, as a deputation from the Commission of the General Assembly, to oppose the passing of the Patronage Bill and of a Bill of Toleration for Episcopalian clergymen in Scotland.[1] In 1717 the Commission of the Assembly sent a deputation to persuade the Whig Government to repeal the Patronage Act. They had audiences of George I. and of the Prince and Princess of Wales, were graciously received and were assured that the Royal Family would be glad of an occasion to serve the Church of Scotland, but they " found " great difficulties were like to be in the way of a

---

(iii.) The patrons, in consideration of their being deprived of their ancient rights, were to receive from the parish six hundred merks, on obtaining payment whereof they were obliged to execute a formal renunciation of the patronage ;

(iv.) The patrons were also to receive all the vacant teinds [tithes]. See Cunningham's *Church History of Scotland*, ii. 234.

[1] The letters of Prof. Blackwell, one of the deputation, are printed in the *Miscellany of the Spalding Club*, vol. i. pp. 195 *et seq.* The petition which they addressed to the House of Lords is printed in the *Carstares Papers*, App. p. 796.

" simple repeal of that Act." [1] Deputations were
sent in later years, and until 1784 the Assembly
annually instructed the Commission appointed at the
close of its sitting "that they should watch for a
" convenient opportunity of applying to the King
" and Parliament for redress from the grievance of
" patronage." [2] Every student of Scottish history
knows that the Patronage Act of 1712 has been
either the cause or the occasion of the ecclesiastical
controversies and divisions which have disturbed the
peace and destroyed the outward unity of the Church
of Scotland.

The Yule Vacance Act of 1712, which repealed
the Act forbidding Scottish Courts to abstain from
sitting on Christmas Day, and on some other days
treated as holidays by the English, but not by the
Scottish, Courts, and which enjoined the Scottish
Courts to hold a vacation from December 20 to
January 10, added by its very unimportance to
its moral significance.   It appeared to be an
attempt to carry out in Scotland ideas cherished
by the Episcopalian Church of England.   It was
with more reason looked upon as a deliberate slight
inflicted upon the religious feeling of Scotland.   The
ill-effect of these Acts as attacks on Presbyterianism
would, to stern Presbyterians, naturally be increased
by the decision of the House of Lords in Greenshields' case, which maintained the legality of Episcopalian worship in Scotland, and must have brought
to the minds of Scotsmen that the right of carrying

---

[1] Diary of the Rev. Wm. Mitchell (one of the deputation) printed
in the *Miscellany of the Spalding Club*, v. pp. 227 *et seq.*
[2] Carlyle's *Autobiography*, ed. 1910, p. 492.

an appeal from the Court of Session to the House of Chapter
Lords, which had slipped into the Treaty of Union VIII.
under an article of curious ambiguity, might make
the decision of ecclesiastical cases arising in the
Church of Scotland depend in the last instance on
the judgement of a Court of which English Archbishops and Bishops formed part.[1]

Two considerations, however, lessen the practical importance of legislation which alarmed even
the most sensible of Scottish Churchmen. The law
re-establishing patronage was the work of Tories
meditating the restoration of the Stewarts, and their
power was terminated by the death of Anne. No
Jacobite ever again held office in Great Britain.
Further, the Patronage Act met with considerably
less strenuous opposition at the time than might
have been expected. The biographer of Robert
Wodrow, the classical historian of the *Sufferings
of the Church of Scotland*, tells us that Wodrow,
" when, contrary to his solemn and matured judge-
" ment, the law of patronage was revived, and a
" decided disinclination to abrogate it manifested by
" the highest legal tribunal in the kingdom, did not
" think it either right or expedient to resist the
" execution of the law, by popular force or by
" ecclesiastical insubordination. He yielded to the
" storm which he could not avert, and on one or two
" occasions he thought it his duty to countenance
" the settlement of an unpopular preacher." [2] As
time went on the Act came to be, first tacitly and

---

[1] In the eighteenth century English Bishops might legally, and
sometimes did actually, vote in the decision of law cases coming
before the House of Lords as a final Court of Appeal.

[2] Wodrow's *History*, ed. Burns, 1836, vol. i. p. 5.

then openly, approved by the successors of Carstares in the leadership of the Scottish clergy. It is certainly not necessary for an historian to decide upon the relative advantages and disadvantages of maintaining the system of Church Patronage in Scotland, but it is a matter of fairness, in judging even of legislation which many persons would now condemn, to recall the undoubted fact that Scottish opinion has greatly varied from time to time on the question whether Church Patronage might not in certain circumstances be a benefit to the Church of Scotland.

(iii.) *Alteration of Law of Scotland.*—The British Parliament occasionally, though not often, altered the law of Scotland. This was in accordance with Article XIX. of the Treaty, which provided for " such " regulations for the better administration of justice " as shall be made by the Parliament of Great " Britain," and with Article XVIII., which declared that " laws which concern public right, policy, and " civil government, may be made the same through- " out the whole United Kingdom," and that laws affecting private right might be changed " for evi- " dent utility of the subjects within Scotland." But Scottish opinion condemned the extension of English law to Scotland. Hence Scotsmen, and especially the Scottish nobility, strongly objected to the extension to the whole of Great Britain of the English law of treason.[1] How much of this feeling has survived in both countries is shown by the practical impossibility of assimilating the Marriage

---

[1] Hume Brown, iii. 143-145 ; Burnet, *Hist. of his own Time,* v. 389-398 ; especially Mackinnon, pp. 367-373.

Law of England and of Scotland, whilst the convenience of maintaining the same Marriage Law throughout the whole of Great Britain is obvious.

(iv.) *The unfair, or excessive, Taxation of Scotland.*—On no point was Scottish feeling more sensitive than on the possible over - taxation of Scotland in a House of Commons in which Scotland was represented by only 45 members. The Act of Union is full of provisions on this subject.[1] "In " the case [indeed] of the land tax . . . Scotland " received the most generous treatment. Great as " was the inequality of the value of land in the two " countries when the Commissioners agreed that " the land tax in Scotland should be less than a " fortieth of that contributed by England, they " were certainly straining a point in favour of the " poorer country. Finally, in the case of malt, it " was concluded that Scotland should be exempt " until the 24th of June 1707, an arrangement " which was to be a bitter source of misunder- " standing between the two nations."[2] In truth it may be said that the most serious and widespread causes of popular dissatisfaction from 1707 to 1760 were at bottom caused by complaints in Scotland with regard to taxation. Nor is it irrelevant to remember that the Scottish Parliament had always, with a strenuousness unknown to the English Parliament, insisted that the King should "live on " his own."[3]

Hence the strenuous opposition of Scotsmen to

---

[1] See sec. 1, Articles VI.-XV., XVIII.
[2] Hume Brown, iii. 107.   [3] See Introd. pp. 14-18, *ante.*

the Malt Tax [1] (1713); to the duty on the export
of linen (1711) [2]; to Walpole's Excise Bill [3] (1733);
and to the appointment of Justices of the Peace in
Scotland, not only as an attempt to extend English
law throughout the whole of Great Britain, but
also, or even more, as the means for enforcing the
collection of customs on foreign imports, especially
wines, and customs which were higher and more
strictly collected in England than they had been in
Scotland.   Hence, too, a matter of great importance,
the popularity of smugglers, who were looked upon
as something like patriots when opposing unpopular
taxation laid upon Scotland by a British Parliament. [4]

As to the connexion between the Union and the
heavy and, as it seemed to Scotsmen, the unfair
taxation arising from it, students of the twentieth
century can from experience form a sounder judgement than could their forefathers of the eighteenth
century.   The nineteenth century has given rise to
many attempts, whereof some have been successful
and others have ended in failure, to transform more
or less independent countries into one united nation.
The cases of failure do not for our present purpose
concern us.   The noticeable fact is that the successful
achievement of national unity, while it never could
produce for a considerable period half the good effects
expected from it, has invariably imposed upon some,
and probably upon all, of the separate countries
which have come to form one State, many unforeseen
sacrifices and almost certainly heavier taxation.   A
student should consider the case of Italy.   There

---

[1] Hume Brown, iii. 150, 151.   [2] *Ibid.* 149.   [3] *Ibid.* 215.
[4] See especially Mackinnon, pp. 354-355, 361-363.

are men still living who can recollect the time when Italy was said to be a merely geographical expression, and consisted of several ill-governed countries which, in spite of common historical tradition, had not been able to form a united and independent nation. After twenty years or more of conflict, foreigners were expelled from the Italian Peninsula, and Italy has attained both unity and independence. But Italy has certainly suffered even in the time of peace from the weight of heavy taxation. There are possibly still living citizens of Rome or of Naples who have sometimes regretted the enjoyment of bad government when accompanied by light taxes. These malcontents, if such exist, have not realised that good administration, judicial purity, and the maintenance of parliamentary government are inestimable blessings, but, like most of the benefits of civilisation, are expensive blessings. This reflection goes a good way to explain, though not to vindicate, the feeling of Scotsmen who between 1707 and, say, 1760 imagined that the political unity of Great Britain had brought more of burden than of benefit upon Scotland.

Third Thought.—Did Scotland suffer from non-representation, or even mis-representation, in the British Parliament?

This is a Thought which refers only to the period between the passing of the Act of Union, 1707, to the passing of the Reform Act, 1832. It must take the form of a query, for it raises a question the answer to which is open to much doubt.

The answer given by almost all Liberals takes the
form of an unhesitating affirmative. This reply is
given with the most force in the words of C. J. Fox,
and summed up with the most impressiveness in the
language of Lecky.

"When we look," said Fox in 1795, "to the
" kingdom of Scotland, we see a state of representa-
" tion so monstrous and absurd, so ridiculous and
" so revolting, that it is good for nothing except
" perhaps to be placed by the side of the English,
" in order to set off our defective system by the
" comparison of one still more defective. In Scotland
" there is no shadow even of representation. There
" is neither a representation of property for the
" counties, nor of population for the towns." [1]

"With scarcely an exception," wrote Lecky in
1882, "the whole political representation of Scotland
" in both Houses of Parliament supported Lord
" North, and was bitterly hostile to the Americans.
" Scotland, however, is one of the very few in-
" stances in history, of a nation whose political
" representation was so grossly defective as not
" merely to distort but absolutely to conceal its
" opinions. It was habitually looked upon as the
" most servile and corrupt portion of the British
" Empire ; and the eminent liberalism and the very
" superior political qualities of its people seem to
" have been scarcely suspected to the very eve of
" the Reform Bill of 1832. . . . The country,
" however, was judged mainly by its representatives,
" and it was regarded as far more hostile to the
" American cause than either England or Ireland.

[1] *Parl. Hist.* xxxiii. 730 ; cited Porritt, ii. p. 5.

" A very able observer, when complaining of the
" apathy and lassitude with which the American
" policy of the Government was generally regarded,
" adds, ' We must except from all these observations
" ' the people of North Britain, who almost to a man,
" ' so far as they could be described or distinguished
" ' under any particular denomination, not only
" ' applauded but proffered life and fortune in support
" ' of the present measures ' "—*i.e.* the measures of
Lord North.[1]

The language of Fox and of Lecky seems at first
sight in itself decisive, and several undeniable facts,
to some of which we have already referred, go far
to support the conclusions of Fox, of Lecky, and,
speaking generally, of Liberals, who have condemned the Scottish representative system under
the Act of Union. These facts may be thus
summarised :

(1) On any democratic view of representative
government the representation of the Scottish people
in the Parliament at Westminster was utterly ineffective and inadequate.[2] To state the facts
broadly, putting aside some unimportant exceptions,
the only classes of Scotsmen represented in the British
Parliament were, in the House of Lords, the Scottish
Peers,[3] and in the House of Commons, persons who
were King's freeholders (tenants *in capite*).

---

[1] See Lecky, *Hist. of England,* iii. 533, 534, citing Annual
Register, 1776, p. 39.

[2] See Chap. I. p. 44, *ante.*

[3] For the sake of simplicity it is well in the discussion of this
Thought to confine our attention, unless the contrary is expressly stated,
to the representation of Scotland in the House of Commons by the
45 Scottish members.

An electoral system which at the beginning of the eighteenth century was inadequate, must have become more and more illusory by the beginning of the nineteenth century.[1] The smallness, further, of the number of the Scottish electors was towards the end of the eighteenth century of much less consequence than the limited class of citizens from whom the electorate was taken. The burgh members were chosen, speaking generally, not by the people of the town, but by the council of each of the burghs, and the council was in almost every case a small body which elected its own members annually, and constantly re-elected them. The law passed under the Act of Union gave Edinburgh one member and divided the remaining sixty-five Royal burghs into fourteen districts, each containing four or five burghs. Each of the burghs making up the districts elected one delegate to elect a Member of Parliament. Hence the election of a Member of Parliament ultimately came into the hands of four or five electors who met together and really chose the Member of Parliament; this must have thrown the election of a

[1] A table constructed after the census of 1821 shows that the county of Aberdeen with a population (apart from the burgh of Aberdeen) of over 100,000 persons had an electorate numbering 188. There were 15 electors in Bute, 19 in Clackmannan, 21 in Nairn, and 23 in Sutherland. The total population of Scotland in 1821 was 2,093,456, of whom about 460,000 were resident in the burghs. The number of registered voters among the remaining population of over 1,600,000 at Michaelmas 1822 was 2986. The 460,000 burgesses had, roughly speaking, an electorate of 1250. It was only in Edinburgh that the actual election was made by the Town Council, consisting of 33 persons; the other 14 representatives of Scottish burghs were elected by 65 delegates, who had been chosen by some 1220 persons who were members of the Town Councils of the 65 burghs divided, for purposes of voting, into 14 groups (*Enumeration of the Inhabitants of Scotland*, pp. 76-78, Glasgow, 1823).

burgh[1] member into the hands of a very small body
easily accessible to the influence of government. The
county electorate always consisted, in name at least,
of King's freeholders, but, by a process of which it is
not necessary here to describe the details, a large
number of nominal or fictitious King's freeholders
were created, who, in fact, almost invariably voted in
obedience to the wish of the landowners, who were
themselves real tenants *in capite* of the King. It
was, however, one of the singular results of the arts
by which the right of voting in the Scottish counties
was made to depend upon legal fictions that a man
might have a vote, or, in fact, many votes, for a
Scottish county, though he had in reality no true
ownership of any land in the county.[2]

(2) The Government of the day did, in fact,
during the eighteenth century exercise very great
influence over the Scottish electorate.

(3) The Scottish representatives, and especially
the elected Peers having seats in the House of Lords,
were to a great extent nominated by the Government
of the day, and as a whole adhered pretty strictly
to the policy, suggested by self-interest, of supporting
the party which held office.

[1] In the similar arrangement made under the Commonwealth, each
group of burghs had a head-burgh at which the election was made.
This precedent was not followed in 1707. The place of election was
to be each burgh of the group in order of seniority, and the delegate
of the burgh at which the election took place had a casting vote.
The working of the system is best described in John Galt's novel, *The
Provost* (1822).

[2] See Appendix A, and compare a Petition drawn mainly by Sir
James Mackintosh, and presented to the House of Commons by Sir
Charles Grey in 1793, with a statement of the mode in which fictitious
votes were created (Adam, *View of the Political State of Scotland in
1788*).

In these circumstances, students may well ask why they should have any hesitation in adopting the conclusions of Fox, of Lecky, and of many critics of the Scottish parliamentary system, and in holding that Scotland suffered in the British Parliament from, at best, non-representation, and often from the mis-representation of the opinion of Scotsmen. The reasonableness of this hesitation lies in the existence of certain considerations, the importance whereof will hardly be denied by any one who has got rid of the two delusions that the wishes of a people are never really represented except under a democratic kind of government, and that representatives who avowedly vote with a sharp eye to their personal interests can never also in effect represent the wish of their electors. These leading considerations which make it impossible to accept the conclusions, for example, of Lecky, with anything like complete acquiescence, may be thus stated :

(1) Under the Act of Union the Scottish repre-sentatives did, in matter of fact, by their policy of supporting the Government of the day, secure for their countrymen the advantages which Scotland hoped to gain from the Union, the security of the Scottish Church, free trade between England and Scotland, at least an equal share with Englishmen in the material benefits of the British Empire, and the administration of Scottish affairs almost ex-clusively by Scotsmen.

(2) Under the Act of Union Scottish members on critical occasions responded again and again to the wish of Scotland, though opposed to the policy of the British Government and to the wish of

England. Thus in 1736 Scotland's parliamentary representatives successfully opposed the legitimate wish of the British Parliament to punish Edinburgh for the monstrous exercise of what we should now call Lynch Law which led to the murder of Porteous. Thus too, in 1826, Scotland's representatives in the Imperial Parliament, under the guidance of " Malachi Malagrowther," the most eminent of Scottish men of letters and of Scottish Tories, resisted and defeated the attempt of a strong Tory Government to enforce one law as to paper currency throughout the whole of the United Kingdom, and defeated it on the mere ground that the withdrawal of £1 notes was, whether expedient or not, offensive to Scottish habits and sentiment.

How, it may be asked, can the doubt of the perfect soundness of the view advocated by Lecky, and other critics of the Scottish Constitution, be explained without imputing to him, and writers who share his opinion, a gross want of judgement ? The answer is easy to find. As long as the questions in which Scotland was mainly concerned affected the rights which Scotsmen asserted under the Act of Union, the Scottish representatives were not in any way a body of men who, whatever their personal selfishness, were deficient in Scottish patriotism, or in other words, in the desire to see Scotsmen fairly treated under the Act of Union. As already pointed out, the policy of supporting the Government in power was on the whole well adapted for securing to Scotland the full advantages of the great Treaty. But as step by step the constitutional and moral unity of Great Britain was secured, the conflict between the rights of Scotland and the rights of England came to an end, and turned into the conflict between two parties, Whigs and Tories, each of which contained Scotsmen and Englishmen. Now, both in Scotland and also in England, the unreformed Parliament was not a body which gave equal representation to each of these two parties. The grievance in Scotland was more intense than the grievance in England. But all reformers, whether Whigs, Liberals, or Radicals, in Scotland as also in England, found that they were defeated owing to the supremacy which the unreformed Parliament gave to their opponents. Indignation at this disadvantage was increased by the long reaction against reform of any kind aroused throughout Great Britain by the cruelties and the violence of the French Revolution. From 1790 onwards, and even more truly from 1815 to 1832, the Whigs, both in Scotland and in England, were unfairly treated. This unfairness, which was greatest in Scotland, excited intense bitterness against the "despotism" of Dundas. The Whig tradition, for it is more than a legend, of this despotic reign of the Tories was grounded on the real, though exaggerated, sufferings of Scottish Whigs who wished to achieve political success in their own country. Lecky and others have, it is submitted, rightly resented the injustice done to the Whigs between 1815 and 1832, but they have with very dubious correctness extended the picture of Tory misrule under Dundas to the whole of the century and more elapsing between 1707 and 1832.

CHAPTER IX

THE GRADUAL ACCEPTANCE OF THE ACT OF UNION

Thought.—Under the Act of Union the people of Great Britain accepted

1. *The constitutional unity of the country, 1707–1760.*
2. *The moral unity of the country, 1760–1805.*

THE GENERAL MEANING AND BEARING OF THE THOUGHT

THE terms and the bearing of this Thought require explanation. The acceptance of the constitutional unity of the country means the acceptance by the vast majority of the people of Great Britain of the political and constitutional arrangements created by the Act of Union, or, to express the same thing in other words, the dying out of any widespread wish on the part of the British people to repeal the Act of Union. The acceptance of moral unity by the British people means their acquiescence in the unity of the country and in the sentiment that the inhabitants of Great Britain formed one united people, at any rate as against foreigners. The acceptance both of constitutional and of moral unity was a necessary condition

295

of the complete success of the Act of Union. Until these conditions were both fulfilled, it could not be affirmed that the Act of Union had attained complete success. It was obviously passed with the hope of creating among the inhabitants of Great Britain the sense of forming, both constitutionally and morally, one united State.

The creation of such constitutional and moral unity was of necessity a matter of time. As has been constantly noted in this essay, hostility between England and Scotland was due to historical causes which, at the beginning of the eighteenth century, had operated for years, and the effect whereof could not be at once removed by any Act of Parliament, however wise its provisions. On the very day when the Act of Union came into force, and for a considerable time after that day,[1] there existed many grounds on which men of good sense and sound judgement might entertain very doubtful hopes of the success of an Act which, on its face, bore the character of a very hazardous experiment in statesmanship. As a matter of fact, very near a century, 1707–1805, elapsed before any man could say with absolute confidence that the policy of union between England and Scotland had been marked by even greater success than boldness.

Our Thought further points out that the political or constitutional unity of the country was achieved a good deal earlier than the moral unity thereof. Nor is this unnatural. A moral feeling often lasts longer than an intellectual conviction. By 1760, few men of judgement could believe that the

---

[1] See Chap. III. p. 137, and Chap. VIII. pp. 257, 261, *ante.*

Act of Union could, or ought to, be repealed. But long after that date there existed Englishmen, such as Dr. Johnson, who disliked Scotsmen, and Scotsmen, such as David Hume, who had no love for Englishmen and liked France a good deal more than they liked England. A writer, however, who describes the course of opinion, and designates the periods during which a form of belief or sentiment prevailed, ought constantly to impress upon his readers that general changes of belief or of feeling do not admit of being divided from one another by any absolutely rigid line of demarcation. The assertion, for instance, that the great body of the British people had by 1760 accepted the political or constitutional unity of Great Britain is, broadly speaking, true. But this assertion is no denial of the undoubted fact that many Whigs accepted such unity long before 1760, and many Tories accepted it between 1745 and 1760. Nor is it a denial of the tradition that even as late as, say, 1800, there may have been found both in Scotland and in England some men who in feeling were Jacobites, and occasionally drank to " The King " over the water."

One additional consideration deserves notice. This work—especially in this chapter—treats of the gradual and finally the complete success of the Act of Union. But this essay is not in any way concerned with a quite different subject, namely, how far under the Act of Union the different parts of Great Britain were well governed. Hence the assertion that the Act of Union was, speaking broadly, a complete success by 1805, does not even imply that the government either of England or of Scotland was at that period a perfectly good and wise system of government. No man of sense can deny that then, and indeed during the whole period of 125 years which elapsed between the passing of the Act of Union and the passing of the Reform Act in 1832, there existed many things under the law and the constitution of Great Britain which required amendment or reform.[1]

FIRST PERIOD—THE ACCEPTANCE OF CONSTITUTIONAL UNITY, 1707–1760

In considering this subject it will be well to consider, first, the resistance to the Act of Union; and, secondly, the final acceptance of political or constitutional unity.

(a) *Resistance to the Act of Union, 1707–1745*

The resistance to the Act is shown by four occurrences.

(1) *Attempted Repeal of the Act of Union in 1713.*—A modern reader is astounded to learn that in less than seven years after the passing of the Act of Union there was introduced into the House of Lords a Bill for repealing the Act; that so far as the number of votes went the proposal was all but carried; that it was supported by the leading Whigs and by many of the men, among others the Duke of Argyll, who had been in 1707 the most zealous of Unionists; and lastly, that the Bill was opposed

---

[1] The scope of this essay brings it to an end in 1832. For the Reform Act almost entirely did away with the parliamentary system of Scotland, which was more or less kept in existence in 1707 by the Act of Union.

and thrown out, as inexpedient and unconstitutional, by the Tories.[1] This appears to afford undoubted proof that the maintenance of the Union had become odious to its best and truest friends. Yet here, as elsewhere, a student of the Constitution must be on his guard against mistaking fictions for facts, and shams for realities. The following words, by an author whose judgement may be trusted, well describe the comic dreariness or the solemn farce which may be the result of parliamentary manœuvres :

" The Union had thus [apparently] been saved " by its enemies, and all but upset, or at least " unsettled, by its friends ; and this would doubtless " be a very remarkable occurrence, were it not evident " that the whole affair was little better than a " solemn farce. It was not conviction, but a regard " for their respective interests, which had induced " the two parties on this occasion to change sides. " As the Union was extremely unpopular in " Scotland, and as a general election was to take " place within a few weeks, the Scottish Whigs, " irritated as they were by the Malt Bill, did not " venture to oppose the motion for repeal when it " was urged upon them by Lockhart. Their Eng- " lish friends professed their readiness to dissolve " the Union, provided that other means, equally " efficacious, could be devised for securing the " Protestant succession ; but their chief object was " to embarrass the Ministry, which was bound to " resist the motion, however welcome to the Tories,

[1] The motion was supported by the Whigs and opposed by the Tories, and the Peers present being equally divided—54 on each side —it was rejected by 17 proxies to 13 (Mathieson, *Scotland and the Union*, p. 293, note 1).

" at a time when its attention was engrossed by
" the declining health of the Queen. Lockhart
" remarks that some of the Scottish Whigs, though
" they affected to approve of it, were evidently
" 'thunder-struck' at his proposal; and the Earl
" of Findlater quite exposed the character of the task
" imposed upon him in the Lords—he showed such
" uneasiness, and 'made so many apologies for what
" 'he was to do.' 'It was very comical,' wrote an
" English politician to Swift, 'to see the Tories who
" 'voted with lord treasurer against the dissolution
" 'of the Union under all the perplexities in the
" 'world lest they should be victorious; and the
" 'Scotch who voted for a Bill of dissolution under
" 'agonies lest they themselves should carry the
" 'point.'"[1]

The more or less unreal attempt to repeal the
Act of Union in 1713 does, however, show that the
Act then had lost much of such popularity as it
may have possessed in 1707.[2]

(2) *The Rebellion of 1715.*—With the history
of the rebellion we are not here concerned. One
may confidently, however, assume that as a body
the Jacobites or Tories who took up arms against
George I. were opposed to the Act of Union on
which His Majesty's title to the Crown of Great
Britain depended. And the success of the rebellion
was nearly as probable as its failure.

---

[1] Mathieson, *Scotland and the Union, 1695–1747*, pp. 292, 293.
[2] A rebellion, it should be remembered, which aimed at the
restoration of the Pretender broke out in 1715. Many Peers may
have felt that their obtaining the favour of a restored King might be
facilitated by proof that they had, though tardily, become opposed
to the Act of Union.

(3) *The Murder of Porteous, 1736.*—This had no direct bearing on the repeal of the Act of Union, but it shows in the strongest manner the unpopularity throughout Edinburgh and Scotland of the King's Government in London. Porteous was murdered at the very moment when he was about to receive a pardon from the Crown. He was guilty at worst of somewhat too strenuously executing the law of the land in respect of a smuggler whose conduct made him popular with the people of Edinburgh. The most ominous part of the transaction is that the murder of a zealous public servant was carried out by some of the most respectable citizens of Edinburgh, and was sanctioned by the public opinion both of the capital of Scotland and of all Scotsmen. The endeavour of the British Government to inflict any substantial punishment upon Edinburgh for a gross defiance of the British Government and for an outrageous violation of the law of the land was brought to nothing by the parliamentary representatives of Scotland. The whole transaction, from whatever side it is looked at, was a far more serious thing than the feeble attempt in 1713 to repeal the Act of Union.

(4) *The Rebellion of 1745.*—The direct and most obvious effect of the rebellion, taken together with the events which occurred between 1745 and 1760 inclusive, was to give a death-blow to Jacobitism, and thereby to bring about the political or constitutional unity of the country. This is the main point which ought here to be considered. But the success of the rebellion in Scotland, and the apathy with which the people of England looked upon the

Chapter
IX.

advance of not more than three or four thousand Highlanders as far as Derby, must be taken as conclusive evidence that the Hanoverian dynasty had as yet acquired little hold on the active loyalty of Great Britain.

(b) *Acceptance of Constitutional Unity, 1746–1760*

The refusal of the English Tories to make the least effort in favour of the Stewarts, and the complete failure of the rebellion, followed by what one may call the conquest of the Highlands, did give a severe and, as it turned out, a final blow to Jacobitism. Much was done towards producing this result before 1760, or even 1745. The Highlands had been provided with roads which made every part thereof accessible to trained troops. The Highlanders were disarmed immediately after 1745. Before 1760 they had under the guidance of Pitt (afterwards Lord Chatham) been enrolled in large numbers in the British armies. The sentiment of what we now call "Imperialism," in the best sense of that word, had been aroused. The growth of the Empire tended both directly and indirectly to turn the eyes of Scotsmen and of Englishmen alike towards Imperial interests, which were clearly dependent on the maintenance of the Union. In 1756 the death of Wolfe and the capture of Quebec excited the same grief and the same sense of triumph throughout the length and breadth of Great Britain. As has been happily said, Burns was the first poet who entered into the spirit of British Imperialism.[1] Even

---

[1] See W. P. Ker, *The Politics of Burns.*

before George III. came to the throne, Murray, a Scotsman, had become the most eminent among English lawyers. The announcement that George III. gloried in the name of " Britain," though it excited censure in England, was in reality a declaration to all Scotsmen, whether Jacobites or Whigs, that every honour that could be gained by a parliamentary career was as open to them as to Englishmen. From 1760 the Union became the political basis of British government, and was, as such, accepted by the British people.

SECOND PERIOD—THE ACCEPTANCE OF MORAL UNITY, 1760–1805

Here again we should dwell upon two matters :

(a) *The Want of Moral Unity in 1760.*—From the accession of George III. to the throne in 1760, and during the earlier years of his reign, there existed a great deal of mutual dislike, not to say hostility, between England and Scotland. Here we come across an apparent paradox. In 1760 the Act of Union had already received acceptance throughout Great Britain, but in that very year the want of moral unity between Englishmen and Scotsmen became more than ever apparent. This paradox, however, admits of easy explanation, and its true causes are worth following out, because they enable us to understand the course of public opinion with regard to the Act of Union. The two leading facts and dates which a student should keep in mind are the complete defeat of Scottish clansmen and rebels in 1746, and the policy of George III. immediately on his coming to the throne in 1760. These two events had their undoubted effect. As already pointed out, they gave to Jacobitism a death-blow which placed the Act of Union absolutely beyond attack. But they also increased the bitterness of feeling between British subjects who dwelt on the south and British subjects who dwelt on the north side of the Tweed. A few facts betray at once the causes, and illustrate the existence of this kind of international feud.

The defeat of the clansmen in 1746 left behind it much of bitterness in each part of Great Britain. Culloden was to Englishmen an undoubted and final victory, but it was a victory preceded by humiliating and startling defeats. Thrice at least had Highland clansmen routed English soldiers. A body of savages, as they seemed to an Englishman, never amounting to more than five or six thousand men, had occupied the capital of Scotland, had advanced, when they numbered not more than 4500 men, to the very middle of England, and then had been allowed to march back to Scotland without delay or defeat. They had filled English Whigs with fear and English Jacobites with hopes of a restoration of the Stewarts and of the overthrow of the Revolution Settlement. If few English Tories had taken up arms for the Pretender, Englishmen, whether Whigs or Tories, had shown little zeal on behalf of the House of Hanover. Fear begets delusions and cruelty. Englishmen believed without reason that the Scottish clansmen had shown the brutality of savages, and with almost equal unreasonableness identified Scottish Lowlanders with Highland

Jacobites, though the Lowlanders were mostly Whigs and the clansmen, guided by loyalty to their chiefs, were hardly Jacobites, since they cared very little whether a Pretender from France or a German Elector was to be King of Great Britain. Englishmen in the main were determined on one thing. The Highlands should be subdued and the clans should be so broken up that no Highland army should ever again march victoriously into England. This resolution was carried out with vigour. But vigour exercised by the Duke of Cumberland meant gratuitous severity and bloodshed. On the other hand, to the mass of Scotsmen who had never hitherto showed sympathy for Highlanders, the march of the clansmen into England seemed to be a Scottish triumph. The gentlemen who were " out in 1745 " became by degrees a sort of Scottish heroes, and " the affair of 1745 "— to use the favourite expression of Sir Walter Scott's father—became a patriotic glory long before it was transformed into a splendid romance by the genius of Sir Walter Scott; and the hatred of the Duke of Cumberland gave new point to dislike of England.

Turn now to 1760. George III. gloried in the name of Britain, and became a king round whom, on the death of Jacobitism, English Tories and Scottish Jacobites could without discredit rally against the Whigs. In truth, the very events which secured the constitutional unity of Great Britain encouraged Scotsmen, whether rich or poor, to flock into England, and whilst it brought men who had been Jacobites and were Tories back into active public life, took away from the great Whig party, which in spirit had ruled Great Britain for well-nigh seventy years, the one main reason for its existence. When the Revolution Settlement and the Act of Union became unassailable, there was no very obvious need for the rule of men specially called upon to defend institutions no longer liable to attack. George III. is said to have described himself at times as a "Revolution Whig." The expression was not altogether misplaced. His ambition was to maintain both the Revolution Settlement and the Act of Union, and also to regain, under the name of influence, the power which both William III. and Queen Anne could more or less exercise as part of the Crown's prerogatives. Take the effect of the fall of Jacobitism (1745) and the accession of George III. (1760) into account, and the want of moral unity between Scotland and England at the latter date becomes perfectly intelligible. Its existence, in any case, during the first ten or twenty years of George's reign is past a doubt.

Londoners assuredly hated the Scotsmen who from 1760 crowded in upon the capital in search of fortune and promotion. It has been well said that "novels never lie." The creator of fiction who paints his own time with any skill tells the truth as to what passes before his own eyes. It is therefore worth while meditating a little on Roderick Random's reception in London. We learn from it the way in which any Scottish adventurer, poor, daring, pertinacious, and (as compared with the mass of Englishmen) well educated, for he could almost always read his Bible and could also write, who had toiled along the road to London in search

of wealth to be gained by ability and perseverance,
was insulted by Londoners. His broad Scots
betrays his nationality. One man calls him a
"lousy Scotch guard"; a hackney coachman makes
his horses stumble so as to bedaub the Scotsman
with mud; the crowd applaud the feat; the victim
runs for refuge to a public-house, and tries to warm
himself by the fire. He is there exposed to unceas-
ing practical jokes. One fellow asks him how long
he has been caught; another pulls his hair amid the
jeers of the company, and the detected North Briton
is hunted out of doors, and is not safe from insult
till he at last flees to some small place of entertain-
ment kept by a Scotsman for Scotsmen.[1] And here
we may note the clannishness which above all things
offended Englishmen. Scotsmen all clung together
and helped one another against English rivals. It
was not the poverty-stricken Scotsman alone who
was liable to insult. Bute,[2] every one admits, was
an incompetent Minister; he was the favourite of
the King, and obtained thereby an eminence to

[1] See *Roderick Random*, Smollett's *Works*, i. pp. 70-72.

[2] The influence of the Bute Ministry upon the English attitude to
Scotland and Scotsmen may be illustrated by a comparison of the references to Scotland in Horace Walpole's Letters before and after 1760.
In 1758 he described the Scots as "the most accomplished nation
in Europe, the nation to which, if any one country is endowed with
a superior partition of sense, I should be inclined to give the preference" (*Royal and Noble Authors*, 2nd ed., ii. p. 201). Similar sentiments are expressed in letters to Principal Robertson (January 18,
1759) and to Lord Hailes (March 25, 1759), although Scottish
members had played a part in the defeat of his father whose memory
he worshipped, and, as he remarked, he had "no reason to be
partial" to Scotland. But after 1760 his comments became bitter,
and the bitterness continued and increased in the years when the
Scottish members were supporting Lord North against the American
colonists.

which his talents gave him no claim. He was believed by the London mob to be in the very worst sense the favourite of the King's mother. For this charge there existed no valid reason. Bute was hated, not because he was supposed to be vicious, but because he was known to be a Scotsman. Wilkes and his *North Briton* deliberately stimulated the popular hatred of every man who came from north of the Tweed, and Wilkes, though he lacked almost every virtue which can be included under the term of character, was an eminent man of letters and did much to form the public opinion of his day. John Home, who had been personally associated with Bute, was in 1769 compelled by Garrick to change the title of a play from " Rivine " to " The Fatal Discovery," and was urged to conceal the authorship; he failed to do so, and the play had to be withdrawn. Junius, whose writings were read far and wide, taught that a Scotsman was by nature a traitor.

" National reflections," writes Junius, " I confess, " are not justified in theory, nor upon any general " principles. To know how well they are deserved " and how justly they have been applied, we must " have the evidence of facts before us. We must " be conversant with the Scots in private life, and " observe their principles of acting to us, and to " each other; the characteristic prudence, the selfish " nationality, the indefatigable smile, the persevering " assiduity, the everlasting profession of a discreet " and moderate resentment. If the instance were " not too important for an experiment, it might " not be amiss to confide a little in their integrity. " Without any abstract reasoning upon causes and

" effects, we shall soon be convinced by experience,
" that the Scots, transplanted from their own
" country, are always a distinct and separate body
" from the people who receive them. In other settle-
" ments, they only love themselves; in England they
" cordially love themselves, and as cordially hate
" their neighbours. For the remainder of their good
" qualities, I must appeal to the reader's observation,
" unless he will accept of my Lord Barrington's
" authority. In a letter to the late Lord Melcombe,
" published by Mr. Lee, he expresses himself with a
" truth and accuracy not very common in his Lord-
" ship's lucubrations. 'And Cockburne, like most of
" ' his countrymen, is as abject to those above him
" ' as he is insolent to those below him.'" [1]

Johnson was the great moralist of his day; he
was a high Tory, and even fancied himself a Jacobite.
He would never have attacked Bute, through whose
hands he received a royal pension. He never would,
in any case, have said a word against George III.
But Johnson's humour was constantly turned against
Scotland, and Johnson's wit was not of a good-
natured character. When Boswell, talking to Burke,
oddly called it " oil," Burke's comment was, " Yes;
oil of vitriol." In the celebrated meeting between
the great moralist and the notorious demagogue they
found a subject of pleasing sympathy in their de-
preciation of Scotland. Even Johnson's exposure of
Macpherson's fraud [2] with regard to Ossian owed part

[1] Junius, i., Preface, pp. xxiv, xxv.   The *Letters of Junius*
appeared between 1762 and 1772.

[2] " Detection her taper will quench to a spark
    And Scotchman meet Scotchman and cheat in the dark."
                    GOLDSMITH, *Retaliation.*

of its energy to the author's joy in exposing the
credulity and the ignorance of Scottish enthusiasm
when it fell in with national vanity. Nor be it
supposed that it was only the mob who felt, or
here and there men of letters who fostered, hostility
between Scotsmen and Englishmen. It did not
indeed affect the conduct of Chatham or of his son.
But as a general rule it did affect the Whig party.
The Whigs were fighting, indeed, a desperate and on
the whole an unsuccessful battle with the King, who
desired to increase his personal power, and who
turned almost instinctively to Scotsmen as valuable
recruits for the "King's friends." They certainly
felt that a King who was the enemy of the Whigs
was a traitor to the cause which ought to be represented by the House of Hanover, and they almost
inevitably fostered, as did Junius, dislike to the
employment of Scotsmen.

" Are you a prince of the House of Hanover, and
" do you exclude all the leading Whig families from
" your counsels ? Do you profess to govern accord-
" ing to law, and is it consistent with that profession,
" to impart your confidence and affection to those
" men only who, though now perhaps detached from
" the desperate cause of the pretender, are marked in
" this country by an hereditary attachment to high
" and arbitrary principles of government ? Are you
" so infatuated as to take the sense of your people
" from the representation of ministers, or from the
" shouts of a mob, notoriously hired to surround
" your coach, or stationed at a theatre ? And if
" you are, in reality, that public man, that king,
" that magistrate, which these questions suppose you

" to be, is it any answer to your people, to say that,
" among your domestics you are good-humoured, that
" to one lady you are faithful, that to your children
" you are indulgent ? Sir, the man who addresses
" you in these terms is your best friend. He would
" willingly hazard his life in defence of your title to
" the crown ; and, if power be your object, will still
" shew you how possible it is for a king of England,
" by the noblest means, to be the most absolute
" prince in Europe. You have no enemies, sir, but
" those who persuade you to aim at power without
" right, and who think it flattery to tell you that
" the character of king dissolves the natural relation
" between guilt and punishment." [1]

The animosity against Scotsmen which certainly
existed in 1760 gradually died away, so that by
1805 the moral union of Great Britain was, as we
shall see, established. The cordiality with which
Beattie was received in London in 1771 and 1773,
the conferment of the honorary degree of D.C.L. by
the University of Oxford, in spite of his being a
Presbyterian minister, and the efforts made to induce
him to take holy orders in the Church of England,
all form a contrast to the experiences of John Home
ten years earlier. Yet the feud of 1760 lasted longer
than one would at first sight suppose. A now forgotten playwright, Charles Macklin, in 1781 produced in London his masterpiece, " The Man of the
World," in which he himself acted the villain and
the hero, Sir Pertinax MacSycophant, which was
originally called " The True-born Scotchman." Its
whole aim was to satirise the successful mean-

[1] Junius, Preface, pp. xxviii, xxix.

Chapter
IX.

ness, the pertinacity, and hypocrisy of a Scottish adventurer. The play obtained a brilliant and popular success.[1]

Nor is it to be thought that Scotsmen did not return the dislike of Englishmen. No Englishman indeed migrated to Scotland in order to make his fortune. Wealth is not to be gained in a poverty-stricken country, and at any rate from 1707 to 1832 few were the posts of public importance in Scotland to which any one but a Scotsman would be appointed.[2] There was no competition, therefore, between Englishmen and Scotsmen at Edinburgh, but the mob of Edinburgh and of the larger Scottish towns was always prepared to support, sometimes by violence, the deference claimed for Scottish national feeling. During the first half and probably till nearly the end of the eighteenth century, eminent Scottish thinkers and writers, such as David Hume, and, in a degree, Adam Smith, were severe and even unfriendly critics of England and English institu-

[1] See *Dict. Nat. Biog.* xxxv. p. 183. Macklin's "Man of the World" may have been a reply to Richard Cumberland's "Fashionable Lover," produced some ten years earlier, in which Cumberland was bold enough to give the leading rôle to an honest Scotch servant. Compare also a remark by John Hall-Stevenson (1718–1785), a friend of Sterne and the author of verses now deservedly forgotten. "Accord-" ing to the [North British] Reviewers, the greatest pleasure that the "whole English nation enjoys, is to see their brethren of North "Britain in their theatres represented as a parcel of scoundrels." Stevenson replied that the English were "not throwing dirt at a "whole nation, but laughing at the folly of a few" (Hall-Stevenson, *Works,* i. p. 93).

[2] The chief exception to this inflexible rule is that for a short period the collection of import duties was confided to English officials, and that for a short time an Exchequer Court was formed over which an Englishman presided as Baron of the Exchequer. See Burton, viii. p. 213.

tions.[1] Indeed the leaders of Scottish thought studied
English writing and English style as foreigners trying
to adopt the language of a country towards which
they felt but moderate sympathy.

(*b*) *The Gradual Progress towards the Establishment of Moral Unity, 1760–1805.*—This movement
began before 1760. Its progress may be traced by
several events.

Consider first the glorious policy of the elder
Pitt's great ministry, 1758-1760. It is best described in his own words spoken on January 14,
1766 :

"I have no local attachments; it is indifferent to
" me whether a man was rocked in his cradle on this
" or that side of the Tweed. I sought for merit
" wherever it was to be found. It is my boast that
" I was the first minister who looked for it ; and I
" found it in the mountains of the north. I called it
" forth and drew into your service, a hardy and
" intrepid race of men ; men who, when left by your
" jealousy, became a prey to the artifices of your
" enemies, and had gone nigh to have overturned
" the State in the war before the last. These men,
" in the last war, were brought to combat on your
" side ; they served with fidelity as they fought with
" valour, and conquered for you in every part of the
" world : detested be the national reflections against
" them. They are unjust, groundless, illiberal, un-
" manly. When I ceased to serve His Majesty as
" a minister, it was not the country of the man by
" whom I was moved, but the *man* of that country

[1] See Bagehot, *Biographical Studies*: "Adam Smith as a Person,"
pp. 271-275.

" wanted wisdom and held principles incompatible
" with freedom." [1]

Chatham built up the glory and the power of England by promoting the moral unity of Great Britain,
and letting every Scotsman know, be he Jacobite
or Whig, that he might take his part in creating
the British Empire; and in this matter justice ought
to be done even to George III.   When he gloried
in the "name of Britain," [2] he probably contemplated obtaining the help of Scotsmen and Jacobites
in increasing or renewing the influence of the Crown.
The words which angered Englishmen announced that
public life at Westminster, and indeed throughout the
whole British Empire, was open as much to Scotsmen
as to Englishmen; and this was a real step towards the
moral unity of the country.   It is more than possible
that the war between Great Britain and the thirteen
Colonies (1776–1783), calamitous though it was,
tended to obliterate ill-will between the north and
the south of Great Britain.   Opinion as to the policy
which ought to be adopted towards the rebellious
colonists was divided in every part of the country.
There does not seem, speaking generally, to have been on
this subject any essential difference of opinion between
England and Scotland.   On the whole, in each country
the war was seemingly popular as long as it promised
success.   No doubt among Englishmen no less than
among Scotsmen there were grave differences between
the wiser men who, with Burke, Hume, Adam Smith,
Horace Walpole, and the merchants of the city of

[1] Basil Williams, *Life of William Pitt, Earl of Chatham*, ii. 189-
190, London, 1913.
[2] The King wrote " Britain," but the word, from the first, was quoted
as " Briton."   See Hunt's *History of England, 1760–1801*, p. 12.

London, saw that success was hardly possible, and that, if gained, it might in the long run be calamitous, and the mass of the British public who were possessed by the thought that the sovereignty of the British Parliament must at all costs be maintained. All that need be insisted upon is that the war with America in no way set Englishmen against Scotsmen, but really brought them together and divided each part of Great Britain into two like parties. It is well to combine this division with a curious sign of popular feeling in 1780, a year made notorious by the Lord George Gordon riots. The circumstance to be noted, for it bears on our present topic, is that the passionate fear and hatred of Papists was as strong in Edinburgh as in London, and indeed stronger. The Parliament at Westminster resisted the pressure of the London mob, but even the authority of the General Assembly of the Scottish Church could not in 1778 withstand the outcry in Scotland against extending to that country a relief to Roman Catholics already granted to them in England, and clearly demanded by the commonest dictates of justice.[1] One more fact is full of significance. The rioters who in 1780 held London for days at their mercy were headed by a half-insane Scottish noble-man. It is incredible that in 1760 a Scotsman would have been the leader or the idol of a London mob.

The year 1784 marks the defeat of the Fox and North Coalition by the King and Pitt on the subject of the India Bill. To no man, except Pitt, can this defeat of the Whigs be attributed more truly than to Dundas. But Dundas had become, and continued to be,

[1] Hume Brown, iii. 349-351.

the leading Scottish statesman.   His tenure of power
is described by Whigs with some truth as despotism.
It was the triumph of a party, but it was the triumph
of the most popular and by far the most influential
of Scotsmen.   Pitt, like his father Chatham, wished to
enlist in the service of Great Britain competent men,
whether they were born south or north of the Tweed.
There were plenty of such competent men in Scotland,
and Dundas preserved for his Scottish followers all
Scottish patronage, and a good part of the patronage
in British India, governed by the East India Company
under the control of the Crown.   It were possible to
date the moral unity of Great Britain from 1784, but
it owes its completion to a far greater event than the
defeat of the Coalition.   The French Revolution, from
1789 to, say, 1793, when war was declared between
Great Britain and France, went near to terminate, if
it did not actually terminate, any moral separation
between England and Scotland.   The men of the twentieth century understand that period better than could
the men who began their experience of public life in
1815.   We know, what many of them gradually forgot,
the condition of opinion created by a war menacing the
independence of this country.   The French Revolution and the war with France created more vehement
differences of party feeling throughout England and
Scotland than could be understood during the mid-
Victorian era.   We have now no difficulty in
understanding how a war, which lasted not for four,
but practically for more than twenty years, blotted
out and terminated every difference connected with
the existence of the Union between England and
Scotland.   There were Tories, there were Whigs, there

were Radicals, there were even Jacobins, both in England and in Scotland in 1805. These names represent the party conflicts of the day, and have no reference to the Union between England and Scotland. It had already obtained moral, no less than political, acceptance by the British people.

We must not forget, though any detailed treatment of the topic is no part of our subject, that the acceptance of the Union in Scotland coincided, and was closely connected, with the growth of commercial prosperity in the eighteenth century. "The "country has been prosperous," wrote Alexander Carlyle, "with an increase of agriculture, trade, and "manufactures, as well as all the ornamental arts "of life, to a degree unexampled in any age and "country."[1] That other circumstances besides the Union contributed to the growth of prosperity is undeniable, but it is not less certain that the trade privileges, which were the main inducement offered by the English ministers in 1707, had a fundamental influence upon Scottish commerce. That influence was not immediately beneficial, for the change from a system of strict protection of Scottish industries brought about a period of economic distress. Yet even at the outset these disadvantages were, to some extent, compensated by the payment of the "Equivalent";[2] for Scottish capital had been depleted by the Darien Scheme; and a sum of nearly £400,000 was a very

---

[1] *Autobiography*, ed. 1910, p. 527.

[2] The Equivalent was a sum of money payable to Scotland under the Treaty of Union, as compensation for the share which Scotland would thenceforth take in the liability for the English National Debt. It was expended in compensating sufferers from the failure of the Darien and similar Companies.

important assistance to the development of·commerce
and industry.   The growth of prosperity, of which
Carlyle speaks, was much more rapid in the West
than in the East of Scotland, and it was not until
the second half of the eighteenth century that the
East Coast towns began to benefit by the Union.
The eighteenth-century revolution in Scottish agriculture was very largely the result of the Union,[1]
and the impulse given in 1707 received fresh strength
after the suppression of the Jacobite cause.

[1] *Scotland and Scotsmen in the Eighteenth Century*, from the MSS.
of John Ramsay of Ochtertyre (1736-1815), vol. ii. chap. x.

CHAPTER X

First Thought.—The permanent success of the Act of Union is shown in—

Chapter X.

(A) *The creation thereby of the United Kingdom of Great Britain, and*

(B) *The preservation thereby of English and of Scottish Nationalism.*

THE CREATION OF GREAT BRITAIN

THE Union of England and Scotland did ultimately confer upon the inhabitants of Great Britain all, and more than all, of the benefits which statesmen of one generation after another had expected to obtain by transforming England and Scotland into one inseparable State governed by one and the same sovereign. One circumstance suffices to prove the truth of this assertion. Most Scotsmen in 1707 held that, as far as Scotland at any rate was concerned, the mere union of the Crowns had on the whole been a failure,[1] and had certainly not brought to Scotland the prosperity which many Scotsmen

---

[1] Compare Graham, *Social Life of Scotland in the Eighteenth Century*, chap. i.-vii.

anticipated from the accession of James in 1603.
When another century had elapsed (1707 – 1807)
there was nobody found in Scotland or in England to suggest that the union of the two countries had not been of great benefit to each of
them; [1] and this is the more remarkable because
the opening years of the nineteenth century were a
time in which party spirit ran high throughout the
whole of Great Britain. On this matter the experience of 1832 is full of instruction. The Reform
Act worked a revolution, though happily for Great
Britain a revolution carried through with the very
minimum of violence, or even of threatened violence;
but, through the length and breadth of the islands,
Whigs and Tories were each filled with revolutionary
or reactionary passion. Yet no leading man, and
assuredly no English or Scottish party, even suggested
the policy of repealing the Act of Union. The unity
of England and Scotland was then held to be the
unshakable foundation of British power and liberty.
Turn the matter which way you will, in the earlier
part of the nineteenth century any fair-minded man
who looked back over the annals of the past hundred
years could see that the Act of Union had doubled
the strength of Great Britain, had enabled the country
to resist the power of Louis XIV., and to withstand
the far greater genius and power of Napoleonic

---

[1] See Scott's letter to Miss Edgeworth, July 18, 1825, *Familiar
Letters*, ii. 311, 312, and letters of Malachi Malagrowther in 1826,
Prose Works, xxi. 374, 375

Scott's protest as Sir Malachi Malagrowther (1826) was meant to
arouse opposition against a supposed slight to Scotland in the abolition of Scottish £1 notes in a Bill passed to-meet the condition of things
in England. But violent as was Scott's language, it fell far short
of any serious suggestion to repeal or modify the Act of Union.

despotism. This was as clear to our grandfathers as it is to-day (1919) patent to ourselves that a united Great Britain supported by the British Empire has enabled us to overthrow the power and the armies of Germany.[1] The Act of Union which created Great Britain laid the foundation of the British Empire.

THE PRESERVATION OF ENGLISH AND OF SCOTTISH NATIONALISM

This subject has received far too little attention.

As regards England.—The slightness of the change introduced into any English institution by the Act of Union, the predominating representation of England in the British Parliament, and the manifest advantages conferred upon England by the political unity of Great Britain, seemed to give, and did give, almost perfect security to English Nationalism. From the nature of things, further, the Nationalism of England was weaker than the Nationalism of Scotland. It was certainly a wise policy to avoid any change in the civil institutions and in the Church of England which might offend English national feeling. But the examination of a difficult topic will be lessened if in considering the present Thought we mainly confine

---

[1] The experience of the nineteenth century suggests the thought that had British statesmen failed to seize in 1707 the one happy opportunity for carrying an Act of Union, the unity of Great Britain might well, like that of Italy or of Switzerland, have been delayed till the middle, and even till near the end of the nineteenth century, and the possible greatness of a British Empire might have remained the daydream of enthusiastic patriotism. Whether it be worth while thus to speculate on what might have been, is a doubtful question, which should probably receive a negative answer.

our attention to the effect of the Union in protecting the Nationalism of Scotland.

As regards Scotland.—The preservation of Scottish Nationalism was a far more difficult and serious matter. As has been stated again and again in this essay, the fear that the Union with England meant the moral conquest of Scotland and the loss of Scottish Nationalism, was, as regards Scotsmen, the true and natural source of opposition to the political unity which was an essential feature of Unionism as understood by the Whigs in both parts of Great Britain. The topic we have in hand is full of perplexity, for one here comes across the confusion caused by the ambiguity and the vagueness of terms such as "Nationalism," "Nationality," "Nation," and the like. On this point the language of Lord Bryce is full both of warning and of help:

"What," he writes, "constitutes a Nationality? "and what is the difference between a Nationality "and a Nation?

"The popular use of the terms is vague, and "any definition that can be given is likely to "be either too wide or too narrow to suit the "facts." [1]

The warning contained in these words lies in the sound statement that over-definition may often cause more misunderstanding than it removes. Their help lies in the indirect suggestion that here, as elsewhere, illustration may, in dealing with speculations in reference to history, give more aid than the attempt to apply logical precision to subjects of popular discourse in which the terms to be used must always

[1] Bryce, *Essays and Addresses in War Time*, p. 127.

have a vagueness whereof a student must take account.

The course pursued in these pages is to examine the two following questions :

Question 1.—What is the meaning of Nationalism, and especially of Scottish Nationalism, as tested by the language of Nationalists ?

It is hardly possible to discover stronger Nationalists, in regard at any rate to their own country, than Walter Scott, and, strange though the juxtaposition sounds, Thomas Carlyle. Scott, more or less imaginatively, revived and represented the tradition of Scottish Jacobites ; Carlyle, half unconsciously, transferred to the nineteenth century the Scottish Calvinism of the seventeenth century.[1] The noblest and by far the most thoughtful among English Nationalists was William Wordsworth. From the language of each of these men much may be learned about the true nature and meaning of Nationalism. Take the following picture of Scott when at the height of his fame and prosperity, and when in full possession of his genius and of his strength. It is worth a hundred disquisitions on the meaning of Nationalism. Scott had been present at a meeting where he had opposed with force and eloquence some reforms or alterations in Scottish judicial procedure.

" When the meeting broke up, he walked across " *the Mound,* on his way to Castle Street, between

---

[1] The creed, political and religious, of Scott might be called Jacobitism without a Stewart King or the possible restoration of a Stewart King, and without the leaning of the later Stewarts to Romanism, whilst Carlyle's religious and political creed has been sometimes termed Calvinism without Christianity.

" Mr. Jeffrey and another of his reforming friends,
" who complimented him on the rhetorical powers he
" had been displaying, and would willingly have
" treated the subject-matter of the discussion play-
" fully. But his feelings had been moved to an
" extent far beyond their apprehension : he exclaimed,
" ' No, no—'tis no laughing matter; little by little,
" ' whatever your wishes may be, you will destroy
" ' and undermine until nothing of what makes
" ' Scotland Scotland shall remain.' And so saying,
" he turned round to conceal his agitation—but not
" until Mr. Jeffrey saw tears gushing down his cheek
" —resting his head until he recovered himself on
" the wall of the Mound. Seldom, if ever, in his
" more advanced age, did any feelings obtain such
" mastery." [1]

Take Scott again in a calmer moment, when
advocating the foundation of the then new Edinburgh
Academy, and dwelling on the noble history of
education in Scotland. Here his Nationalism comes
fully out, and in its best form. He reminded his
audience in 1824 that " at no moment was the study
" of that beautiful language [Greek] so interesting
" as at present, when the people among whom it
" was still in use, were again, as he trusted, about to
" emancipate themselves from slavery and barbarism,
" and take their rank among free nations." But he
adds that " he would have the youth taught to
" venerate the patriots and heroes of their own
" country, along with those of Greece and Rome;
" to know the histories of Wallace and Bruce, as
" well as those of Themistocles and of Cæsar; and

[1] Lockhart's *Life of Scott*, i. (ed. 1838), 299.

" that the recollection of the fields of Flodden and
" Bannockburn, should not be lost in those of Platæa
" and Marathon." [1]

Here Scott joins hands with Carlyle, and the latter
gives to Scott's wish its grandest and profoundest
meaning :

" A heroic Wallace, quartered on the scaffold,
" cannot hinder that his Scotland become, one day,
" a part of England; but he does hinder that it
" become on tyrannous unfair terms a part of it.
" . . . If the Union with England be in fact one
" of Scotland's chief blessings, we thank Wallace
" that it was not the chief curse." [2]

Hear now William Wordsworth. He blends together the two aspects of Nationalism. " Who," he
asks, " does not rejoice that former partitions have
" disappeared — and that England, Scotland, and
" Wales are under one legislative and executive
" authority ? " [3] . . . He bids us " look upon
" Scotland and Wales : though, by the union of these
" with England under the same Government (which
" was effected without conquest in one instance)
" ferocious and desolating wars, and more injurious
" intrigues, and sapping and disgraceful corruptions
" have been prevented; and tranquillity, security,
" and prosperity, and a thousand interchanges of
" amity, not otherwise attainable, have followed ;—
" yet the flashing eye, and the agitated voice, and
" all the tender recollections, with which the names
" of Prince Llewellin and William Wallace are to

---

[1] Lockhart, *Life of Scott*, iii. 217.
[2] Carlyle, *Past and Present*, Book i. ch. ii.
[3] *Convention of Cintra*, pp. 163, 164.

" this day pronounced by the fireside and on the
" public road, attest that these substantial blessings
" have not been purchased without the relinquishment
" of something most salutary to the moral nature
" of Man : else the remembrances would not cleave
" so faithfully to their abiding-place in the human
" heart." [1]

Weigh the words of these Nationalists, and you
have the true meaning of Nationalism more clearly
placed before your mind than by any subtle definition.   It means the love of a special country by
the inhabitants thereof as their homeland.   They
love this home, be it England, Scotland, or Wales,
its religion, its institutions, its laws, its traditions,
its history, its heroes, and above all its spirit, with
a love resembling the affection which a man feels
for his family, for his father, for his mother, for his
brothers and sisters.   The love, it is true, may
originate in various causes, in community of race,
of language, of religion, or of history, but whatever
its origin, this attachment of a man to his own
country is itself a matter of moral value.   It is at
once the cause and the result of patriotism.   If
two nations really wish to unite into one State
they will desire, if they understand the nature of
man, that they shall each preserve as much of the
noble spirit and traditions of their separate nationality
as may be compatible with the wider sense and the
extended patriotism which ought to bind together
all the citizens of the one politically united country.

Question 2.—What was the effect of the Act of

[1] *Convention of Cintra*, p. 170.   The whole of pp. 163-170 are
worth study.

Union in preserving the spirit of Scottish nationalism
in the various spheres of national life?

National Independence.—Here the Act, it must
at once be admitted, deprived Scotsmen of something
to which for centuries they had attached the highest
value. After the Union, Scotland could no longer
determine her own course of action independently
and in defiance of the wish of England. It is vain
to deny that this was a great and, as it seemed, to
many Scotsmen, an unwarrantable sacrifice. Before
the Act had passed into law, Scotland had, theoreti-
cally at least, the right at any moment to declare
war upon England, or, in alliance with France,
attempt an invasion of England. But this right
was of less value than it sometimes appeared. When
England was prosperous and united, Scotland
declared war at the certainty of great loss and
subject to the possibility of great peril. Flodden
had its lesson as well as Bannockburn. And,
as we have seen, the union of the Crowns was
all but as fatal to true national independence as
the union of the Parliaments, for it involved something too like subjection to the Government in
London, and this often meant the interference
of English ministers in Scottish affairs. But the
parliamentary union of the kingdoms, both theo-
retically and in fact, was a very different thing from
the subjection of Scotland to England. It was, as
its very name proclaimed, a treaty whereby England
and Scotland alike became members of the one State
of Great Britain, wherein no doubt England, to use
a modern expression, was the predominant partner.
But partnership made on fair terms is an essentially

different thing from subjection or servitude. It is important, however, not to underrate the extent of the real, and still more of the apparent, sacrifice made by Scotland in accepting a union of Parliaments, or an incorporative union, to use the language of 1707, instead of a federative union. For, unless this is understood, the legitimate fear of English tyranny felt by patriotic Scotsmen becomes incomprehensible, and the boldness as well as the wisdom of Whig statesmanship will not meet with its fair appreciation. To see that the sacrifice of Scottish independence need not mean the loss of Scottish Nationalism was at the beginning of the eighteenth century a sign of the most statesmanlike foresight.

The Administration of Scottish Government.— Important legislation, such as an Act settling the descent of the Crown, or strokes of statesmanship, such as the declaration of war or the making of peace with a foreign country, might well affect the habits or the happiness of Scotsmen far less than what may be called, in a narrower sense, the administration of Scottish affairs in Scotland. Now in Scotland, from 1603 onwards, and also after the Union, the administrative government of Scotland has generally been, and for the most part still continues, in the hands of Scotsmen. Deviations from this practice have been and are few, and the exceptions to this statement, *e.g.* by the appointment of Englishmen as Judges in Scotland during the Interregnum, prove the rule. They are warnings against a dangerous error ; they are not precedents which any British Government would be tempted to follow. Nor, it may be added, does any course of conduct tend more directly towards

the protection and encouragement of Nationalism Chapter
than adherence to the principle that the administra- X.
tion of public affairs shall be placed in the hands
only of the natives of the country where a Government exercises its power. Even the Stewarts rarely
attempted to place the management of Scottish
government in the hands of Englishmen; a Scottish
tyrant or a Scottish bigot would, they felt, be likely
to give less offence to Scotsmen than would an
energetic and fair-minded Englishman who failed to
understand the feeling of a country with which he
was not connected by descent or education. The
care with which this conviction has been followed
since the Union is the more remarkable when con-
trasted with the free admission of Scotsmen to every
form of governmental or official life throughout Great
Britain, or the British Dominions.

Law.—Scotland since, as before, the Union, has
been governed by the law of Scotland, grounded on
Roman and upon feudal law. No doubt the law of
Scotland, in common with the law of every civilised
country, has been altered, and presumably amended,
during the two centuries which have elapsed since
1707. But it remains as distinctly the law of Scotland as the law of England remains the law of England. Much less attempt than one would have
expected has been made to assimilate the laws of
each country to one another, and this even where
diversity has caused considerable evil. Thus in the
marriage law there has been no attempt at obtaining
one law for the whole of Great Britain.[1] The remark

[1] Compare the Marriage (Scotland) Act 1856 (19 & 20 Vict. c.
96, s. 1), which makes the residence of *one* of the parties in Scotland

applies also to the law as to the legitimation of children born out of wedlock, by the subsequent marriage of their parents. Such assimilation as has arisen is one of the beneficial effects of the House of Lords being a final Court of Appeal from the decisions both of the Scottish Court of Session and of the English Courts of Common Law and of Equity.

The Church.—The National and Presbyterian Church of Scotland was, before the Act of Union, and continued, after it, to be, the creation, and, in the main, the representative of Scottish Nationalism.

The Act which created the United Kingdom of Great Britain did much more than pay respect to the national Church of Scotland. It did all that legislation could do to guarantee the Church's existence. It provided against, and in fact, by its support of the Church of Scotland, made impossible, a restoration of the Stewarts which would have threatened Scotland with the revival of Episcopacy. So excessively careful were the authors of the Act of Union to link together the political unity of the Kingdom with the maintenance of the national and Presbyterian Church of Scotland that they gave to that venerated body additional security. They made provisions for the security of the Church of Scotland unalterable,[1] and also provided that Professors in the Scottish Universities should subscribe to the Confession of Faith.[2]

---

for twenty-one days prior to the marriage requisite for a valid marriage in Scotland. See Dicey, *Conflict of Laws*, 2nd ed. p. 617.

[1] See Act of Union, s. 2.

[2] See Act of Union, ss. 2, 3, 6. This requirement was abolished in 1853. See 16 & 17 Vict. c. 89, s. 1.

The Act of Union did, one may add, in truth strengthen the position of the Scottish national Church by introducing into the life of Scotland a kind of toleration which, at any rate in a Protestant country, was absolutely required by the spirit of the eighteenth or nineteenth century, and might not have been as easily obtained under a purely Scottish Parliament. Episcopalians are in Scotland as much, from a legal point of view, Nonconformists as are Dissenters in England. No one will now deny the need for ensuring to Scottish Episcopalians as much of toleration as was extended to Dissenters in England. Something more than this also was necessary. It is inconceivable that after the Union the execution of Aikenhead for blasphemy should have been allowed to take place at Edinburgh, and few are the critics of the Act of Union who will regret that the Act, indirectly at any rate, made the repetition of such monstrous intolerance an impossibility.

There is much to be said against the legislation under which Church Patronage was revived. It is, as already pointed out,[1] a notable but exceptional instance of the breach by the British Parliament of the spirit, and possibly of the terms, of the Act of Union. But, as should be noted, there is hardly any parallel in British legislation to this defiance of the principles of the Act. It would have been far better, a modern critic feels, if the Act for the revival of Patronage, passed by Tories who hoped to carry through on the death of Anne the restoration of the Pretender, had been repealed when the Revolution Settlement was secured by the accession of

[1] Cf. pp. 280-282, *ante.*

George I. to the throne of Great Britain. But the omission to carry out in this matter the spirit of the Act of Union is accounted for, though not politically justified, by the circumstances that many Scottish Presbyterians approved in their hearts of the system of Patronage as promoting the appointment of educated and more or less liberal-minded men as ministers of the Church of Scotland, and that the Crown and many private patrons exercised their patronage, in a large proportion of instances, in accordance with the wishes of the parishioners of a vacant parish.[1]

Consider, however, the whole position of the Church of Scotland under the Act of Union, and it will become impossible to deny that in the ecclesiastical sphere the Church possessed both a theoretical and a practical authority which pre-eminently kept alive Scottish Nationalism.

Education, Language, Literature, and Thought.
—*Education.* The system of parish schools in Scotland depended in 1707 on the Act for Settling of Schools[2] passed in 1696. The Act was in reality the work of the Church. The teaching was actually given by the parish schoolmaster, and the Presbyterian ministers were, as a class, closely connected with the parish schoolmasters. In short, the parochial education of Scotland was in one way or another the achievement of the national Church, and of the

---

[1] "Till 1750, much the greater part of churches were settled "according to the letter or spirit of the Act of 1690, even when a "presentation was got" (Ramsay of Ochtertyre, *Scotland and Scotsmen*, vol. i. p. 74). On the relation between the Patronage Act and the English view of Parliamentary sovereignty, see pp. 22, 243-44, *ante.*

[2] 1696, c. 26, A.P.S. x. 63.

combined action of the Presbyterian ministers and Chapter
X.
Presbyterian schoolmasters; and it afforded elementary education to the mass, not only of the working
class, but also of the gentry of Scotland. The educa-
tional system was grounded upon knowledge of the
Bible and of the doctrines of Presbyterianism. It
was in no way checked or interfered with by the Act
of Union. It immensely favoured the growth of political and moral unity throughout the whole of Great
Britain. The authorised version of the Bible, published in 1611 under the authority of James, was a
work accepted by every Protestant, whether Presbyterian or Episcopalian, as well in the northern as
in the southern part of Great Britain. This version
of the Bible was admittedly written in the clearest
and noblest English. It was read, and has been constantly read by every English and Scottish Protestant
sufficiently educated to read any book. It was, at
the time of the Union, accepted throughout the
whole of Great Britain as the accurate rendering of
the verbally inspired word of God. The religious,
the moral, the social, and the political effects of such
a Bible hardly admit of exaggeration. It made
Englishmen and Scotsmen ultimately speak, read,
and write one and the same language, and it linked
together the religious ideas of all British Protestants.
Further, the Presbyterian Church of Scotland performed, from the Protestant standpoint, the great
national service of spreading Presbyterianism throughout Scotland, and reducing gradually the number of
Roman Catholics in the Highlands, which at the time
of the Revolution and of the Union was great. With
the religious effects of this effort we are not here at

all concerned; what does concern any man who investigates the results of the Union is that the labours, whether of clergymen or of schoolmasters in the Highlands, did most certainly tend to extend the influence of Lowlanders in the northern parts of Scotland, and also to increase the number of persons to whom the Union of Great Britain became gradually more and more acceptable. Then, too, the national system of elementary education did create in Scotland a far greater number of citizens, in proportion to the population of that country, capable of reading and writing than the number of such persons who at the time of the Union were to be found in England. The Universities, no less than the parochial schools of Scotland, were under the influence of, and, by the Act of Union itself, closely connected with the national Church. Even in the parochial school a Scotsman might learn, and often did learn, a good deal of Latin. By the middle of the eighteenth century the universities of Scotland had attained deserved fame, which did not at that time belong to either university in England. The language of a distinguished Englishman of great knowledge and of marked insight is on this point decisive. Walter Bagehot thus writes of the universities of Scotland at the time when Adam Smith held the Professorship of Moral Philosophy in the University of Glasgow :

" The Scotch universities had then, as now, several " professorships very fairly paid, and very fairly " distributed. The educated world in Scotland was " probably stronger a century ago than it ever was " before or since. The Union with England had " removed the aristocracy of birth which over-

" shadowed it before, and commerce had not yet
" created the aristocracy of wealth which overshadows
" it now.   Philosophical merit had therefore then in
" Scotland an excellent chance of being far better
" rewarded than it usually is in the world.   There
" were educated men who cared for philosophy, and
" these people had prizes to give away." [1]

Language.—The intense nationalism of Scotsmen,
generated and kept alive mainly by conflicts with England, certainly told upon the literary work of Scotsmen both before and after the Act of Union.   One
must, however, draw a rather marked distinction, at
any rate from the time of the Union of Crowns,
between the language or tongue spoken by Scotsmen
and Englishmen, and the language read or readable by
the educated inhabitants of each country.   In one
sense, indeed, the same language was spoken (if for
the present purpose we except the Highlands of
Scotland), both say in London and in Aberdeen.
But it may be allowable to doubt whether a cockney
would even at the beginning of the eighteenth
century have understood the language addressed to
him by an Aberdonian, or whether an ordinary
Scotsman, even if he came from Edinburgh, would
have easily followed remarks made to him—probably
jeers—by an ordinary Londoner.   When James came
to the throne of England his Scottish accent, or in
other words his broad Scots, perplexed courtiers
anxious to catch every word of wisdom falling from
royal lips.   The practical difference between the
spoken language prevalent in the north and in the
south of Great Britain assuredly did, for a time,

[1] Bagehot, *Biog. Studies*, pp. 274, 275.

impede the political as well as the moral unity which the Act of Union tended to produce.

Literature and Thought.—Towards the middle of the eighteenth century Scotsmen of the highest literary eminence formed the so-called Select Society " to promote the right reading and speaking of " the English language." To use the words of a Scottish writer, " all that was intellectually " strongest in Scotland felt that her proper place " in general literature could only be attained by " learning an adept use of the tools of the literary " trade, and that the most essential of these tools "·was English style, and not any pedantic or per- " verse preservation of the vernacular."[1] The consequence of these conscientious efforts to learn English, of which the Select Society was the outward and visible sign, is that Scottish men of letters, such as Adam Smith and most emphatically Robertson, came to write very good bookish English, but not precisely the natural English of the best English writers, who had learned it from babyhood and from their nurses.[2] Horace Walpole somewhere gives an account of the first call he received from Robertson, whose works were greatly admired. Walpole wondered that Robertson, whilst he wrote good English, spoke a tongue which he (Walpole) could hardly understand. Johnson loved Robertson but would not talk of his

---

[1] Craik, *A Century of Scottish History*, i. 478. Cf. a remark by Ramsay of Ochtertyre (i. 169): "The Scots of the seventeenth " century had neglected, while it was in their power to improve, their " own language. Nothing remained for their descendants but to " acquire that of their ancient rivals, who had brought theirs to a " degree of perfection."

[2] See Bagehot, *Biographical Studies*, pp. 294, 295.

book.[1]   He found his style " a mass of wool covering
" a very little gold," [2] and somehow men of judgement in England did not appreciate Scottish men of
letters during the middle of the eighteenth century
at the worth which their own countrymen attributed to them.   This fact in part accounts for the
significant circumstance that literary Scotsmen were
in the middle of the eighteenth century very deficient in knowledge of or sympathy with England.
Between 1750 and about 1790, Scotland, on account
to some extent of the peace and ultimately the
prosperity created by the political unity of Great
Britain, produced for the first time a literary school
which fairly claimed originality and influence throughout England and also throughout the leading countries
of Europe.

" At that time the recollection of the old rivalry
" between the two countries had by no means died
" away ; there was still a separate Scotch philosophy,
" and a separate literature ; and when it happened,
" as it perpetually did, that Scotch writers were not
" thought so much of in England as they thought
" they ought to be, they were apt to impute their
" discredit to English prejudice, and to appeal to
" France and Paris to correct the error.   Half
" Hume's mind, or more than half, was distorted by
" his hatred of England and his love of France.   He
" often could not speak of English things with
" tolerable temper, and he always viewed French
" ones with extravagant admiration.   Whether Adam
" Smith altogether liked this country may perhaps
" be doubted—Englishmen then hated Scotchmen so

[1] Craik, i. 405.   [2] Contrast the opinion of Buckle, iii. p. 19, *n.* 30.

" much—but he had no kind of antagonism to her,
" and quite understood that in most economical
" respects she was then exceedingly superior to
" France. And this exceptional sympathy and
" knowledge we may fairly ascribe to a long and
" pleasant residence in England. For his great
" work no qualification was more necessary ; *The*
" *Wealth of Nations* would have been utterly
" spoiled if he had tried (as Hume incessantly
" would have tried) to show that, in industrial
" respects, England might not be better than
" France, or at any rate was not so very much
" better." [1]

The points, however, which are worth notice as
bearing upon the way in which the Act of Union
affected Scottish literature are these : The first
blooming of Scottish literature from about the middle
of the eighteenth century is due to the political unity
of Great Britain ; it was no doubt in its mode of
expression influenced by the reasonable effort to
give expression to Scottish thought and feeling in
thoroughly English language, but—and this is the
point which ought to be pressed home—the thoughts,
the ideas, and the feelings which in the middle of the
eighteenth century found expression in the writings
of Scotsmen everywhere bear the impress of Scottish
education and of Scottish training in the widest sense
of that term. This literature, therefore, was in reality
the outcome of Scottish Nationalism, though some of
its forms were affected by English models, and the
greatest of Scotland's men of letters had at that time
studied not only the language but the thoughts and

[1] Bagehot, *Biographical Studies* (1899), p. 273.

the sentiments to be drawn from the then far ampler Chapter
X.
stores of English literature.

The influence of the *Wealth of Nations*, delivered in
the shape of lectures attended, heard, and admired by
an audience of students at Glasgow, and published in
1776, shows that, well before the end of the eighteenth
century, and before the reaction against the French
Revolution had created perfect unity between Scotland and England, Scottish writers and teachers had
exercised a profound effect upon public opinion in
England. The intellectual impulse given by Scotland
was, in fact, remarkable in many departments of
thought and investigation. " In a sarcastic sentence,"
says Professor Hume Brown, " Voltaire has indicated
" in what lay her significance for the other nations.
" ' It is an admirable result of the progress of the
" ' human spirit,' he wrote, ' that at the present time
" ' it is from Scotland we receive rules of taste in all
" ' the arts—from the epic poem to gardening.' The
" words were ironically meant, but they point to what
" was an indisputable fact."[1] In Philosophy, Hume's
Treatise of Human Nature, Reid's *Inquiry into
the Human Mind*, and, though it has not survived
criticism more dispassionate than it received at the
time, Beattie's *Essay on Truth*; in Literature,
Macpherson's *Ossïan*, the novels of Smollett, and the
poems of Thomson and Collins; in History, the
works of Robertson and Hume; in Criticism, the
writings of Lord Kames and Hugh Blair; the discoveries of William Cullen and John Hunter in
Medicine, of Joseph Black and Sir John Leslie in
Chemistry, of James Hutton in Geology, and of

[1] Hume Brown, iii. 373.

James Watt in Engineering—all these works exercised an influence which was not confined to the United Kingdom, for the writings of most of these men were translated into various European languages, and their effect became known throughout the civilised world. The contact with English life and thought which can be traced in their biographies, and not less in their bibliographies, shows that the intellectual nationalism of Scotland in the spheres of teaching, of learning, and, generally, of thought, was certainly not impeded, but, we may say with confidence, was considerably stimulated, by the Union between the two countries.

Turn now to a second manifestation of Scottish Nationalism in the world of letters. As typical examples thereof between, say, 1780 and 1840 take Burns, Scott, Lockhart, Brougham, Jeffrey, and many more writers whose names will occur to our readers. This second flowering of Scottish letters, at any rate as regards Scott, affected the literature not of Great Britain only, but of the whole civilised world. It is inspired by Scottish Nationalism. It were hardly an exaggeration to say that Scott's poetry and Scott's novels were written with a view of setting before the world the romance of Scottish history; and his genius enabled his works to attain their end. One side of Scottish life at least became known to the whole civilised world. Burns, no doubt, is known nowadays mainly to Scotsmen, by whom he is carefully studied. He is conventionally admired by Englishmen, by whom his poems are sometimes not understood and, sometimes at least, unread. But no one doubts that his poetry owes

much of its force to Scottish Nationalism. Now
from this state of things flows one indubitable result :
At the time when the greatness and originality—we
may say the life and the energy—of Scottish thought
and sentiment, in short of Scottish Nationalism, was
revealed to the whole world, the Act of Union had
accomplished the moral as well as the political unity
of Great Britain. It may be doubted whether a single
eminent Scotsman from 1780 to 1832, or for twenty
years later, felt or expressed the least desire for the
breaking up of the Union between England and
Scotland. Scott, in spite of his unswerving loyalty
to any really Scottish institution, even though it
were represented by Scottish one-pound notes,
frankly and as a man of good sense recognised
the benefits of the Union to both parts of Great
Britain. If one may venture to refer to a period
lying beyond the scope of this treatise, one may point
out that Thomas Carlyle, accustomed as he was to
grumble at everything admired by his contemporaries,
found his religious and political hero in Cromwell,
who forced Union upon Scotland at the point of
the sword. Carlyle has not a word to say in favour
of parliamentary government, and you will find in
his pages no regret expressed for the destruction
of the Parliament of Scotland. He apparently
acquiesced in the Act of Union though it was the
work of the Whigs, and felt that it in no wise interfered with the true nationalism of Scotland.

Matters specially affecting Scotland.—In the
working of the Act of Union it has been well understood by the British Parliament that the policy,
though not the words, of the Act should make the

British Parliament and Government pay deference to Scottish opinion on matters which exclusively, or mainly, concerned Scotland. Curious evidence of the spirit with which the Act has been on the whole worked with regard to Scotland may be found in the very pamphlet where Scott, as Malachi Malagrowther, goes nearest to an attack on the Union. The violence of his feeling is unmistakable. He suggests an alliance against the English Government between Scottish and Irish members of the House of Commons. He comes very near to the credit, or discredit, of having invented and advocated parliamentary obstruction. Yet "Malachi" himself appeals in 1826 with confidence to the justice of England. He admits what is strictly relevant to our subject, the immense increase in the English goodwill to individual Scotsmen.

"Times are," he tells us, "much changed since " the days of Wilkes and Liberty, when the bare " suspicion of having come from north of the Tweed, " was a cause of hatred, contempt, and obloquy. The " good nature and liberality of the English seems now " even to have occasioned a reaction in their senti- " ments towards their neighbours, as if to atone for " the national prejudices of their fathers. It becomes " every Scotsman to acknowledge explicitly, and with " gratitude, that whatever tenable claim of merit has " been made by his countrymen for more than twenty " years back, whether in politics, arts, arms, profes- " sional distinction, or the paths of literature, it has " been admitted by the English, not only freely, but " with partial favour. The requital of North Britain " can be little more than good wishes and sincere kind-

" ness towards her southern Sister, and a hospitable
" welcome to such of her children as are led by curiosity
" to visit Scotland. To this ought to be added the
" most grateful acknowledgement."[1]

He admits that on the whole the spirit of the Act
of Union had been hitherto observed. What he does
urge, with, as Scotsmen thought, some truth, is that
the Government's Bill for abolishing £1 notes in
Scotland broke through the understanding which
had grown up that Scottish affairs should, even in
regard to legislation, be treated with great deference
for the public feeling of Scotland. The Government
of the day, a Tory Ministry, withdrew the obnoxious
provisions of the Bill with regard to the currency,
and Malachi Malagrowther's agitation came to an end,
and Scott dismissed his patriotic anger.

Examine these various spheres of action in which
nationalism is likely to appear. It will be found
that in every one of them, except where the Act
abolishes the political independence of Scotland, the
terms of the Act of Union and its working support
and protect the true nationalism of Scotland.

A circumstance which in reality bears witness to
the success of the Union between England and Scotland has, one may suspect, of recent years suggested
the thought that something to preserve Scottish
Nationalism should be done by legislation. People
notice, what is certainly true, that the permanent
peace, or rather unity, throughout the whole of
Great Britain, combined with the whole course of
scientific invention in the creation, *e.g.*, of railways,

[1] Malachi Malagrowther on the Currency, Scott's *Prose Works*,
xxi. 359.

steamboats, aeroplanes, telegraphic inter-communica·
tion, whether by wire or wireless, has resulted in
bringing every part of the world, and certainly every
part of Great Britain, nearer to each other. The
inevitable consequence of changes which no legislation can permanently prevent is that the distinctions
and the different characteristics between one part of
Great Britain and another are dying out. Unity
tends in one sense towards uniformity. It is now
more than eighty years since Lockhart published in
1838 the last volume of his *Life of Scott*. He
noticed even then that whatever stamped Scotsmen
as a separate distinct people was destined to be
obliterated. "The amalgamation of the sister coun-
" tries on all points has already advanced far and
" will soon be completed."[1] This process of assimilation has after all gone on less rapidly than Lockhart anticipated. It has affected England no less
than Scotland. To state the same fact from another
point of view, the close connexion between the different parts of one island and the constant inter-
connexion of their inhabitants by marriage is producing a character which, whether for good or for
bad, is not precisely the same as that of the Englishmen or of the Scotsmen of 1707. But one effect, and
an inevitable result, of good government and absolute
peace under the Act of Union, taken together with
the changes which have brought each part of Great
Britain more closely together, is that the celebrity
or the eminence of particular localities and the
inhabitants thereof is less marked than it was some
two cénturies ago. Edinburgh has not lost its charm

---

[1] Lockhart, *Life of Scott*, i., preface, p. vii.

or its intelligence, yet it is all but incredible that Edinburgh, or any other town in Great Britain, including London itself, should ever have again the pre-eminence which made Scotsmen a century ago describe Edinburgh as the modern Athens. So, the existence in England of minor cities which had a special fame and character of their own, such as was possessed at one time by Norwich and Lichfield, is now all but an impossibility. This dying away of separate local centres of intellectual power is, like all changes, not without its loss. But one should never forget the warning of Burke, that the man who quarrels with the nature of things goes very near to fighting against the decrees of Providence. One may venture to say that some of the cries for so-called Home Rule are nothing better than lamentations over the way in which the growth of civilisation, by the very benefits which it extends, limits the personal and relative eminence both of individuals and of individual countries. The Act of Union is thus treated as open to censure because it has attained the very objects for the sake of which it was passed, the unity, and therefore the peace and the prosperity, of Great Britain.

Second Thought.—The success of the Act of Union is almost without a complete historical parallel.

The people of many countries have, in the course of history, annexed to themselves lands and their inhabitants by the mere force or right of conquest. The nations which have done this have often

succeeded in making the conquered people become
the fellow - citizens, and even very loyal fellow-
citizens, of their conquerors. A good number of
instances of such success may be found in the con-
quests made by France. There is little doubt, for
example, that the inhabitants of Alsace and Lorraine,
whatever we may say of the means by which these
provinces were united to France, became loyal subjects
of the French monarchy, and even more loyal citizens
of the French Republic and the Empire. Savoy had
no desire in 1814 to be separated from France, and
apparently had little objection to be reunited to the
so-called Empire of Napoleon III. The peculiarity
of the Union between England and Scotland is this :
Statesmanlike considerations had for centuries pointed
out to the statesmen of each country that the people
of Great Britain would gain much by being brought
under one more or less centralised government which
should rule the whole island. But from the time
of Edward I. and his ill-starred attempts to conquer
Scotland the two countries had become divided from
one another by the most embittered nationalism.
Each had gained victories over the other. Neither
force nor negotiation had availed to bring about
any permanent union. At last the two countries
had by a happy chance come under the rule of one
and the same king, though otherwise remaining on
most points separate and completely independent
countries. This piece of good fortune was, as every
reader of this essay may see, neutralised by new and
very bitter causes of dislike, not to say hatred,
between the inhabitants of the north and the south
of Great Britain, begotten by the events of the

seventeenth century. At the beginning of the Chapter eighteenth century, British statesmen, both Eng- X. lishmen and Scotsmen, came to the determination to try whether they could not achieve a union by simple bargaining without the use either of menace or of force. The idea was the more difficult to carry out because the inhabitants of each country were on each side determined to preserve their own national character. The policy of Unionism was by most contemporaries pronounced a chimera. Yet it succeeded, and in the course of about a century really unified two hostile nations and made them what they are now, the united State of Great Britain. The parallel to such a triumph is hard to find. The history of the relations between the Scandinavian States shows that even the strongest and most obvious self-interest will with difficulty produce unity between countries separated by historical causes. We may also bear in mind the slowness with which Switzerland has become one State instead of twenty-one more or less independent cantons, or the imperfect constitution which bound together the Commonwealth of Holland. The successful conversion of the thirteen American Colonies, after they had obtained independence from Great Britain, into a true nation under the name of the United States, was a success resembling that achieved in the eighteenth century by the authors of the Act of Union. But one may well doubt whether, in any one of these cases, the triumph of statesmanship was achieved against so much difficulty, or with such complete success, as in the case of Great Britain. Meanwhile the work of the Whigs in 1707 stands a lasting monument of successful British statesmanship. The Act of Union was indeed unpopular. It achieved, however, most deserved success. For it was designed and passed by parliamentarians of great energy, foresight, and patience. This triumph of legislative wisdom was achieved not by any concession to popular enthusiasm for federalism, for nationalism, for self-determination, or whatever might be the catchword of a day, or even of a generation, but by determined efforts, made by statesmen endowed with sound sense, to provide for the true interest both of England and of Scotland. These thoughtful leaders spent year after year in constructing a scheme for union which, though unpopular, exactly met its end, and has survived for centuries the now forgotten censures and invectives of rhetoricians as eloquent as Lord Belhaven and as patriotic and also as wrong-headed as Fletcher of Saltoun.

Fairness to Englishmen makes it right to dwell upon one quality or habit which has contributed more than any other English virtue both to the success of the Act of Union and to the greatness of the British Empire. Englishmen have committed (as witness their dealings with the thirteen Colonies which brought about the independence of the United States) many errors in colonial government. The history of Scotland, both in the century which preceded and in the century which followed upon the Act of Union, exhibits many blunders in their dealings with the inhabitants of Scotland. England has certainly not shown the capacity for successful annexation of foreign countries which has been displayed now and again by France. But Englishmen have clung to one idea which has been fruitful in good results. It is the equality of all British subjects when in England. This has been promoted by the rule, open though it be to criticism, that any man born in England, or now in the British Dominions, is a British subject. This has prevented the permanent existence within England of different classes ruled by different laws. It has also gradually produced the further result that a British subject of whatever race, descent, or religion will possess in England, or we may say now in the United Kingdom, the same political rights as an Englishman. This ideal has its disadvantages. Still, adherence to it immensely facilitated the working of the Act of Union. Great though the unpopularity of Scotsmen was, every man born in Scotland found lucrative and honourable careers open to him in England. It is to be regretted that British Colonies have found it very difficult, whether rightly or not, to carry out in their own territory the principle established for the advantage of every British subject in England. The success of Whig statesmanship in carrying the Act of Union was greatly facilitated by the conviction, even of Scotsmen, that, on the Union of the Parliaments, every British subject would have in England the rights and privileges of a natural-born Englishman.

EPILOGUE

First.—The tradition of statesmanship in favour
of uniting the whole of Great Britain, into one
single State ruled by one sovereign, stretches over a
period of at least four hundred years, extending from
the accession of Edward I. (1272) till about the middle
of the reign of Anne (1707). It is easy to see how this
tradition arose. As civilisation advanced both in
England and in Scotland any statesman of either
country could hardly fail to dream at least of the
day when unity of government would give to the
whole island which we now call Great Britain
safety from invasion by foreigners, and also bestow
upon its inhabitants a power among the States of
Europe which they could never acquire as long as
Englishmen and Scotsmen continued to be distinct
and even hostile nations. Edward I., who is naturally
considered by Scotsmen as nothing better than a
defeated tyrant, was from an English point of view
one among the greatest of English kings. He was
at any rate one among the first to dream this dream
of complete unity throughout the whole British
Islands. His policy in Scotland was the same as his
policy in Wales. The end he proposed to himself was
noble. The method he first imagined for achieving

Epilogue. it, namely, by marriage between the heiress of the Scottish and the heir of the English Crown, was a step in the right direction. Its success was rendered impossible by ill-fortune. Edward's error is that he then adopted a wrongful and ineffective plan for attaining a good object. His attempt to subdue Scotland by force deferred the complete political union of Great Britain for four centuries.

Second.—Readers must bear in mind a fact which is constantly referred to in this essay. This circumstance, which governed the whole history of the Act of Union, is the way in which the intense nationalism of Scotland, on the one hand, and, on the other hand, English pride in the national power of England, overbalanced for a long time the statesmanship which foresaw in the unity of Great Britain the true foundation of British independence and of British prosperity. The strength of the obstacles which the attempt at any kind of union was forced to overcome is best shown by the failure to attain it by rulers of no common ability. In the middle of the sixteenth century a Scots man of letters [1] had already pointed out that a union of the Crowns created by marriage gave the best chance of forming a union of the whole of Great Britain, and Henry VII. had already laid the foundation of this policy. But neither the rough wooing of Henry VIII. (1544) nor the invasion of Scotland by the Duke of Somerset, followed by the defeat of the Scots at the battle of Pinkie, had any other effect than to increase the hostility of Scotsmen and Englishmen. The sagacity and the experience of James, supported by the immense advantage of his having become the

[1] John Mair, or Major. See Chap. III. p. 115, *ante.*

lawful King of each part of Great Britain, availed him little when he tried to convert the unity of the Crowns into a complete unity of the countries. The rout of Scottish armies by Cromwell did at last establish the armed supremacy of England, and for a time made it possible to unite the two countries under one Commonwealth (1652–1660). The Restoration of 1660 dissolved the unity of the countries into the old Union of the Crowns, and Charles II., while really desiring to achieve a unity of the Parliaments, found himself unable to give effect to his desires. The Revolution of 1688, though, as we have seen, it was a real step towards absolute political unity, did not, in spite of William the Third's ardent Unionism, attain its end. Anne was nominally the means of achieving a result which her eminent predecessors had failed to attain. But the success of Anne is really the triumph of Whig statesmanship which carried through the Act of Union in 1707. Here, however, we must not overlook one striking fact. The Act of Union was passed through the wisdom of English and Scottish statesmen. It is more than doubtful whether, had it been practicable in 1707 to submit the Act of Union to a referendum, as we now call it, in which every Englishman and Scotsman could give his vote, it would have been possible to obtain a popular sanction for the wisest Act ever sanctioned by a Scottish or an English Parliament.

Third.—The passing of the Act of Union was favoured by some circumstances which may be called accidents, by the action of some English rulers who preceded Anne, and, as already pointed out, by the current of events from the accession of

Epilogue. James VI. to the Crown of England as James I. (1603).

Favourable Accidents, or Luck.—By these expressions are meant events which were not the result of policy, and yet in the long run promoted the political unity of Great Britain. Such, for example, was the failure of any of Henry the Eighth's children to leave issue. At the beginning of Henry's reign the likelihood of a Stewart becoming the lawful heir to the English Crown was, comparatively speaking, small. It was again pre-eminently lucky that a Stewart King should first become King of Scotland and next become King of England. If, for instance, the designéd marriage between Edward VI. and Mary Queen of Scots had been carried into effect, their son would have had a legal claim to the throne of Scotland. But it would have been much harder to enforce than was the claim of James VI. of Scotland to the throne of England. The difference may be put thus : The accession of a Tudor to the throne of the Stewarts would have seèmed to Scotsmen the victory of England and the subjugation of their own country. The accession of James Stewart to the throne of Elizabeth was for Scotsmen a victory for Scotland. It opened to Scottish nobles a prospect of sharing the increased wealth of their King; it opened to the Scottish people the hope of sharing in the trade and the prosperity of England. This popular expectation was more or less disappointed, but it certainly facilitated the acquiescence of James's Scottish subjects in the union of the Crowns. It was again a piece of good luck that Anne should be ruler of England and of Scotland at a time when the Treaty for a Union was laid before the Scottish Parliament. It was much easier for Scotsmen to accept a proposal coming from a Stewart Queen whom nobody supposed to be a tyrant* than it would have been to accept a plan of union recommended either by William III., a Dutchman unacquainted with Scottish habits, or than it would have been to acquiesce in a union proposed by a foreigner such as George I., who never in any circumstances could have aroused the enthusiasm either of Englishmen or of Scotsmen. One may possibly add as a fortunate circumstance that the avowed Romanism of James II. of England and of his son, for once in the course of history, made the Episcopalian clergy of England and the Presbyterian ministers of Scotland almost equally dread a Restoration which endangered at once the National Church of England and the National Church of Scotland.

The Influence of preceding Rulers.—Though up to the time of Anne the difficulty of establishing a complete political union between the two parts of Great Britain turned out insuperable, yet there were at least five among the rulers of both countries who took very considerable steps towards the creation of perfect union. Henry VII. was a king of known prudence. In nothing did he show his foresight more distinctly than in arranging the marriage between his daughter Margaret and James IV. of Scotland. This is one of those political strokes which are justified by events. Henry VII., further, did nothing by the use or threat of violence to injure the possible effect of his pacifying and uniting policy.

James, from the moment of his succeeding to the English crown, fixed his whole heart upon bringing about the unity of his separate and divided kingdoms. He was a man to whose sagacity both his contemporaries and posterity have found it hard to do anything like justice. His undeniable faults, weaknesses, or vices were patent. He lacked personal dignity ; he is supposed to have been wanting in physical courage ; he had none of the special qualities which secured to all the Tudors popular respect and often admiration. His tactlessness and his tastelessness gave grounds for accusations which might not unfairly be brought against him. He was in England substantially a foreigner ; he talked English in the form of broad Scots ; he was a really learned man, and he had gained a good deal from painful experience. He further lacked all that knowledge of parliamentary government which was of immense service to all the Tudors. He was impatient, and he was also weak. Yet for all this James was in many respects a noteworthy statesman, and his statesmanship enabled him to favour the policy of Unionism. He was a pedant, but he was something much more than the most learned fool in Christendom. He had indeed mastered the learning and the literature of his day, but he had also gained instructive lessons from perpetual conflicts against the severe dogmatism of Scottish preachers and the reckless audacity of Scottish noblemen. In spite of James's shortcomings —and they were great—his career in Scotland, even before he became King of England, was marked by practical success. He was constantly insulted and humiliated by the leaders of the Scottish Church. But he on the whole defeated them. After his strength was more than doubled by his obtaining the

crown of England his triumph over the Scottish
clergy was past a doubt. If he had lived longer,
or if Charles I. had inherited the experience and
the sagacity of his father, the policy of James might
have established a form of moderate Episcopalianism
as the National Church of Scotland. As an ardent
champion of Unionism he failed to attain his end.
But it must be admitted that the end he aimed at
was the right one. He was aided no doubt by the
genius of Bacon. But. it is a considerable praise for
any monarch to say that he adopted the policy
advocated by one of the wisest men of his age. A
censor might perhaps say that the greatest service
rendered by James to the people of Great Britain
consisted in his birth, for he thereby brought into
existence the union of the Crowns. He did much
more than this. His succession to Elizabeth was
the result of careful and crafty policy on the part of
James. His indifference indeed about the execution
of his mother is revolting, though it is a little difficult
to determine what ought to be the feelings of a son
towards a mother who had never shown him any
affection and was deemed by James himself and by
all his contemporaries to be his father's murderer.
It remains true, however, that to retain the goodwill
of Elizabeth was an essential condition towards
bringing about the union of the Crowns. James's
policy, in short, made him the willingly accepted ruler
of England no less than of Scotland. He showed
imprudence and impatience in some of the methods
on which he relied for passing an Act of Union. Yet
we must weigh against such blunders the success
which he attained in furthering the practical unity

Epilogue. of his northern and his southern kingdom.   It was something to establish officially the term Great Britain as the name of one country.   It was a still greater step to establish legally, and through the mouth of a judge so venerated by what may be called the Liberals of the day as Coke, the principle, which even now has a good deal of value, that every man born in the king's dominions since the accession of James is a subject of the British Crown.   James in his best moments perceived that, even if things were left alone, the real union of Great Britain would come of itself.   He perceived with rare prescience the great benefit which would accrue to his kingdoms from mutual free trade, and also the ardent desire of Scotland to obtain freedom of trade throughout the whole of England and her Dependencies.   What is of even more importance, by the use of the Royal prerogative he did a good deal towards establishing free trade between England and Scotland.[1]   It confirms one's belief in James's sagacity that he was in financial matters in advance of his age.   He obtained an English judicial decision which established the king's right to tax goods imported from abroad into England. The judges who gave judgement in 1606 in favour of the Crown [2] did not give an unconscientious judgement or take an erroneous view of the common law as it then stood.   Englishmen have long perceived the danger of increasing during the seventeenth century the prerogatives of the Crown.   But Parliament has, from an historical point of view, been too apt to

[1] See T. Keith, *Commercial Relations of England and Scotland, 1603–1707*, p. 34.

[2] See Bates's case, 2 State Trials, 371.

imagine that prerogatives of which we now see the inexpediency were at all times opposed to the common law of England. It may well be suspected that even economists, if such there were, of 1606, and certainly the mass of the English people, considered that money levied in England on the importation of foreign goods was in truth, as it certainly was in appearance, money paid by foreigners for the benefit of the English Crown and people. The discovery of this fact, or at any rate this way of looking upon import duties, has induced at least one federal State to place the taxation of imports wholly in the hands of the federal Government. Contrast Bates's case with the demand of Charles I. for ship-money and you measure the difference between the sagacity of James and the stupidity of Charles. Cromwell did actually during the Commonwealth form a parliamentary union of Scotland and England, and indeed of Ireland also, under the title of "The Commonwealth of England, " Scotland, and Ireland, and the Dominions thereunto " belonging." This was a splendid achievement; it was made possible by Cromwell's rout of the Scottish armies first at Dunbar and then at Worcester. But just because it was the fruit of victory and of conquest this parliamentary union could not stand. It was opposed to the whole national sentiment of Scotsmen. It had a permanent effect: it gave to Scotland free trade, and inspired after the Restoration that desire for the renewal of free trade which in 1703 made all Scottish Whigs, and probably some Scottish Jacobites, feel that a parliamentary union which they disliked was made tolerable because it restored the Cromwellian freedom of trade. Charles II.

proposed, and possibly desired, a closer union between England and Scotland, but does not seem to have regretted that his effort in this respect failed. William III. was from the Revolution of 1688 onwards the earnest advocate of an Act of Union, but he too failed in giving effect to the policy of which he approved. He, however, by allowing the development of what we have termed the Constitution of 1690, formed for the first time a Scottish Parliament of sufficient political power, when supported by a General Assembly[1] of great moral authority, to perform the arduous task of creating for Great Britain one common Parliament which should soon obtain the tacit assent and, after about a century, gain the complete constitutional and moral support of the British people.[2]

The Current of Events.—The general course of history and of opinion between the years 1603 and 1707 is, as pointed out again and again, the true and essential cause of the final passing of the Act of Union; and here it is worth while to note that because success was mainly due to alterations in public opinion, the failure of such men as James, Cromwell, and William III. to effect a permanent union between England and Scotland was in reality almost inevitable until certain alterations of public opinion had finally taken place. One example will suffice to show our meaning. How could James have carried through with success an attempted parliamentary union as long as Englishmen and Scotsmen, among whom you may include James himself, believed

---

[1] See Chap. II., Seventh Thought, p. 90, *ante*, and Eighth Thought, p. 96, *ante*.

[2] See Chap. X. p. 319, *ante*, First Thought.

that the unity of a State involved the creation of a National Church of which all the citizens of a State should form a part ?[1] Cromwell had probably more or less perceived that such civil unity was not necessarily bound up with ecclesiastical unity. But whether he had in this respect entirely reached the enlightened views of a writer like Andrew Marvell or of the Whigs who carried the Act of Union may be doubtful. The Whigs at least had in 1703 perceived—and perhaps they did not go further—that the existence of a Presbyterian Church in Scotland and of an Episcopalian Church in England was not really inconsistent with all the Protestants of Great Britain becoming loyal to the Crown and to the Constitution of Great Britain.

Fourth.—Under Queen Anne the Parliamentary Union of England and Scotland, and thereby the United Kingdom of Great Britain, was finally constituted. This of course was in substance the work of the Queen's ministers, who were the leaders of the English and Scottish Whigs. The one thing which any student of the Act of Union should constantly bear in mind is the extraordinary wisdom with which the Act was framed. It was based upon a real contract between the separate Parliaments of the then separate kingdoms of Scotland and England. The whole aim of the men who drafted the contract was to give the English and the Scottish people the benefits which each of such people mainly desired to receive under the Treaty and the Act of Union. Hence inevitably resulted the further effect that the men who drafted the Treaty of Union care-

[1] See Chap. VIII. pp. 257-259, *ante.*

Epilogue. fully left every institution in England and every
institution in Scotland untouched by the Act, provided
that the existence of such institution was consistent
with the main objects of the Act. Hence the extraordinary success of the Act. It destroyed everything
which kept the Scottish and the English people
apart; it destroyed nothing which did not threaten
the essential unity of the whole people; and hence,
lastly, the supreme glory of the Act, that while
creating the political unity it kept alive the
nationalism both of England and of Scotland.

APPENDIX A

FICTITIOUS VOTES

A PETITION presented to the House of Commons in 1793,
and drawn up by Sir James Mackintosh (cf. Porritt, ii.
p. 155), thus describes the system of creating fictitious
votes:

" By the remains of the feudal system in the counties
" the vote is severed from the land and attached to what is
" called the superiority. In other words, it is taken from
" the substance and transferred to the shadow; because,
" though each of these superiorities must, with a very few
" exceptions, arise from land of the present annual value of
" four hundred pounds sterling, yet it is not necessary
" that the land should do more than give a name to the
" superiority, the possessor of which may retain the right
" of voting notwithstanding he be divested from the
" property; and, on the other hand, the great landlords
" have the means afforded them, by the same system, of
" adding to their influence without expense to themselves by
" communicating to their confidential friends the privilege
" of electing members to serve in Parliament. The process
" by which this operation is performed is simple. He who
" wishes to increase the number of his dependent votes,
" surrenders his charter to the Crown, and parcelling out
" his estate into as many lots of four hundred pounds per
" annum as may be convenient, conveys them to such as he
" can confide in. To these, new charters are upon applica-
" tion granted by the Crown, so as to erect each of them
" into a superiority, which privilege once obtained, the

" land itself is reconveyed to the original grantor, and thus
" the representatives of the landed interest in Scotland may
" be chosen by those who have no real or beneficial interest
" in the land " (*Commons Journals*, xlviii. p. 740).

There is evidence that this process had begun before the
Union, but it received a great impetus from an Act of 1743
(16 Geo. II. cap. 11). A claim to a vote based upon a
40s. freehold had, in accordance with that Act, to be
proved by a return or retour (or by a record of a retour
preserved in Chancery) dated before September 16, 1681.
The effect of this restriction was that the sale of any portion
of a 40s. land, even if the portion retained by the vendor
far exceeded a 40s. land of old extent, destroyed a vote ;
neither the vendor nor the purchaser could claim a vote,
whatever their respective proportions of the land might be.
Lands returned before 1681 at 40s. or more of old extent
could therefore, if sold in portions, be capable of conferring
a vote only by the alternative method of showing that one
or more of the portions were worth £400 of valued rent.
Such valuations were freed by the Act of 1743 from any
proof of an original valuation by the old extent, and they
were made by the Commissioners of Supply, from whose
decisions appeals could be taken to the Court of Session.
Actual sales resulting in the subdivision of lands into free-
holds, each of which provided a qualification of £400 a
year, constituted of course a legitimate extension of the
franchise, but the system developed into a means of creating
fictitious votes by the transference of mere superiority.
The test of a freehold was a title held directly from the
Crown, and this title was independent of any pecuniary
interest in the property. A tenant-in-chief who had sold
the actual property in the land might still retain the
superiority or *dominium directum* and remain a freeholder ;
the actual possessor of the lands held the *dominium utile*,
but was merely a vassal. There were several methods of
creating a vote based on mere superiority (cf. Wight on
Elections, vol. i. bk. iii. c. 2) ; the most common devices
were variations of the system described in Sir James
Mackintosh's petition. A tenant-in-chief (T) made a

APPENDIX B

CHRONOLOGICAL TABLE

March 19. Death of Alexander III. of Scotland.

April 2. Appointment by the Great Council of Scotland of Guardians or Regents for the infant Queen Margaret, the "Maid "of Norway."

November 6. Treaty of Salisbury for the marriage of Queen Margaret to the eldest son of Edward I.

March 17. Confirmation of the Treaty of Salisbury by a Scottish Parliament (Treaty of Brigham).

September 26. Death of Queen Margaret, aged about eight years.

May 10. Edward I. claimed the right of settling the disputed succession to the Scottish throne.

June 3–6. The claimants to the throne admitted Edward's right to decide the succession.

November 17. Award by Edward I. in favour of John Balliol as a vassal King of Scotland.

96. Rebellion of John Balliol against his English Overlord.

July 10. Abdication of John Balliol. The Kingdom of Scotland under English military occupation.

98. Guardianship of William Wallace.

July 22. Defeat of Wallace and partial resumption of English military occupation.

English scheme for the administration of Scotland as part of the Kingdom of England.

March 27. Coronation of Robert Bruce.

June 24. Battle of Bannockburn.

July. First known instance of the presence of Commissioners of the burghs in a Scottish Parliament.

May 4. Treaty of Northampton acknowledging the Independence of Scotland.

4, March 4. Rejection by the Scottish Parliament of a proposal made by King David II. to acknowledge Prince Lionel of England as heir to the throne.

collusive grant of land in feu to a friend (F 1) and thus deprived the land of any pecuniary value. He then granted a liferent of the bare superiority to a second friend (F 2), after which F 1 resigned the feu and reconveyed it to T. The result was that F 2 as a liferenter of a superiority of a 40s. land or of a land worth £400 a year was entitled to a vote. The Act 12 Anne, cap. 6, provided that an elector might be called upon to take an oath denying any collusive arrangement, and the terms of the oath were made more stringent in 1734 (7 Geo. II. cap. 16), for the voter could be asked to swear that his title was not nominal, fictitious, or created merely as a qualification for a vote, and that he held the lands as a true and real estate for his own use and benefit. Refusal to take the oath involved the removal of a voter's name from the list of freeholders, and a conviction for taking it falsely amounted to perjury. The Court of Session in 1768 sanctioned the practice of putting searching questions to freeholders who took the oath, but a series of decisions of the House of Lords, two years later, were interpreted as disallowing such interrogatories, and the only restriction upon the creation of fictitious votes depended upon the conscience of the voter.

No scrupulous man could obviously take the oath where his interest was nominal, and Dr. Somerville tells in his *Memoirs* (p. 177) how in 1780 he refused to accept such a qualification:

"It was foreseen that the votes would run near, and " great exertions were made by the friends and dependants " of both the families [of the candidates, Lord Robert Ker " and Gilbert Elliot], and several new voters were brought " on the roll by the transfer of superiorities or what were " truly called fictitious votes. In the beginning of the " contest, Sir Gilbert Elliot [the father of the candidate] " made me an offer of a superiority, which I declined with- " out a moment's hesitation, as I had done a year before " when Lord Somerville intimated his intention of confer- " ring the same privilege, merely for the purpose of making " it subservient to my own personal interest. I was so

Appendix
A.

" sincerely attached to Sir Gilbert Elliot that the means of
" serving him would have been a more cogent motive for
" compliance with his desire than any prospect of advantage
" to myself. But the trust oath was an insurmountable
" obstacle to the gratification of my wishes."

A later decision of the House of Lords, on an appeal
from the Court of Session in 1790, allowed interrogatories
to be put, but a subsequent finding of the Court of Session,
confirmed by the House of Lords in 1792, declared that
such investigations and interrogatories could be made only
when objection had been taken within four months of the
enrolment of the freeholder (Wight, ii. pp. 95-110). The
nature of the questions and answers may be understood
from a reply quoted by Wight:

" I consider myself bound in honour not to vote in the
" county of Aberdeen against the candidate patronised by
" the Duke of Gordon, but I do not consider myself in
" honour bound to vote for such candidate. I entertain
" this feeling . . . not merely because I derive my qualifica-
" tions from His Grace, but also in consequence of other
" circumstances wholly foreign from the present cause.
" With regard to renouncing the liferent in question, I
" think myself bound in honour, as I am disposed in
" inclination, so to do whenever His Grace expresses a
" wish to that purpose."

This reply led to the removal of the voter's name from
the roll of freeholders.

The years between the decisions of the House of Lords
in 1770 and 1790 were the great period of fictitious votes,
and a confidential report upon the political opinions, family
connexion, and personal circumstances of the voters in
Scottish counties, prepared in 1788 for the managers of the
Whig party, reveals the high proportion of fictitious votes
in certain counties before the decision of 1790. In Aberdeenshire, out of a total of 178 votes, 44 were controlled
by the Duke of Gordon and 33 by the Earl of Fife; in
Banffshire, out of a total of 122 votes, 37 were controlled
by the Duke of Gordon and 50 by the Earl of Fife; in
Inverness-shire, out of a total of 103 votes, 31 were con-

trolled by the Duke of G
six landowners; in Kinros
16 were controlled by Mr
a total of 124 votes, 43
Gordon and 12 by Mr. I
shire, out of a total of 77
Earl of Fife and 21 by the
of a total of 20 votes, 8
of Cawdor and 3 by Mr. I
a total of 12 votes, 8 were
These are the most notorio
in Midlothian there were
not controlled by any of th
total of 93; in Fife, 127
of 187; in Forfarshire, 64
out of 75; in Kincardine
121 out of 161. Some eff
may be seen in the reduct
at the General Election of
the Banffshire voters from
Report from which we are
" holders in several of th
" [1790] Michaelmas meet
" all nominal and fictitious
" believe that their examp
" other counties of Scotland
of Scotland, ed. Sir Charles
1790 it became distinctly
votes.

1367, September. First recorded instance of the appointment of Lords
of the Articles.

1427–8, March 4. Meeting of Parliament in which Acts were passed
for the election of a Speaker by the Commons and for
permitting the smaller "barons" in the shires to send Commissioners to Parliament in commutation of their obligation
of personal attendance.

1542, December 14. Accession of Queen Mary at the age of one week.

1543, March–August. Treaty for the marriage of Queen Mary to
Edward, Prince of Wales.
December. Denunciation of the Treaty by the Scottish Parlia-
ment and renewal of the alliance with France.

1547–8, January. Offer of a Union by Protector Somerset after his
victory at Pinkie (Sept. 10, 1547).

1560, August. The smaller "barons" attended Parliament, for the
first time' for many years, and claimed the right to speak
and vote.

1585, December. The smaller "barons" claimed to be allowed to send
Commissioners to Parliament.

1587, July. Act creating the 40s. franchise for freeholders in the
shires ; establishment of the Scottish Constitution as it existed
in 1603 ("the Constitution of 1603").

1602–3, March 24. Accession of James VI. to the English throne as
James I.

1603–4, March 19. Speech of King James in the English Parliament
advocating a Union of the Kingdoms.

1604, June 2. Bill for appointing Commissioners passed by the
English Parliament.
July 11. Commissioners appointed by the Scottish Parliament.
November 15. The King's Proclamation assuming the style of
King of Great Britain.
December 6. Report of the Commissioners.

1606, November 21. The House of Commons began to discuss the
Report.

1606–1612. The royal control over the selection of the Lords of
the Articles became complete.

1607, March 31. Speech of King James advocating the Union.
May 2. Bill for the abolition of hostile laws introduced into the
Commons.
August 11. Report of the Commissioners accepted by the Scottish
Parliament conditionally on its being adopted by the English
Parliament.

1608, June. The Chancellor and ten out of twelve judges decided
that a Scottish "post-natus" was not an alien in England.
Abandonment of the discussion of the Union proposals by the
English Parliament.

1640, June 6. Act ordering that the Lords of the Articles should be
chosen freely by each of the Three Estates.

Appendix
B.

1651, September 30. Bill for the annexation of Scotland introduced into the " Rump " Parliament.

October 28. Declaration of the " Rump " Parliament in favour of a Union with Scotland.

1652, February 12. Scottish shires and burghs instructed to send representatives to Dalkeith to assent to the English Parliament's proposals of Union.

February–March. Assent of a majority of the representatives to the English proposals.

March 25. "Declaration of the Parliament of England in order to the uniting of Scotland into one Commonwealth with England " adopted by the "Rump" Parliament.

April 13. Bill for the Union introduced into the Rump Parliament.

August. Meetings of Conventions of representatives of Scottish shires and burghs to elect twenty-one Deputies to confer with the English Parliament about the machinery of the Union.

October 1652–April 1653. Discussions between the Scottish Deputies and Committees of the English Parliament.

1653, March 2. The English Parliament fixed at thirty the number of Scottish representatives in the United Parliament.

April 20. Expulsion of the Rump before the Bill for Union had been passed.

June 8. Five Scotsmen nominated to sit in " Barebones' " Parliament ; four attended in July.

October 4. Bill for a Union introduced.

December 12. Dissolution of Barebones' or the Little Parliament without passing the Union Bill.

December 16. Publication of the Instrument of Government of the Commonwealth of England, Scotland, and Ireland and the Dominions thereunto belonging.

1654, April 12. Ordinance by the Lord Protector for uniting Scotland into one Commonwealth with England.

May 4. Proclamation at Edinburgh of the Protectorate and the Union.

June 27. Ordinance for Distribution of the Elections in Scotland.

September 3. Meeting of the United Parliament.

December 22. Bill to sanction the Ordinance of Union introduced.

1655, January 22. Dissolution of the first Protectorate Parliament without passing the Union Bill.

1656, August. Elections in Scotland for the second Protectorate Parliament.

September 17. Opening of the Parliament.

October 25. Bill introduced to legalise the Union.

1657, April 28. The Ordinance of Union of 1644 passed by Parliament.

1658, January 20. Meeting of the "Other" or Upper House nominated by the Lord Protector in accordance with the Humble Petition and Advice. Four members were summoned from Scotland, but there is no record of their attendance.

February 4. Dissolution of the second Protectorate Parliament.

September 3. Death of Oliver Cromwell.

December 14. Scotland ordered to send thirty members to the Parliament summoned by Richard Cromwell.

1659, January 27. Meeting of Parliament.

April 22. Dissolution of the Parliament of Richard Cromwell.

May 7. Restoration of the "Rump" Parliament, which regarded as invalid everything done since April 20, 1653.

July 27. Bill for a Union of Scotland with England introduced into the "Rump" Parliament.

November 15. Representatives of Scottish shires and burghs met General Monck in the Parliament House at Edinburgh.

1660, March 16. Dissolution of the restored Long Parliament without passing the Union Bill.

1663, June 18. Royal control over the selection of the Lords of the Articles restored.

1668, January–July. Commissioners from both countries discussed a commercial treaty but failed to agree.

1669, October 19. Meeting of a Scottish Parliament especially summoned to discuss Union proposals made on the initiative of Charles II.

King's speech to the Parliament of England recommended a Union.

October 22. The King asked by the Scottish Parliament to appoint Commissioners.

1670, April 11. Act of the English Parliament empowering the King to appoint Commissioners.

September 14. Meeting of the English and Scottish Commissioners in the Exchequer Chamber at Westminster.

November 14. Adjournment of the Commission, which failed to agree and was never reassembled.

1689, March 16. Letter from William of Orange read in the Scottish Convention, expressing the pleasure with which he had received from Scotland letters in favour of a Union and his concurrence in the suggestion.

March 21. A Union recommended in the King's Speech to the Parliament of England.

March 23. Reply from the Scottish Convention expressing desire for a Union.

April 23. Nomination by the Scottish Parliament of Commissioners to treat of a Union.

April 24. Letter from the Scottish Convention to King William asking that English Commissioners should be appointed.

Appendix
B.
——— 1690, May. Abolition of the Lords of the Articles and establishment of " the Constitution of 1690."

1700, February 12. Union again suggested by King William in a reply to an Address from the House of Lords.

February 16–28. Bill for appointing Commissioners to treat with the Scottish Commissioners " for the weal of both Kingdoms " passed by the House of Lords.

March 5.. Bill read by the Commons for the first time, and rejected on the second reading.

1701, June 12–24. Committee appointed by the House of Lords to report on previous negotiations for Union.

1702, February 28. Message from the King to the English Parliament recommending " a firm and entire Union."

March 11. The English Parliament invited by Queen Anne to " consider of proper methods towards attaining a Union."

May 6. Royal Assent given to Act of the English Parliament empowering the Queen to appoint Commissioners.

June 9. Union recommended in the Queen's letter to the Scottish Parliament.

June 25. Act of the Scottish Parliament empowering the Queen to appoint Commissioners.

October 27. Meeting of the English and Scottish Commissioners at the Cockpit at Westminster.

1703, February 3. Adjournment of the Commission, which had failed to agree and never reassembled.

May 6. Opening of the First Session of the " Union Parliament " (Scotland).

June 1. Act of Security introduced in the Scottish Parliament.

August 17. Act anent Peace and War introduced in the Scottish Parliament.

September 9. Recall by the Scottish Parliament of the powers given to the Scottish Commissioners for Union.

September 10. Intimation made by the Queen's Commissioner to the Scottish Parliament that he was not authorised to give the Royal Assent to the Act of Security, which Her Majesty wished to take into further consideration. Royal Assent given to Act anent Peace and War.

September 16. Close of the First Session of the " Union Parliament " (Scotland).

1704, July 6. Opening of the Second Session of the " Union Parliament " (Scotland).

1704, August 5. Royal Assent given to the Act of Security.

August 28. Close of the Second Session of the " Union Parliament " (Scotland).

1705, February. Act passed in the English Parliament for " the effectual securing the Kingdom of England from the apparent dangers that may arise from several Acts lately passed in the Parliament of Scotland," and for empowering the Queen to

appoint Commissioners for Union in the event of similar
action being taken by the Scottish Parliament.

June 28. Opening of the Third Session of the "Union Parliament" (Scotland).

September 21. Royal Assent given to an Act of the Scottish Parliament empowering the Queen to appoint Commissioners to treat of Union. Close of the Third Session of the "Union Parliament" (Scotland).

December 21. Royal Assent given to an Act of the English Parliament repealing certain clauses of the Act of 1705 for securing the Kingdom of England.

1706, February 27. Scottish Commissioners appointed by the Queen.

April 10. English Commissioners appointed by the Queen.

April 16. First meeting of the Commissioners of both Kingdoms in the Council Chambers in the Cockpit.

April 25. Agreement reached on three main principles : (*a*) an incorporating Union ; (*b*) freedom of trade ; (*c*) the Hanoverian Succession.

May 25. Agreement reached on questions of Customs and Excise, and on other taxes.

May 29. Agreement reached on questions of Scottish Courts and jurisdictions.

June 7. Proposal by the English Commissioners that the number of Scottish representatives in the House of Commons be 38.

June 11. Conference asked by the Scottish Commissioners on the question of the number of representatives.

June 12. Conference.

June 14. Insistence by the Scottish Commissioners on a larger number than 38 as essential to carry the Union.

June 15. Proposal by the English Commissioners that the number of Scottish representatives in the British Parliament be 45 in the House of Commons and 16 in the House of Lords.

June 18. Acceptance of this proposal by the Scottish Commissioners.

June 26. Acceptance by the Scottish Commissioners of the English Commissioners' proposal that the amount of the Equivalent payable to Scotland as compensation for increased financial liability be £398,085 : 10s. Four Commissioners of each nation appointed to draw up the Articles of Union.

July 16. Draft of the Articles of Union read separately to the two bodies of Commissioners.

July 22. The Articles of Union signed and sealed.

July 23. The Articles of Union presented to the Queen.

October 3. Opening of the Fourth Session of the "Union Parliament" (Scotland). Recommendation in the Queen's Speech to adopt the report of the Commissioners. Articles of Union presented and ordered to be printed

1706, October 14. A Fast Day appointed by the Commission of the General Assembly for prayer that the discussion of the Treaty of Union might be brought "to a happy issue."

October 15. First discussion of the Articles of Union in the Scottish Parliament.

October 17. Presentation in Parliament of an Address from the Commission of the General Assembly urging the House "to do everything necessary for securing the true Protestant religion and Church government presently by law established in this kingdom."

October 23. Anti-Union riot in Edinburgh.

October 24. Troops brought into Edinburgh by order of the Privy Council.

October 30. First discussion of the Articles of Union concluded.

November 2. The First Article read as a motion to be put to the vote. Lord Belhaven's famous speech.

November 4. The First Article approved by 116 votes to 83. Principle of an Incorporating Union accepted.

November 12. Act passed for "the security of the true Protestant religion and government of the Church as by law established."

November 15. Second Article of Union approved by 120 votes to 57; the succession of the House of Hanover accepted.

November 18. Third Article of Union approved by 113 votes to 83; the creation of a Parliament of Great Britain accepted. Attack upon the Lord High Commissioner on his return from the Parliament House to Holyrood House.

November 19. Fourth Article of Union (Freedom of Trade) approved by 154 votes to 17.

November 29. The militia clause of the Act of Security (1704) suspended by the Parliament because of serious anti-Union riots in Glasgow, Dumfries, and elsewhere.

November 30. Act passed "against all musters and rendezvouzes during the present session of Parliament."

December 3. Queen's Speech recommending the Articles of Union to the English Parliament.

December 31. Motion to insert in the Eighteenth Article a clause exempting Scotsmen from the English Sacramental Test "in all places of the United Kingdom and dominions thereunto belonging," rejected by 83 votes to 74.

1707, January 7. The numbers of Scottish representatives in the two Houses of the British Parliament as proposed in the twenty-second Article of Union accepted by 114 votes to 73.

January 15. Act read for ratifying the Articles of Union as modified by the Scottish Parliament and for inserting in the Act of Union the Act for the Security of the Church.

January 16. Act "ratifying and approving the Treaty of Union of the two Kingdoms of England and Scotland" passed by 110 votes to 68.

January 28. The Scottish Act of Ratification read in the House of Lords and in the House of Commons.

January 31. Bill for the Security of the Church of England introduced in the House of Lords.

February 4. Bill for the Security of the Church of England passed by the Lords.

February 5. Bill for the Security of the Church of England received by the Commons.

Act passed in the Scottish Parliament for "settling the manner of electing and summoning the representatives for Scotland to the Parliament of Great Britain."

February 11. Bill for the Security of the Church of England passed by the Commons. Bill for an Union ordered by the Commons.

February 13. Election by the Scottish Parliament of Scottish representatives in the two Houses of the first Parliament of Great Britain.

Royal Assent to the Act of the English Parliament for the Security of the Church of England.

Instruction by the House of Commons to insert in the Bill for an Union the Act of Security for the Church of England and the Act passed by the Scottish Parliament for the Security of the Church of Scotland.

February 28. Bill for an Union passed by the House of Commons.

March 4. Bill for an Union passed by the House of Lords.

March 6. Royal Assent to Act of Union in the English Parliament.

March 19. Presentation to the Scottish Parliament by the Lord High Commissioner of an exemplification under the Great Seal of England of the Act of the English Parliament ratifying the Treaty of Union. The exemplification read and recorded.

March 25. Close of the Fourth Session of the "Union Parliament" and last meeting of the Scottish Parliament. Adjournment of the Parliament to April 22.

April 29. Proclamation by the Queen ordering that the existing English Parliament, with the addition of the Scottish representatives, should constitute the first Parliament of Great Britain.

May 1. Act of Union came into force.

October 23. Meeting of the first Parliament of Great Britain.

APPENDIX C

LISTS OF COMMISSIONERS, 1604–1706

(1) COMMISSIONERS OF 1604

(a) English Commissioners.

The Lord Chancellor (Lord Ellesmere).

The Lord Treasurer (Earl of Dorset).

The Lord High Admiral (Earl of Nottingham).

Earl of Southampton.

Earl of Pembroke.

Earl of Northampton.

Bishop of London (Richard Bancroft ; afterwards Archbishop of Canterbury).

Bishop of Durham (Tobias Matthew ; afterwards Archbishop of York).

Bishop of St. Davids (Anthony Rudd).

Lord Cecil (Secretary of State ; afterwards 1st Earl of Salisbury).

Lord Zouche (President of the Council of Wales).

Lord Monteagle.

Lord Eure.

Lord Sheffield (President of the Council of the North).

Lord Clinton (afterwards 3rd Earl of Lincoln).

Lord Buckhurst (M.P. for Sussex ; afterwards Earl of Dorset).

Sir Francis Hastings, Kt. (M.P. for Somerset ; a Puritan leader).

Sir John Stanhope, Kt. (M.P. for Newtown, I.W. ; afterwards 1st Lord Stanhope of Harrington).

Sir John Herbert, Kt. (Second Secretary of State ; M.P. for Monmouthshire).

Sir George Carew, Kt. (afterwards Ambassador to the Court of France).

Sir Thomas Strickland, Kt. (M.P. for Westmorland).

Sir Edward Stafford, Kt. (M.P. for Queenborough ; formerly Ambassador to the Court of France).

Sir Henry Nevil of Berkshire, Kt. (M.P. for Lewes ; formerly Ambassador to the Court of France).

Sir Richard Bulkley, Kt. (M.P. for Anglesey).
Sir Henry Billingsley, Kt. (M.P. for City of London; Lord Mayor in 1596 ; translated Euclid into English).
Sir Daniel Donne *or* Dunn, Kt. (Dean of the Arches ; M.P. for Oxford University).
Sir Edward Hoby, Kt. (M.P. for Rochester ; a scholar and a favourite of King James).
Sir John Savile, Kt. (Baron of the Exchequer).
Sir Robert Wroth, Kt. (M.P. for Middlesex).
Sir Thomas Chalmer, Kt.
Sir Robert Mansel, Kt. (M.P. for Carmarthenshire ; Admiral and Treasurer of the Navy).
Sir Thomas Ridgeway, Kt. (M.P. for Devon ; afterwards Baron Ridgeway and 1st Earl of Londonderry).
Sir Thomas Holcroft, Kt. (M.P. for Cheshire).
Sir Thomas Hesketh, Kt. (M.P. for Lancaster).
Sir Francis Bacon, Kt. (M.P. for St. Albans; afterwards Lord Chancellor and Viscount St. Albans).
Sir Lawrence Tanfield, Kt. (M.P. for Oxfordshire ; afterwards Chief Baron of the Exchequer).
Sir Henry Hubbard, Kt.
Sir John Bennet, Kt., LL.D. (Judge of Prerogative Court of Canterbury ; impeached 1621).
Sir Henry Withrington (*or* Widdrington), Kt.
Sir Ralph Gray, Kt.
Sir Thomas Lake, Kt. (M.P. for Launceston ; Latin Secretary to King James ; afterwards Secretary of State).
Robert Askwith, Merchant (M.P. for York).
Thomas James, Merchant.
Henry Chapman, Merchant.

(*b*) Scottish Commissioners.

The Lord Chancellor (Earl of Montrose).
The High Constable (Earl of Erroll).
The Earl Marischal.
Earl of Glencairn.
Earl of Linlithgow (7th Baron Livingstone; cr. Earl of Linlithgow in 1606).
Archbishop of Glasgow (John Spottiswood).
Bishop of Ross (David Lindsay).
Bishop of Caithness (George Gladstanes; afterwards Archbishop of St. Andrews).
Prior of Blantyre (Commendator of the Priory; afterwards 1st Lord Blantyre).
Lord Glamis (afterwards 1st Earl of Kinghorn).
Lord Elphinstone (formerly Lord High Treasurer).
Lord Fyvie (President of the Court of Session; afterwards Lord Chancellor and 1st Earl of Dunfermline).

Lord Roxburgh (afterwards 1st Earl of Roxburgh).

Lord Balmerino (Secretary of State; afterwards President of the Court of Session).

Lord Scone (afterwards 1st Viscount Stormont).

Sir James Scrimgeour of Dudhope, Kt. (Hereditary Standard-Bearer ; M.P. for Forfarshire).

Sir John Cockburn of Ormiston, Kt.

Sir John Home of Coldingknows, Kt.

Sir David Carnegie of Kinnaird, Kt. (afterwards 1st Earl of Southesk).

Sir Robert Melville of Murdocarnie, Kt. (afterwards 1st Baron Melville of Monimail).

Sir Thomas Hamilton of Binnie, Kt. (afterwards 1st Earl of Haddington).

Sir John Leirmonth of Balcomie, Kt. (M.P. for Fife).

Sir Alexander Straton of Lauriston, Kt. (M.P. for Midlothian).

Sir John Skene of Ourriehill, Kt. (Lord Clerk Register; editor of the Laws of Scotland).

John Sharp of Houston, Lawyer.

Thomas Craig, Lawyer (the greatest Scottish Feudalist).

Henry Nesbit, Merchant (M.P. for Edinburgh).

George Bruce, Merchant (afterwards Sir George Bruce of Carnock).

Alexander Rutherford, Merchant (M.P. for Aberdeen).

Alexander Wedderburn, Merchant (Town Clerk of Dundee ; M.P. for Dundee).

(2) COMMISSIONERS OF 1670

(a) English Commissioners.

Archbishop of Canterbury (Gilbert Sheldon).

Lord Keeper of the Great Seal (Sir Orlando Bridgeman).

Duke of Buckingham.

Duke of Ormonde.

Earl of Manchester.

Earl of Essex.

Earl of Anglesey.

Earl of Carlisle (1st Earl).

Viscount Fauconberg.

Bishop of Durham (John Cosin).

Bishop of Chester (John Wilkins ; one of the founders of the Royal Society).

Lord Arlington (Secretary of State).

Lord Widdrington.

Lord Townshend (Sir Horatio Townshend, 1st Baron and 1st Viscount).

Lord Ashley (afterwards 1st Earl of Shaftesbury).

Sir Thomas Clifford, Kt. (afterwards 1st Baron Clifford of Chudleigh).

Sir John Trevor, Kt. (Secretary of State; M.P. for Great Bedwin).

Sir Heneage Finch, Baronet (Attorney-General; M.P. for Oxford University ; afterwards 1st Earl of Nottingham).

Sir Robert Carr, Baronet (M.P. for Lincolnshire).

Sir Richard Temple, Baronet (M.P. for Buckingham ; Commissioner of Customs).

Sir Thomas Osborne, Baronet (M.P. for York ; afterwards 1st Earl of Danby and 1st Duke of Leeds).

Sir Thomas Littleton, Baronet.

Sir Leoline Jenkins, Kt. (Judge of the Admiralty Court; M.P. for Hythe ; Lawyer and Diplomatist).

Sir Thomas Higgons, Kt. (M.P. for New Windsor; Diplomatist and Author).

Sir Edward Booley, Kt.

(*b*) Scottish Commissioners.

The Lord High Commissioner (Earl of Lauderdale).

Archbishop of St. Andrews (James Sharp).

Earl of Rothes (Lord Chancellor).

Earl Marischal (Lord Privy Seal ; 8th Earl ; grandson of a Commissioner of 1604).

Earl of Atholl.

Earl of Home.

Earl of Dunfermline.

Earl of Lothian.

Earl of Tweeddale.

Earl of Kincardine.

Bishop of Dunblane (Robert Leighton).

Bishop of Galloway (James Hamilton).

Sir Archibald Primrose (Lord Register ; afterwards Justice-General ; judicial title, Lord Carrington).

Sir John Nisbet (Lord Advocate and a Lord of Session ; judicial title, Lord Dirleton).

Charles Maitland (Lord of Session ; title, Lord Haltoun ; afterwards 3rd Earl of Lauderdale).

Sir James Dalrymple (Lord of Session ; title, Lord Stair ; afterwards 1st Viscount Stair).

Sir John Baird (Lord of Session ; title, Lord Newbyth).

William Erskine.

Sir Robert Murray (Lord of Exchequer and Deputy-Secretary; one of the founders of the Royal Society).

Sir Archibald Murray of Blackbarony (M.P. for Perthshire).

Sir Robert Sinclair of Longformacus (M.P. for Berwickshire).

Sir Alexander Fraser of Durris (M.P. for Kincardine).

Sir William Bruce of Balcaskie (M.P. for Fifeshire).

Sir Andrew Ramsay (Provost of Edinburgh ; M.P. for Edinburgh).

Sir Patrick Murray (afterwards Receiver-General to William II.
and Mary II.).

(3) COMMISSIONERS OF 1702

(a) English Commissioners.

The Archbishop of Canterbury (Thomas Tenison).
The Keeper of the Great Seal (Sir Nathan Wright).
The Archbishop of York (John Sharp).
The Lord High Treasurer (Lord Godolphin).
The President of the Council (Earl of Pembroke).
The Keeper of the Privy Seal (Marquis of Normanby).
Duke of Devonshire.
Duke of Somerset.
Duke of Newcastle.
Earl of Carlisle (3rd Earl; grandson of a Commissioner of 1670).
Earl of Jersey.
Earl of Burlington.
Earl of Nottingham (Secretary of State; son of a Commissioner
of 1670).
Duke of Rochester.
Earl of Marlborough (Captain-General of the Forces).
Earl of Scarborough.
Bishop of London (Henry Compton).
Sir Charles Hedges (Secretary of State).
Sir John Holt (Chief Justice of Queen's Bench).
Sir Thomas Trevor (Chief Justice of Common Pleas; afterwards
1st Baron Trevor ; son of a Commissioner of 1670).
Sir John Leveson Gower (Chancellor of the Duchy of Lancaster).
Sir Christopher Musgrave, Baronet (M.P. for Totnes).
Sir John Cooke, Kt. (afterwards Dean of Arches).
Robert Harley, Esq. (M.P. for New Radnor; afterwards 1st
Earl of Oxford).
Charles Godolphin, Esq.
Samuel Clark, Esq.
Dr. Stephen Waller.

(b) Scottish Commissioners.

The Lord High Commissioner (Duke of Queensberry).
The Keeper of the Great Seal (Marquis of Annandale).
Duke of Argyll.
Marquis of Lothian (Justice-General).
Earl of Seafield (Secretary of State).
Earl of Lauderdale (5th Earl; a Lord of Session; son of the 3rd
Earl, a Commissioner in 1670).
Earl of Leven.
Earl of Hyndford (Secretary of State, 1696–1702).

Viscount Tarbat (Secretary of State, 1702–1704 ; afterwards 1st Earl of Cromarty).

Viscount Stair (afterwards 1st Earl of Stair ; son of a Commissioner of 1670).

Viscount Rosebery (afterwards 1st Earl of Rosebery ; son of a Commissioner of 1670).

Lord Boyle (afterwards 1st Earl of Glasgow).

Sir Hew Dalrymple (President of the Court of Session ; M.P. for North Berwick).

James Stewart, Lord Advocate.

Adam Cockburn of Ormiston, Treasurer Depute (afterwards a Lord of Session as Lord Ormiston).

Sir John Maxwell, Justice-Clerk (judicial title, Lord Pollock).

James Murray of Philiphaugh (Lord of Session as Lord Philiphaugh ; afterwards Clerk Register).

James Falconer of Phesdo (Lord of Session as Lord Phesdo ; M.P. for Kincardineshire).

Sir James Stewart of Bute (M.P. for Bute ; afterwards 1st Earl of Bute).

Archibald Douglas of Cavers (M.P. for Roxburghshire ; afterwards Receiver-General).

Sir David Dalrymple, Solicitor-General (M.P. for Culross).

Sir David Cunningham of Milncraig (M.P. for Lauder).

James Smollett of Bonhill (M.P. for Dumbarton).

Patrick Johnstone, Provost of Edinburgh (M.P. for Edinburgh).

Hugh Montgomery, Provost of Glasgow (M.P. for Glasgow ; afterwards 5th Baronet of Skelmorlie).

John Scrimgeour, Provost of Dundee (M.P. for Dundee).

John Allardyce, Provost of Aberdeen (M.P. for Aberdeen).

(4) THE COMMISSION APPOINTED IN 1706

The asterisk denotes membership of the Commission of 1702.

(a) English Commissioners.

*Archbishop of Canterbury (Thomas Tenison).

Lord Keeper of the Great Seal (William Cowper ; afterwards 1st Earl Cowper).

*Archbishop of York (John Sharp).

*The Lord High Treasurer (Lord Godolphin).

*The President of the Council (Earl of Pembroke).

*The Lord Privy Seal (Duke of Newcastle).

*Duke of Devonshire.

*Duke of Somerset.

Duke of Bolton.

Earl of Sunderland.

Earl of Kingston.

*Earl of Carlisle (3rd Earl ; grandson of a Commissioner of 1670).

Earl of Orford.
Viscount Townshend (2nd Viscount; son of a Commissioner
of 1670).
Lord Wharton.
Lord Grey.
Lord Poulett (created 1st Earl Poulett in 1706).
Lord Somers.
Lord Halifax.
The Speaker of the House of Commons (John Smith).
Marquis of Hartington (M.P. for Yorkshire; afterwards 2nd
Duke of Devonshire).
Marquis of Granby (afterwards 2nd Duke of Rutland).
*Sir Charles Hedges (Secretary of State).
*Robert Harley (Secretary of State; afterwards 1st Earl of
Oxford).
Henry Boyle (Chancellor of the Exchequer; afterwards 1st
Baron Carleton).
*Sir John Holt (Chief Justice of Queen's Bench).
*Sir Thomas Trevor (Chief Justice of Common Pleas; after-
wards 1st Baron Trevor; son of a Commissioner of 1670).
Sir Edward Northey (Attorney-General).
Sir Simon Harcourt (Solicitor-General; afterwards 1st Viscount
Harcourt).
*Sir John Cooke.
*Dr. Stephen Waller.

(b) Scottish Commissioners.

*The Lord Chancellor (Earl of Seafield).
*The Lord Privy Seal (Duke of Queensberry).
Earl of Mar, Secretary of State.
Earl of Loudoun, Secretary of State.
Earl of Sutherland.
Earl of Morton.
Earl of Wemyss.
*Earl of Leven.
*Earl of Stair.
*Earl of Rosebery (son of a Commissioner of 1670).
*Earl of Glasgow (Treasurer Depute).
Lord Archibald Campbell (cr. Earl of Islay in 1705; afterwards
3rd Duke of Argyll).
Viscount Dupplin (afterwards 6th Earl of Kinnoull).
Lord Ross (William, 12th Earl of Ross).
*Sir Hew Dalrymple (President of the Court of Session).
*Adam Cockburn of Ormiston (Lord Justice-Clerk).
Sir Robert Dundas of Arniston (a Lord of Session).
Robert Stewart of Tillicoultry (a Lord of Session).
Francis Montgomery (M.P. for Ayrshire, a member of the Privy
Council).

*Sir David Dalrymple (Solicitor-General ; M.P. for Culross).

Sir Alexander Ogilvie of Forglen (Receiver General; M.P. for Banff; appointed in 1706 a Lord of Session under the title of Lord Forglen).

*Sir Patrick Johnstone, Lord Provost of Edinburgh (M.P. for Edinburgh).

*Sir James Smollett of Bonhill (M.P. for Dumbarton).

George Lockhart of Carnwath (M.P. for Midlothian).

William Morison of Prestongrange (M.P. for Peeblesshire) .

Alexander Grant, yr. of Grant (M.P. for Inverness-shire).

William Seton, yr. of Pitmedden (M.P. for Aberdeenshire).

John Clerk, yr. of Penicuik (M.P. for Whithorn ; afterwards a Baron of the Exchequer).

*Hugh Montgomery (formerly Provost of Glasgow).

Daniel Stewart.

Daniel Campbell of Ardentinny (M.P. for Inveraray).

INDEX